PENGUIN BOOKS

THE FAT LADIES CLUB

Facing the First Five Years

The Fat Ladies Club

Facing the First Five Years

***

HILARY GARDENER, ANDREA BETTRIDGE,
SARAH GROVES AND LYNDSEY LAWRENCE

PENGUIN BOOKS

PENGUIN BOOKS

Published by the Penguin Group
Penguin Books Ltd, 80 Strand, London WC2R ORL, England
Penguin Putnam Inc., 375 Hudson Street, New York, New York 10014, USA
Penguin Books Australia Ltd, 250 Camberwell Road,
Camberwell, Victoria 3124, Australia
Penguin Books Canada Ltd, 10 Alcorn Avenue, Toronto, Ontario, Canada M4V 3B2
Penguin Books India (P) Ltd, 11 Community Centre,
Panchsheel Park, New Delhi – 110 017, India
Penguin Books (NZ) Ltd, Cnr Rosedale and Airborne Roads,
Albany, Auckland, New Zealand
Penguin Books (South Africa) (Pty) Ltd, 24 Sturdee Avenue,
Rosebank 2196, South Africa

Penguin Books Ltd, Registered Offices: 80 Strand, London WC2R ORL, England

www.penguin.com

First published 2003
1

Set in 11/13 pt Monotype Bembo
Typeset by Rowland Phototypesetting Ltd, Bury St Edmunds, Suffolk
Printed in England by Clays Ltd, St Ives plc

Naturally, we dedicate this book to our families; after all, if it wasn't for them, there wouldn't be a Fat Ladies Club. But also, now that we truly understand what a tricky job being a good mum is, we have to dedicate this book to our very own mums – Mary, Lenia, Evelyn and Margaret – for a job well done. No words could thank you all enough for everything you have done for us.

Acknowledgements

We would like to thank all of Annette's family for their continued support and interest in our Fat Ladies Club.

And once again we would like to thank Mary Green, Hilary's mum, for her fantastic illustrations.

Contents

The Who's Who of
the Fat Ladies Club xi

Where Are We Now? 1

Here Comes the Sad Bit 34

Braving It Again . . . and Again 67

Eat, Drink and Will We Ever Be
Merry Again? 103

Sleep and Sex 133

Flab and Fashion 163

Toilets and Tantrums 190

Ground, Swallow Me Up! 221

Waving Goodbye – Off to School 245

So What's Next? 268

The Who's Who of the Fat Ladies Club

Hilary Gardener – *Gobby Girlie*. Hilary is the learning disability nursing farmer's wife. She now has three children. Molly is nearly five, Isabella, known as Ella, is nearly three and Alfie is only ten weeks old.

Andrea Bettridge – *Goalie Girlie*. Andrea is the Arsenal fanatic police officer. She now has two sons, Max and Sam. Max is just turning five and Sam is nearly three.

Sarah Groves – *Gorgeous Girlie*. Sarah is currently the only true member of the Fat Ladies Club as she is five months pregnant with her third child, but still manages always to look immaculate. Jack, her eldest, is about to turn five and Eloise will soon be two.

Lyndsey Lawrence – *Genius Girlie*. Lyndsey is the brainy scientist who is currently on maternity leave with her second daughter, Caitlin. Caitlin is three months old and her big sister, Bethan, is now nearly five.

Where Are We Now?

Five years can seem an absolute lifetime and yet no time at all. It is impossible to believe how much has happened in our lives over the past few years, both exhilarating and devastating, but the Fat Ladies' friendships have been cemented through it all.

One huge loss for us was the death of our fellow Fat Lady, Annette, two years ago. This has left a gaping hole in our little girlie gang. Her absence from our lives is painfully evident as five become four to write this book.

So why are we writing a sequel then? That is a question that we frequently ask ourselves. It is not because we feel that we're a font of all knowledge on raising preschool children, and it certainly isn't because we're the gurus of childcare whose example should be followed by all. If you think it's because we have too much time on our hands, well nothing could be further from the truth. If we thought it was an impossible mission to accomplish the completion of the first book, then this one really will be nothing short of a miracle. Then again, one thing we have learnt over the past few years is that mothers really are expected to be miracle workers. We rapidly have come to realize that the primary skill of motherhood is the ability to juggle ten balls, along with three samurai swords and a couple of flaming batons for good measure – all while simultaneously standing on our heads singing 'Old MacDonald Had a Farm', of course.

Recently we looked back at photos of us all with our precious newborn first babies. We looked so young, with not a grey hair in sight, which is more than can be said for now. We are looking older, even if we're not acting any wiser! I don't think any of us will ever feel we're 'grown up' – well, definitely not 'responsible adults' anyway ... We now have at least two children each, along with demanding careers and husbands, to name but a few of our 'juggling balls'. And we've each had some of those tricky flaming batons and samurai swords chucked into our lives to test us to our limits and ensure that those grey hairs just keep on coming.

So we decided to write this sequel because, once again, we wanted to give the 'no-holds-barred', true-life version of events in those early years – the juggle of preschool parenting, getting it right, getting it wrong, the guilt and the giggles. We are certainly not aiming to compete with the literary expertise of the likes of Dr Green of *Toddler Taming* fame. There will be no do's and don'ts, no deep psychological reasoning for using different techniques of discipline, just our open and honest account of all those tear-your-hair-out occasions when you severely question exactly who is the child. Hopefully it will just make you laugh out loud and realize that you are not alone on those guilt-ridden nights when you tuck up your child, kiss them good night and sit back to make a plan as to how you're going to do it better tomorrow.

Hilary

* * *

I can safely say that on the ageing front I have come off the worst. If it wasn't for the fantastic invention of hair dye, I reckon that I'd be snowy white by now. When all the children look back at photos of the Fat Ladies Club when we first met, they don't even recognize who I am. Clearly, having three children has taken its toll on me far more than I had realized.

I am still married to David, the farmer, and we now have three

Hilary, Molly, Ella and Alfie

children. But I'm rapidly becoming more of a Margot Leadbetter than a Barbara Good when it comes to hands-on help around the farm. Since being pregnant with Molly, five lambing seasons ago, I haven't been able to help with any lambing at all. Each year I seem either to be pregnant, and therefore not allowed anywhere near the flock for fear of contracting toxoplasmosis, or to have a young child in tow, so I am more of a hindrance than a help if I start trying to get my hands dirty. For the first few years this was totally frustrating, but I'm rapidly turning into someone who is happy not to have sheep poo on her green wellies.

Molly, similarly, is a bit of a girlie – Barbie pink and farming really do not go together. She loves the idea of going to the farmyard, she loves the outdoors and she thinks that all her Christmases have come at once when she gets to have a ride on her Dad's quad bike with him, but give her a lamb to hold and see the look of total disgust come over her face at the prospect of being pood on. At the age of two and a half, Isabella (our little Ella) is the complete opposite. Nothing gives her greater pleasure than to be lying down in a pen of lambs or running through a flock of sheep and being covered in dung of any description. Alfie, our little fella, is only a few weeks old and has yet to appreciate that there is, in fact, life beyond the boob.

Farming has changed pretty dramatically over the past few years, but that is an entirely different story. The biggest change for us has been the fact that David has had to close the pig farm, as it was no longer financially viable. This was a bit of a demoralizing phase for him, after seeing it built up, but I have to say that, for the children and me, it was a blessing in disguise. As I sat with him, desperately trying to maintain a look of sympathetic understanding, the Margot in me was secretly cheering at the prospect of no more eye-watering pig pong in the garden all summer. No more hanging the washing inside even in a heat wave for fear of the oil-based stench infiltrating every fibre of our clothing. No more evil overalls loitering in my porch and no more foul-smelling husband lounging around in the evening saying, 'I can't smell anything,' when I'm gagging at the prospect of even entering the same room as him! Pigs may be cute, they may even be one of the cleanest animals by nature, but it has to be said that they don't half pong. As you have possibly gathered by now, I was quite glad to see them go. Summers in the garden have since taken on a whole new meaning.

I am still working as a community learning disabilities nurse, but this is now on an extremely part-time basis. After having Molly, I returned to work on a three-day week. From my perspective this worked really well; I loved having my professional identity, as well as my parental identity, and felt that the hours were perfect. Molly, however, was never enamoured with my return to work. Initially I had a friend childminding for me. This seemed to be the perfect solution; she simply included Molly in her own family's life. Even though Molly was only seven months old when I went back, boy did she give her a hard time! She screamed to the point of vomiting every time I left the room throughout the introductory weeks, and then on my first day back at work she literally screamed all day. When I arrived home, my poor childminder was totally at the end of her tether and broke down in tears. The guilt I felt was horrendous, first towards my precious little girl, for abandoning her, but mainly towards my childminder for inflicting such a headstrong little madam on her. It turned out that Molly had a throat infection, though, and my guilt nearly made me quit work there and then. I took annual leave for the rest of that first week back at work, and then we started the battle of abandonment once more. Thankfully my childminder had the patience of a saint and persisted with my wilful little girl. It took four weeks before Molly finally conceded to childcare and came home carrying a little storybook inside which were the words: 'For my Molly Miggins, thank you for our first lovely day together, love Debbie'. Things then went pretty smoothly for a couple of years. Molly became quite settled into the routine of two days with the childminder and one day with my mum, which was never perceived as childcare by Molly, merely a treat. She even coped with a change of childminder at the end of the first year. However, she always made sure that the actual parting was sheer torture. She would cling around my neck and let out blood-curdling screams as she was pulled away. This always got to me and would start affecting me from the night before. I was just glad that it was only two days a week that we had to go through this heart-wrenching experience. At least I knew that she had a lovely time once the initial parting was over, otherwise I couldn't have coped at all.

Once Ella was on the scene I returned to work again when Molly was two and a half, this time putting them both into a day nursery. This worked wonders on Molly – she loved it, never cried when I left her and seemed to be in her element. It felt as though a huge weight had been lifted from my shoulders, until Ella decided to play the 'Let's emotionally torture Mum' game and clearly hated being in the 'baby room'. We stuck it out, using up every hour of annual leave to bide my time until she could go up into the one-year-olds' room because I knew she would love it there, and sure enough she did. I had four whole weeks of both children being happy in their childcare before Molly moved up a room, too, and the nightmare started all over again. Two months later – two years and eight months after returning to work from my first maternity leave – I finally threw in the towel and admitted defeat. I could cope no longer with the emotional turmoil of juggling my career and childcare. As I sat down with the managers of the nursery telling them that I was removing my children, I sobbed. I felt a total failure as both a parent and a professional, and with the permanent preoccupation with those two aspects of my life I also felt that I was doing a pretty appalling job of being a wife. Once we decided that we should call it quits with my career, it felt fantastic. I was all set for some evening's shelf stacking to bring in some extra cash and was ready to start doing one job, being a mother, well for a change.

As it turned out, my managers and colleagues were not as prepared to see me leave as I was. They drew up a plan for me to work just one day a week, in order for me to be able to use my mum for childcare. So this is what I have been doing for the past year or so. Working a mere seven and a half hours a week is heaven – it's just enough to keep my hand in and my brain ticking over, and I actually take home more money than I did working the three days because I don't pay childcare. I only wish I had done this from the outset. I am currently on maternity leave again, but intend returning when Alfie is four months old. I only hope that my mum will be able to cope with juggling all three children, the school runs and my disabled father on this one day a week. It's going to be tough for her, but don't we all have a secret belief that our mums are, in fact, Wonder Woman? So I'm sure that mine will manage.

Even working one day a week, I do still find that it interferes with my busy social life. Before having children, I couldn't imagine what full-time mums could possibly find to fill their days; I am loath to admit that I, too, do find it a struggle to fit in those irritating little essentials like cooking, cleaning and food shopping. Admittedly my diary is mainly filled with a flurry of activities for the children: ballet, swimming, playgroup pick-up, friends to play, kinder gym – and so the list goes on. Simply remembering where you're meant to be, when and for which child would be a challenge for your average member of Mensa, let alone a spongy-brained mum! And I haven't yet had to add the anticipated boy activities that Alfie is bound to throw in to the weekly timetable in years to come. What with all of this, and desperately trying to fit in the occasional fitness or social activity of my own, I can safely say that my weeks are full and my brain and body can take no more.

Have I changed since having children? Now that is a question that would be answered differently depending on which friends or family members you asked. If you consulted my old hockey club friends, they would say that without a doubt I have changed completely – especially to the friends who have not yet joined the parenting club. I no longer frequent the clubhouse, but when I do go it is usually with the children for an hour in the bar after David has played, so I am preoccupied by keeping an eye on the children rather than propping up the bar. I no longer play hockey at all and have absolutely no desire to go outside and face the midwinter elements adorned in a hockey skirt and shin pads again. I do feel a bit of an outsider at the club now. It's a bit like going back to the student union bar at college after you've left. The atmosphere is the same, the drinking games haven't changed, but you are no longer part of it. This all sounds very dismal and depressing, but I have to say that I don't miss it at all. I have kept in touch with some close friends from the club and we regularly socialize with them, just not in Astro boots and bandannas.

Other than my extradition from the hockey club, I don't think I have changed at all. I'm still a motormouth who never knows when to 'put it in neutral', I still have far too many opinions on far too many subjects, and I still stress about my weight, but can't bear the thought of cutting down my food intake.

Our social life has changed, though. David and I rarely go out for a bevy together now, but tend to have people around to ours to eat instead. This must be a nightmare for our guests, as they are not only a captive audience for my motormouth which has been deprived of adult interaction all day, but they are also subjected to my cooking, and I am no Jamie Oliver, to put it mildly. This transition to home socializing rather than restaurants and pubs is largely because it saves on the hassle of finding a baby-sitter. Even when we go to other people's houses, we ship the entire family with us and plonk them on any bed going, then ship them home again in the dead of night. Our children have always done this and are great at staying asleep while they are transported around the countryside. That is the one huge down-side of living out in the sticks; it is just impossible to get a baby-sitter. Our house is known to the children in the local area as the haunted house, which they dare each other to run up to. So, for most local teenagers, the prospect of baby-sitting in it would be on a par with inviting them to spend an evening in the Hammer House of Horrors! I can't say that I miss the weekly post-hockey pub crawl, followed by a curry and a fight for the only taxi likely to be able to take us home before dawn. In fact, I am ashamed to admit that I much prefer the home entertainment routine, which really does make me sound like a sad thirty-something, doesn't it?

The other thing that I have discovered about myself is that I do seem to have a need for full-on involvement in whatever activities I join. When I was part of the hockey club, I could never just be a member; I was ladies' chairperson, manager of the under-19s girls team and one of the mainstays of the social committee. Obviously I've dropped all this but I am now an active member of the playgroup fundraising committee and in charge of the village church's Sunday school, and I also run a monthly after-school children's church service called the Sunshine Service. I have no idea how I managed to get myself so involved in the church, but the other Fat Ladies have nicknamed me the Vicar of Dibley. I went to church as a child and helped in Sunday school as a teenager, but have had very limited involvement since then. When Annette died, I did have a desire to start going to church occasionally and I started taking my girls, too. I really wanted my children to just have a good basic Christian background, knowing the Bible stories, the kiddie hymns, but also having fun. Before I knew it, I was volunteering to provide exactly this service for the village. I even ended up doing the full nativity service for the church last Christmas. I tell you, Dawn French, move over. Here comes Hilary Gardener!

So yes, my life has changed, and when I look back now I realize that these changes have been quite dramatic, but definitely for the better. I love being a mum, even though I really don't think I'm very good at it. My priorities and what gives me pleasure in life may have changed, but I am still me, with the same sense of humour and fun that I have always had, and I am happy to say that I really do love my life just the way it is.

Andrea

* * *

I would like to start by saying that I can proudly boast that I do not have a single grey hair yet. This is just as well because, when I listen to Hilary and Sarah discussing the pros and cons

Andrea, Max and Sam

of semipermanent versus permanent colour and the cost-effectiveness of home colouring versus the expense of salon intervention, I feel that I would be destined for a major cock-up and end up with green hair if I had to embark on such girlie activities.

Unfortunately, I don't think it will be that long before I do join the others on the greying front though, as I am in the process of going through one of the most stressful times of my life. Yes, I hate to admit it, but I am the statistical one in five (from our little gang) whose marriage is breaking up. I am someone who took my marriage vows very seriously and when I said 'til death us do part' I meant it, so the decision to separate was not mine. I really did not ever imagine myself in the position I am currently facing. It's amazing how we never know what is around the corner. I thought I had learnt this from the speed Annette's illness took hold and killed her, but once again I am gobsmacked by an unexpected twist in my life. Only nine months ago, as Bruce and I walked into Highbury giggling with excitement at the prospect of watching Arsenal's opening match of the season, I remember thinking how lucky I was to be married to someone who was with me all the way in the overzealous Arsenal supporting stakes. Our friends perceived our marriage to be one of the closest, yet here I am, my single mortgage approved, house sale agreed, waiting for the chain to complete and move into my new little home with my boys. So how has this happened? Last year, Bruce built up his own business in electronic computer components, and it is doing incredibly well. Basically he has fallen in love with his business and no longer sees me as part of his new life. I'm not sure what would be worse, my husband leaving due to having an affair with another woman, having an affair with a man or simply having an affair with his own desires to do well. Any of these would hurt. I just don't have the luxury of having someone else to blame! The sad thing is that being the sort of person I am, I am not even managing to be angry at him. I think that I am just so grateful that he is not also falling out of love with his children that I am forgiving him for what he is doing to me. I'm sure this must make me a right mug, but that's me. He is still as devoted as ever to his boys and fully intends to continue being the hands-on dad he has always been.

On a more cheerful note, I am still just as obsessed with Arsenal now as I have ever been, and I think that parts of my life over the past five years have mirrored my team's highs and lows. Season 97–98 was a huge high on both fronts, as this saw the pre-season arrival of Max, our first son, followed by Arsenal doing the double and winning the Premiership and FA Cup when he was just ten months old. The poor lad didn't know what had hit him when the final whistle blew in the FA Cup Final. The sight of both his parents leaping around the sitting room like a pair of kangaroos on acid was all a bit frightening for him, and his bottom lip took on a decided wobble. Fortunately, this didn't have a long-term damaging effect on his football-supporting abilities, but, after being dressed in an Arsenal Babygro from the day he was born, he really didn't have much choice in life about liking football.

Prior to that big win for Arsenal, Max had had to watch every televised match of the season with us, and he soon mastered the fact that when lots of men in red run around on television Mummy and Daddy do lots of shouting. Max must have thought, 'Sometimes they go quiet and grumpy, which is called losing, but I like it best when they get very excited and take me out for a treat at the end – this is called winning.' It's hardly surprising then that by the age of eighteen months he understood the concept of football and he, too, was thrilled when Arsenal won. What with this early armchair spectating and many a Sunday on the sideline with my friend Lizzie, watching Mummy play football, I am proud to be able to say that Max is now a fully fledged 'junior Gunner'. His favourite player is Freddie Ljungberg; he loves to sing Freddie's song and recently announced that he wants a red Mohican just like his idol. That's something that will have to wait until the summer holidays, as I don't think his school would approve! Max has tons of enthusiasm for sport and loves kicking a ball around in the back garden wearing his kit. Whether he has the dexterity or sporting prowess to be a decent player is another question. I fear he is too much like his father, in which case his preoccupation with cleanliness will outweigh his sporting instincts. Already he is the sort of child who, the minute he gets the tiniest amount of dirt on his bright white shorts, will come running in crying as though a world catastrophe had occurred and will not calm down until his shorts are spotless again.

If Max takes after his dad, then my other son, Sam, at two and a half, is already showing strong signs of being like me in personality. We are both the sort of people who are generally cheerful, but also extremely clumsy. If there is something to trip over, knock against, drop or fall off, you can guarantee that Sam or I will be successful in doing exactly that. He has shown early signs of inheriting my sporting ability too, though, and really does appear to have an eye for the ball with no concerns for the 'Persil challenge' on his whites.

He's so like me, I only hope that he doesn't also inherit my painful obsession with promptness. I was born five weeks early and, unless I turn up at a venue at the very least five minutes early, I always panic about my punctuality. Sam was also born five weeks early, so I'll just have to wait to see whether there is any truth in the theory that punctuality traits are related to the promptness of your birth.

My pregnancy with Sam did mirror my team's performance that season in many ways. Arsenal developed a trend of being the bridesmaid; the excitement of the day was there, but they ended up finishing second and, to top it all, the bride was Manchester United. Similarly, all the excitement of my pregnancy was there, but it was overshadowed by the constant fear of losing the baby. The whole pregnancy was not at all straightforward, but I'll save the details of that for later. Then, after going to watch Arsenal play, my waters broke six weeks early. Sam was born a week later, and it has to be said that he has proved far easier on the outside. I often wonder if my waters had actually gone at the Arsenal match whether I would have been given an honorary season ticket for life.

On the work front, I did return to work as a police officer when Max was seven months old. I didn't realize how much of a dent in my confidence the break and birth had made until I was faced with an interview for my new post as a community officer. At the time I had ten years experience under my belt and prior to my maternity leave had worked on a drugs unit, yet I still felt like a rookie again. Fortunately, my past reputation got me through the board, which just left the adrenaline-pumping prospect of having to make my first arrest again. Things that I had done two years earlier without even a second's thought were suddenly daunting first experiences.

I was so nervous in the weeks leading up to my return to work that I'm relieved that I did not have the same problem as Hilary when it came to leaving Max at his nursery. I originally went back full time, and Max spent three days at a local nursery; he was looked after by Bruce's mum for one day and Bruce for the other. He settled into nursery so well. We had a few tears for about two days, but after that he would smile and wave me goodbye. When I picked Max up, I would usually spot him before he spotted me. It was a fantastic feeling to see the joyous look on his face as he recognized me and came toddling over. I was soon to find out that he also didn't mind who took him or picked him up – a good job really because the local criminals were unaware that I was a new mum with childcare concerns. I had a really busy first few weeks back at work – it was great to plunge straight into the thick of things and rebuild my confidence as an officer, but I did have severe guilt pangs with the amount of times either Bruce or my friend Lizzie had to be called on at short notice to collect Max for me.

The nursery was great in lots of ways, but it did have one drawback and that was the speed at which an outbreak of an infection would spread. During his first month, Max had conjunctivitis, 'hand, foot and mouth' (which completely shocked me as I confused it with foot and mouth, which is a whole different ball game), not to mention a permanently snotty nose and chesty cough. He would catch the condition at the nursery, but then be 'expelled' whilst he recovered. The dose of conjunctivitis was during my first week back, and I just couldn't bring myself to ask for time off so soon, so Max went to stay at my mum's in Somerset until he was better. This worked fine, except that it was the first time I had been apart from him and I found it really upsetting. I got revenge on my mum, though, for all those years of constant overconcerned phone calls whenever I was ill; I must have rung her every hour on the hour to check on him!

I was enjoying my new role at work, but after six months I took the difficult decision to reduce my hours to four days a week and then, after the birth of Sam, to three days a week. I realized that I was missing out on spending any quality time with my boys, and before too long they would be grown up and I would have missed it. I say that this was a difficult decision because I have always loved my choice of career and by reducing my hours I think I was accepting that I was definitely putting it on hold for a while. The police service has become much better in recent years in encouraging part-time working for female officers, and I had superb support from my supervisors. Unfortunately, though, there will always be an opinion amongst some officers that we should not be doing frontline policing part time, and I have had to bite my tongue at some of the comments from these dinosaurs. I often feel I have to work way beyond the call of duty just to keep the female flag of capability flying. Despite all this, I am so glad I did make this decision, as this has always left me with at least one day in the week just for the children and me. We go swimming, meet up with friends or just hang out together, which we have always loved.

Where my career will go from here is something I frequently wonder about. Part of me had planned to start climbing the rungs of the police force ladder again, and recently I even considered sitting my sergeant's exam, but an even bigger part of me can now see a potential end to this career as a frontline officer. I didn't think I would ever say that, but an incident at work a couple of years ago made me sit back and reflect on my future. During an arrest I was hit in the face with my own handcuffs, which left me with a permanent scar above my top lip. Max, in particular, found this extremely upsetting, and for a while he didn't want me to go to work in case I was hurt. His reaction really affected me and made me realize that there was no longer just me to consider. So I decided to 'return to school' and get qualified. After taking an evening class in law last year, I am proud to say that at the tender age of thirty-two I took my first A level. I thoroughly enjoyed training my brain to study again and proved to be a bit of a swot who always got her essays in on time, of course! When I went to sit the exams, I did feel extremely old. As all of the seventeen-year-old college day students filed in I felt as though I was the granny in the corner who drastically increased the average age in the room.

When it came to the results, I was so excited I couldn't wait for the post, so I went and stood in line with all the other students, waiting for my brown envelope. If I had felt conspicuous in the exam hall, I must have stood out like a sore thumb as I waited in amongst these grunge-clad teenagers, wearing my police uniform. When I opened my envelope and found that I had passed, my excitement level was equal to theirs, though, and I squealed with the best of them. I did receive a few strange looks as I bounced around congratulating and hugging anyone and everyone, but no one had the courage to ask who the hell I was. Perhaps they thought I was doing an extremely poor job of undercover surveillance and had forgotten the essential rule for blending in: don't wear your uniform!

Having had this one studious success, I have now embarked on an Open University course, with a view to getting a degree. I do not have any definite plans for what I will do with this in the future, but, if I continue to focus these studies on law, it will hopefully help me find an alternative to frontline policing that is still within the criminal justice system.

This brings me up to the present day, and now my life and my team's success could not be more different. I am definitely in one of the most difficult phases of my life to date as I prepare to start life as a single mum. Arsenal, on the other hand, is unstoppable and has just won the double again. During all of these ups and downs, the Fat Ladies have certainly become great buddies. I love popping up to Sarah's house for a chat, which is so convenient as she lives ten yards from the police station, or phoning Hilary just to annoy her husband by talking about nothing in particular when we will be meeting in ten minutes, then phoning or e-mailing Lyndsey to tell her the same thing. I love being godmother to Ella, Hilary and David's second daughter and Sam's 'friend girl', as he calls her, and I love it that Sarah rang me at work this morning before nine o'clock to congratulate me on Arsenal's win last night. As well as knowing what colour the team plays in now, she even knows a couple of players' names!

Lyndsey

* * *

As I sit here putting pen to paper, or more accurately finger to keyboard, I am having a huge sense of *déjà vu*. Once again I am on maternity leave, nursing a three-month-old baby girl, Caitlin,

Lyndsey, Bethan and Caitlin

and desperately trying to gear my brain back into writing. Bethan, who is now approaching the grand old age of five and a real 'girlie girl', adores her long-awaited baby sister. She sees her as an addition to her extensive Barbie collection and insists that I dress Caitlin from head to toe in pink, flowery dresses. Needless to say I try my best to leave the dressing until Bethan is safely out the door and well on her way to school, but then I have to deal with the wrath of the Princess of Pink at a quarter past three each day if her baby sister's attire is not entirely to her liking!

Tim, my Welsh husband, has become even more painfully patriotic. I thought you were supposed to mellow with age, but Tim just gets worse and worse. He would argue that I have simply become less tolerant, as there have been many occasions when my patience levels have plummeted and I have ended up hurling caring marital comments such as 'If it's so damn great there, why don't you go back?' However, I have the full backing of my sisters-in-law, who have nicknamed him the Victor Meldrew of Welsh advocacy.

Fathering two daughters hasn't yet tainted Tim's rugby passion either, and he still makes frequent trips down the M4 to the Millennium Stadium in Cardiff, which of course always end in tears. I think the bonus of a day's escape from the family does help to ease the pain of the frequent Welsh losses.

My tolerance of this rugby love was somewhat tested earlier this year when Tim thought that it would be no problem at all to make the nine-hour round trip down to Cardiff the day before Caitlin's due date. He genuinely thought that I was being unreasonable when I pointed out that the logic of 'I'll have my phone on vibrate in my pocket' would not instantly beam him back into our sitting room should my labour start, even if he did manage to hear what I was saying over the sound of 65,000 singing rugby fans. There was no way I was going to entertain his alternative suggestion, which was, of course, for me to go with him to Wales. This, he thought, would not only solve his problem of proximity for the birth, but would also have the added bonus of his second child being born in Wales. Sibling rivalry is going to be interesting enough to manage without one waving the English flag whilst the other is a miniature Welsh dragon-obsessed clone of its father. So Tim begrudgingly accepted that this was one game he would have to watch on television. As it turned out, Caitlin arrived bang on time and in four hours flat, so my paranoia was not unfounded. He would barely have made it back over the Severn Bridge, let alone to the hospital.

What else has changed in our lives over the past few years? Well, we moved house just after Bethan's second birthday, to a small village in Oxfordshire. Whilst it makes us more accessible to the M40, which is our main route to work, the reason for deserting the Berkhamsted area and the bosom of the Fat Ladies Club was plain and simple – house prices. On Bethan's arrival, our small semidetached Hertfordshire house was quickly overrun by her equipment, so once I returned to work it felt like a good idea to upgrade whilst we had two salaries coming in. To do that in Herts, however, right on the whopping-house-price commuter route to London, proved impossible on our budget and so we looked westwards. We are currently facing the prospect of another move, though, as my job has relocated back into the heart of Herts. The toss-up between downsizing home and being closer to work or travelling 120 miles a day is one we can realistically address after I return to work from my current maternity leave. The thought of making poor Bethan start a new school when she has only just settled into her present one is enough to make me at least attempt to endure the gruel of the daily drive. The really frustrating thing is that halfway through the journey I will literally have to drive past our old house. Now that really will be a daily kick in the teeth to think that I would have been home forty minutes earlier if we hadn't moved.

On the subject of work, I did return to my post as clinical trials manager for a pharmaceutical company when Bethan was six and a half months old. I remember it vividly: the sleepless nights deciding on appropriate childcare and then, once back, the guilt trips of leaving my precious baby in the hands of strangers. I eased myself back into the work scene by initially going back on a three-day week. I then extended this to four days when Bethan was ten months old, with the aim of being full time by her first birthday. Childcare was a painfully tough decision, but we eventually decided on a nursery. However, I just couldn't cope with the 'handing over' process each morning, no matter how welcoming the smile at the nursery doorstep. It simply ripped me apart and killed any ability of my postnatal spongy brain to concentrate and contend with work issues. We soon settled into a 'Good Cop, Bad Cop' routine where Tim took her each morning and I had the pleasure of the afternoon pick-up.

At work I found myself clock watching, and for the first time since school I was almost waiting for the sound of a bell ringing for home time! I would get in extra early in order to leave extremely promptly the second my daily hours of employment were over. This was totally alien to both me and my colleagues, as I work in an environment of people who live to work rather than work to live. I openly admit that I had been one of them before Bethan was born. My desire to be with my daughter certainly unleashed assertiveness skills which meant I was able to ignore the raised eyebrows and accentuated watch reading as I packed up for the day. I knew that no matter what anyone else thought of my time keeping I was doing my job well, but that I also had my priorities right. The second I left the office, my brain switched to Bethan, and I wanted to be with her instantly. I would practically run to my car, then race through the 25-minute journey to the nursery. The staff couldn't get the door open fast enough for my liking. I just wanted to find my child, sweep her into my arms and not be parted from her for another second.

Bethan, on the other hand, seemed to take it all in her stride. She enjoyed herself and flourished in the nursery environment. Even with the change of nursery at two and a half, when we moved, she settled very quickly. Recently she has started school, bringing to an end her nursery life, but she can't quite let go. We've had to send letters to the children at nursery, telephone them to allow her to say 'hello' and even make an occasional visit for her to update them on school life. She misses both her carers and the other children alike, which, for a guilt-ridden working mum, is such a relief. It shows that we at least got her preschool childcare right, and it made her transition to school very easy.

Once I was into the routine of working again and knew that Bethan was happy at nursery, I have to admit that I did enjoy the adult company and responsibility of my job. If I am totally honest, the childfree hours of not having to plan the next feed or activity were a welcome change, too. Despite all this, once I was back to a four-day week I knew that I couldn't face the full-time five-day week again, which had not been planned. I managed to persuade my boss that I could do the job in four days, but of course I ended up doing five days work. It was just that I had to pack it into four days, so my days got longer. Tim and I had to switch roles, and I became the Bad Cop doing the morning drop-off, whilst Tim was Good Cop doing the 6 p.m. pick-up. This meant that I wasn't getting home until after seven most nights, but I would rather that than give up my precious day off with Bethan. I vowed it was a day to be together, and housework and food shopping trips would have to be shared with Tim at the weekend. Bethan and I really did pack it all in to Fridays, starting with the forty-minute drive over to Fat Ladies Land for swimming with Molly, Max and Jack. This was followed by an extremely rowdy McDonald's lunch with the children running riot whilst we caught up on all the gossip over a McChicken sandwich and diet cola. Oh, how our lives have changed! Then we would trek back over to Oxfordshire for ballet and tap lessons with Bethan's two best friends from nursery. We would leave the house about 9.30 a.m. and not return from our frantic socializing until about 5.15 p.m., utterly exhausted (me, not Bethan). On occasion, I would find myself wondering if I were in fact a masochist and perhaps that extra day at work would be easier than this routine.

Having said that, I am really going to miss our frantic Fridays together now that Bethan has started school. She began shortly after I commenced my current maternity leave, so I have not yet had to experience those precious days off without my little girl.

I have a couple of months left before I return to work, and I must say that the thought doesn't thrill me. I am really enjoying being a full-time mum, and the timing of Caitlin's arrival, although later than we had hoped, has actually proved to be perfect. It has meant that I have been able to be around to settle Bethan into school life, as well as having the daytime hours to really enjoy Caitlin as though she were my first child. Being able to be there for Bethan at the school gate each day is wonderful. It's a luxury that full-time mums don't realize that they have. My plan is to return to a three-day week only this time, but whether I can realistically cram my full-time job into these hours is something to be tested. I really do not want to compromise this brief time zone of early years' parenting any further than this, so I am determined to make it work.

The childcare aspect once again terrifies me. What with me working so far away, Caitlin needing full-time care and Bethan needing school runs, our only option seems to be a nanny – so the search is on. How on earth do you select someone who you don't know from Adam to look after your precious children? At least at a nursery if the main carer is having an off-day then other staff can intervene. More importantly, your child has the social interaction with all the other children. We are facing the prospect of Caitlin being mainly on her own with the nanny whilst Bethan is at school, and, at seven months old, she's hardly going to be in a position to let us know if the nanny has not been nice. That *Nannies from Hell* documentary is one that has stuck in my mind like a bad nightmare for years. I can really understand why those parents set up the surveillance cameras now. It's not just that you don't want the nanny to be cruel, it's more that you want to know that your precious baby is getting as much love and attention when you are not there as she does when you are. I hoped it would be easier second time around, but how wrong I was. I'll see how I go at work for three months, then we'll take it from there.

I am not so concerned about Bethan because the hours with the nanny will be far fewer and she can verbalize any upset. Anyway, she has fitted so well into village life and as she seems to be developing quite an extensive little social network I suspect that her after-school social calendar will be quite full, and she will barely notice my absence in those three days. It is strange for us to see our daughter truly considering the place where she lives, and not just the house, to be her home, as Tim and I have always led quite a nomadic and isolated lifestyle. We tend not to build huge social networks in the area we live owing to our long working hours, but rely on the company of long-standing friends who are dotted about the country.

On the subject of our social life – what's that? Since Bethan came along, this has taken a plummet. Not that we were huge partygoers or out every night, but now we are both out for the count by 9.30 p.m. on weekdays and may really live a little by staying up until 10 p.m. on a Saturday night! We do still frequently have friends to stay for the weekend, but it is a bit embarrassing to be dozing off before the TV Watershed when your guests have travelled 300 miles for an evening of your company.

These past five years have certainly had their moments,

but I think that Tim and I both agree that, whilst parenting has been our toughest challenge yet, we wouldn't want it any other way.

Sarah

* * *

And so it falls to me as the only official 'FTM' – that's 'full-time mum' – of the group to bare my soul regarding all the ups and downs of the past five years whilst I have been toiling under this prestigious title. It seems an awfully long time ago since we wrote

Sarah, Jack and Eloise

the first book, and that was all about our real-time lives at that stage. It is now going to be a Herculean challenge to dig up all those memories of what has happened in my life since the birth of my first child, Jack. Added to this is the fact that I'm older, have another child, Eloise, and am currently four months pregnant with our third child, leaving me effectively with a lot less time on my hands. This has left my mind spinning at the very thought of embarking on a second book. But here goes.

As any FTM reading this will understand, when anyone asks, 'What do you do all day?' or 'What do you do with all that time?' you simply stare aghast at the notion that the person can actually believe that they are asking a valid question. It is almost as if the person thinks that if you don't dress up and commute to an office environment every day then somehow your existence is quite worthless. Yet, when pushed, you feel incapable of giving a comprehensive response, and it just ends up with you desperately trying to justify yourself . . . 'Well, err, umm,' and your mind goes into overdrive thinking of all those tasks you accomplish in a day, but which don't seem significant enough to mention. Somehow, preparing for, going through the act of, washing up after and fumigating the kitchen following every mealtime, not to mention dealing with the tantrums which often accompany these thrice-daily occasions, doesn't seem a feasible explanation of a mother's day well spent. Neither does the loading or unloading of the washing machine, the ironing and hoovering, the food shopping and nappy changes, which also come under the job description. And God forbid if you happen to mention frivolous pastimes such as 'going to the gym' or 'mother–toddler groups' because then you're entering into 'Well, it's alright for some!' territory, which seems to earn you disdain rather than the acknowledgement that you're actually looking for. I now find myself having to account for five years of such an existence – daunting or what! You'd better sit tight for a blow-by-blow account of a thousand whites washes and hundreds of stress-filled days of the FLC FTM.

Joking aside, I have to say that I wouldn't change my current role in life for anything: I firmly believe that I am doing the right thing for myself and my children, and I love being able to spend time doing puzzles or having tickling fights with Eloise whenever I want. Eloise is just over eighteen months old now and the absolute spitting image of her brother; there is no doubt at all that they both came from the same mould. She is fast displaying her independent little character, with plenty of feminine charm, yet somehow she always manages to get grubby within seconds of me dressing her. This has given rise to many a laugh at my expense because the other Fat Ladies seem to think that I am always so immaculate. It gives them great pleasure to see that I have ended up with the grubbiest little girl! Rather than being a prima ballerina, I think Eloise is destined for more tomboyish pursuits. I also love being able to pick Jack up from the school playground at the end of every day. He is now approaching five years old and is just like his father in both looks and temperament. He is very headstrong and knows exactly what he wants to do, and when, which can sometimes be a real battle. My mother recently witnessed a mild argument between Tim and me, and remarked afterwards that she had noticed that Jack argues in exactly the same style as his father. Great – what hope have I got? Does that mean that I am destined for a life of arguments in my household that already have a preordained conclusion so that, even if my adversary is not always right, he is certainly *never* wrong? I will just have to sharpen up on my subtlety skills if I am to survive. I have to say, however, that my little Jack does look so handsome and grown up in his 'big boy's' striped school blazer, and I'd much rather he have a strong personality than none at all. I feel very privileged to be able to be at home and help form their early years as best I can: I am just grateful that

Tim and I started a family well before my salary and 'career path' ever became an issue for me. I feel lucky that our lifestyle hadn't reached the point at which we relied on the second income. I can't begin to imagine the traumas over childcare that the others have had to go through. I count myself extremely fortunate in being able to fulfil one of those hugely important roles in life that is sadly so underrated.

Up until Jack was two and a half, we were living an existence of permanent commuters, between England and Spain. Tim's posting to San Sebastian, in Northern Spain, when I was heavily pregnant with Jack, lasted three years in the end. During that time, I always felt that as soon as I had unpacked my bags either in Berkhamsted or in San Sebastian, it was time to repack and fly back to my 'other' place of residence. It was strange leading a sort of double existence, leaving home here to go back to home 'there', with a different routine in each place and different things to occupy my time. We became such pals with a local firm of taxi drivers that took us regularly to and from Heathrow that even now, two years on, they still hoot me in town as they drive past and ask after 'little Jack'. In Spain, we had a steady stream of visitors come over to see us, for weekends and weeks at a time, which was always a source of company for me in a place where I was a bit of a Norma No-Mates who didn't speak the lingo. I did have fun trying to master this new language and became quite competent in the markets at ordering my fish, meat and vegetables, but didn't quite make it beyond polite social niceties to a decent 'chatty' level, which is why I valued our visitors so much!

When back in the UK, I would spend two mad weeks fitting all my social life into a tight schedule, as well as trying to maintain Jack's interests at heart. Fortunately he was too young, at eighteen months old, to be forming his first memories. Otherwise I might have had a child on my hands who was growing up resenting any form of coffee or lunch with friends due to a huge concentration of them inflicted on him in his early years. It would always seem like a welcome rest to return to the relative calm of San Sebastian, where I could count the number of my acquaintances on one hand. I used to talk to the neighbour across the hall who only ever nodded at me and scuttled off without muttering so much as a '*Buenos dias*', and I did chat in very broken Spanish to the people running the *guarderia* (nursery) where I used to take Jack a few mornings a week, so that I could go to the gym.

Jack wasn't enamoured with the idea of nursery and would be practically climbing out of the person's arms screaming for me as I turned my back to leave. They always reassured me, as they generally do, that he calmed down seconds after I had left, but I always felt *so* heartless forcing him to go to these unfamiliar people who didn't speak a word of English – and all because I wanted to go to the gym. How selfish was that? It wasn't even as if I were going to work or to the doctor's, or something equally unavoidable. Still, I persevered so that I could have that all-important time to myself, but also so that Jack had some social interaction with other children, which I felt he lacked drastically in Spain – even if it was with children who only spoke to him in Basque! However, he did seem to get along happily with them: it's quite amazing how inconsequential a language barrier can be for children when it can be totally crippling for adults.

It wasn't until Hilary and Molly came to visit us, and I took Jack along to a morning's session, that I began to have a few doubts about the place. Hilary observed that all the staff in the place were men and that the guy who greeted Jack was wearing a long, beige raincoat, or 'Flasher Mac', as she called it. Admittedly, he had only just arrived for work, and it was raining, but this was instantly dodgy in Hilary's opinion and of course started me wondering if I were unwittingly depositing my child at some paedophile club three times a week. However, I put it down to her overactive imagination and overexposure to social problems back in England. The fact that the credentials of the place had been checked over by a reliable Spanish colleague of Tim's reassured me enough to continue taking Jack there.

I have to say that Hilary's notion that she has come off worst on the ageing front is far from true. It was when I was in Spain and slightly dubious about going to the hairdresser's for a cut, let alone a colour, that I decided to attempt the *au naturel* look by letting the grey grow through. I foolishly hoped that I might turn out looking maturely elegant rather than prematurely gaunt, but soon realized that being a brunette meant that grey shows up big-time when it starts coming through in bunches. There was nothing for it: I had to swot up on my Spanish hairdresser vocab and bite the bullet. After all, the term 'henna' must be universal. What I found out to my horror is that the term 'henna' might indeed be universal, but the length of time it is left on the hair obviously isn't. After forty-five minutes sat with the henna product on my hair, fifteen minutes of which was spent underneath one of those heated head units which are normally reserved for ladies wanting blue rinses, the lady finally took me to the sink to wash it off. She then sat me down on the chair ready to cut my hair and removed the towel. The effect struck me dumb – my hair had turned from dark brown with flecks of grey to bright, positively luminous red. Yes, scarlet. '*Es roja!*' was all I was able to stutter to a very calm hairdresser who was standing rubbing my hair with a towel with a contented smile on her face, which read 'job well done'. I couldn't believe that they would be happy with such an effect and demanded that they try to wash it out. Five scrub washes and a haircut later, I finally left to rejoin the friends who had been looking after Jack. Their faces said it all – I think they realized that it really wasn't necessary to verbalize the fact that I looked like a cross between a Belisha beacon and a gobstopper, for fear of triggering floods of tears that were evidently brewing. So strong was the colour that friends back in England who hadn't seen me for ages were still commenting on my new red hairstyle for months afterwards! Needless to say, since moving back to England, I feel in much safer hands when it comes to covering up my signs of ageing, which, I have to say, is something of a regular necessity. To ram the point home further still, Jack recently asked me whilst staring deep into my face, 'Mummy, what are wrinkles?' I would love to say at this point that he was asking the question because he had never seen any before; however, as I fobbed him off with some waffle about ageing, I surreptitiously headed off to the bathroom to inspect just how visible my crow's-feet had become.

We moved back to Berkhamsted when Jack was reaching two and a half, that age when nurseries and schooling suddenly become an issue. It seemed a shame to be leaving an existence where we were able to spend some time here at home and the rest on the Northern Spanish coast, eating out in fantastic restaurants and enjoying the Continental lifestyle. But, in hindsight, the timing of Tim's job move was perfect. I was expecting again, and, having suffered a couple of miscarriages during the time we had been commuting, I was happier staying put in one place to give the pregnancy its best chance. I was more than pleased not to have to try my hand at the commuting by air with *two* young children! Jack then started at a local school's nursery at the same time as Max, just a couple of months before Eloise was born that summer. I can hardly believe that he and Max will be starting in year 1 this year, as grown-up five-year-olds, and Eloise will possibly be beginning at a slightly earlier age than Jack (just over two) at the same nursery. I'll hate to give up that one-on-one time I have with my little girl, but it will certainly be a good idea for her to have gained a bit of independence before our third child arrives. I still think of her as my 'baby' and forget that she's almost two, with a determined little mind of her own which I think will benefit from some form of social nursery environment. After all, Andrea's Sam is already doing his three mornings there, so she won't be lonely.

In the meantime, I have found several ways of keeping the old brain cells ticking over, in the form of one or two projects. The largest of these has to be a major purchase we made when Jack was one year old and has pretty much been our family project ever since. Having always felt akin to the French culture, and most importantly its food and wine, I suppose it was only a matter of time before we bought an old French ruin to renovate. Our much-loved wreck is in a deeply rural part of France, in La Haute Marne, not far north of Dijon, and has become a regular retreat for us during most of the school holidays. I can let my creative skills loose down there, from decorating and curtain making to gardening, and making tarts with the fruit from the trees in the garden. Time permitting, it's a haven for artistic expression. In another bid to activate the grey matter last year, I took up a psychology course which, if nothing else, has persuaded me that I would like to study it at greater depth, probably when the children are a bit older and I have more time to devote to the subject.

Looking back at what I have been up to for the past five years, I have to admit that I am thoroughly enjoying life as an FTM, despite the obvious daily challenges such as finding myself at the beck and call of my husband when he gets home in the evening just after I have managed to get the children off to bed, whilst simultaneously preparing the supper. I still have a long way to go in perfecting that instantaneous and seamless switch – which real domestic goddesses manage to pull off – from snot-and-food-embalmed kids' punchbag to all-listening, all-understanding voice of sexually attractive – and interested – wife. Some nights all you really want to do after putting the children to bed is flop in front of *EastEnders* with a bottle of wine and a packet of crisps.

Fortunately, Tim is starting a new job in a couple of months time, which will mean a bit more international travel for him – and a bit more free-evening time for me! He has recently been on leave between jobs which has meant that he has been able to appreciate at first hand the stress levels that can be reached being at home with children all day. I think comments such as, 'Well, cancel a couple of coffee mornings this week and you might be able to fit in a trip to B&Q for me!' were always designed to provoke, but will now begin to ebb away, I hope. He now understands the need for us FTMs to have the occasional excuse to be able to whisk the pram out of the house, straight past the Hoover and the ironing board, and find solace for a couple of hours talking with other like-minded mothers whilst your toddler wrecks somebody else's house!

Here Comes the Sad Bit

It would have been lovely to say that we do not have enough material to write a chapter with such a depressing title, but unfortunately that is far from the truth.

When the five of us had our first children our lives were all pretty rose-tinted. We all had healthy incomes, happy homes and contented marriages. We also all had solid circles of friends and family, and had straightforward first pregnancies with happy, healthy babies at the end. What more could we want, and what could possibly go wrong for five such fortunate friends? We really were the epitome of Enid Blyton's Famous Five, 'with lashings of ginger beer'.

The fact that there are only four of us giving our life updates in the first chapter meant, for us, that this chapter simply had to cover the person missing from our club. To not do so would feel as though we were simply brushing Annette's death under the carpet, which is something we would and could never do.

As if this weren't enough, we have all also had various other tragedies thrown into our lives over the past five years, just to make sure that those 'rose-tinted glasses' aren't simply broken, but well and truly shattered. The huge plus that we can pull out of all of this is that, as each of us has had to endure our low points, the Fat Ladies' friendships has become even stronger.

So if you are prone to suffering from overemotional outbursts, this is the chapter to skip. If not, take a deep breath and get ready to face our soul-searching, tear-jerking 'sad bits'.

Hilary

*** *** ***

I'm going first again for this one, as I am the one who seemed to get the ball rolling when it came to things not running quite so silky smooth for the five of us. For me, parenthood coincided with a string of medical problems. None too traumatic or horrific, but certainly not what I needed at that point in my life. First, my pregnancy with Molly saw the grannyfication of my lower body! My legs and feet became a feature that even a lady in her eighties would quite frankly be disappointed with. I developed a delightful array of varicose veins and a fantastic bunion on my left foot. The varicose veins I remain the proud owner of, as I have not yet got around to surgical intervention for these, but the bunion soon became a major priority to sort out. Not only was it excruciatingly painful to walk any distance, but also I couldn't get shoes, of any passable style for a lady in her early thirties, that fitted. When I found myself genuinely considering doctoring my shoes by cutting a hole and letting the offending bunion stick out, as my nan had done for so many years, I realized that surgery was no longer merely an option, but was essential. When Molly was eleven months old, and I was extremely broody, I accepted that the conception of a second child would have to wait a couple of months until my foot was straight and I was painkiller-free. I had never left my little girl overnight before and the worry of leaving her far outweighed my fear of the general anaesthetic and the pain I was promised afterwards. The surgery went extremely smoothly, and Molly thrived in the arms of her 'Dan' (her word for Gran). I came home after two days with a knee-length plaster cast and was given strict instructions to rest and not fully bear weight on that leg. They say that nurses are the worst patients, and I have to hold up my hands and acknowledge that I am up there with the best of them. The word 'rest' is simply not in my vocabulary and, as I wasn't told to keep the foot off the ground completely, I felt that walking with a decent limp met with the doctor's instructions. To top it all, we were moving house a week later and David was in the middle of harvest and therefore unable to help with the packing, so my options for rest really were nonexistent. In the heat of summer, the stitches beneath the plaster on the 'resting' leg became so itchy that I was even considering tearing off the plaster with my bare hands and attacking them with a Brillo pad. In hindsight, I probably would have done myself far less damage if I had done exactly that. Instead, despite my medical knowledge, I used the stem of a flower from the Fat Ladies' 'Get well soon' bouquet to ram down the plaster and attack the offending stitch. It has taken me four years to admit to this out-and-out stupidity – I haven't even dared to tell David until this very moment. All I can think is that the itch seriously affected my cognitive skills for that brief moment. I mean, they don't let cut flowers anywhere near medical wards because of the risk of staphylococcal infections, so to physically rub one across an open wound was up there in the top ten blatantly barking moments of my life.

Two days later I noticed that my foot began to smell disgusting. At first I thought it was just cheesy unwashed feet, but when the smell became so bad that I wanted to leave my leg in another room, I knew things weren't great. The day before our move I felt like someone from the living dead. I smelt like a rotting corpse, so I got my mum to take me back to the hospital to get it sorted before the big move. The doctor cut off the plaster and, as he peeled it back, he and the nurse both visibly retched at the stench that wafted out and immediately admitted me and put up an IV antibiotic drip. I felt extremely sorry for myself to say the least, as I lay in hospital for a whole week while David and Molly

*Ramming the stem of a flower down my plaster to relieve an
itch has to be one of my most blatantly barking moments*

moved home. My mum and David soon fell into a neat little routine of caring for Molly, and after only a couple of days she couldn't have given two hoots whether she saw me or not. I had given her my all for the past year, 24/7, and the harsh reality of the fact that my child was totally fickle and my role as her mum was dispensable was gutting. As the icing on the cake, I didn't really have any sense of what or where my home was because of the move. When I did eventually go home, it felt as though I was a guest in David and Molly's house at first. I had to ask where things were kept and how things were done in the new house. I'm sure that during my stay the hospital staff must have thought I was mentally unstable, too. Prior to being a parent, I could deal with life logically and eloquently. Now, however, I seem to break down and blub at all the most inopportune moments. I couldn't conduct a sensible conversation about my medical condition without my voice rising an octave and tears welling up to the point that my nose dripped. I'm just one of those people who hates not being in control; when I knew I had done it to myself with that bloody carnation, there was a huge percentage of self-castigation as well as self-pity. This pathetic example of motherhood hit an all-time peak when I was told that the wound was too bad to reapply the plaster and so I would not be able to leave hospital in time for Molly's first birthday. All attempts to disguise my emotional outbursts were abandoned, and eventually the doctor agreed to reapply the plaster, leaving a window for the wound to be dressed through each day.

It was great to be home, but I still really should have been prescribed tranquillizers to ensure that the instruction to 'rest' was adhered to. I made it to Molly's first birthday party, though, which she shared with Bethan – although it was frustrating organizing the event from a chair whilst wielding a crutch to direct my poor mother-in-law to achieve all the tasks I couldn't accomplish myself. It was one of those magical mothering moments to see my first-born blow out the candle on her first birthday cake.

This foot fiasco set back by three months my mission to try for child number two. In the great scheme of things, this is no time at all, but my hormones were raging. Annette's bonny bump was blooming and Sarah had just announced that she was pregnant again, so those three months seemed more like years. We started trying two months after Molly's first birthday and I fell pregnant immediately. Life was back on track. But then in week eight I lost the baby. I don't know which is worse, a miscarriage with your first or one after you already have children. I'm sure whichever you experience it feels pretty devastating. Having not miscarried my first, I can't comment on that, but miscarrying my second certainly did feel like I was losing a child. We knew what that foetus had the potential to become because she was looking at us every day, in the form of Molly. I decided I needed to get away before trying again, and so I rang Sarah in Spain and booked a flight for Molly and me to go to spend a week with her. It was just the job – it rained nonstop, but we just sat eating and chatting for the whole week, while Jack and Molly ran riot around her gorgeous apartment. I even found it strangely therapeutic to embark on some maternity retail therapy, by proxy! Sarah was sixteen weeks pregnant, so we trawled the smartest maternity boutiques in San Sebastian as I helped her invest in all sorts of classy outfits for her ever expanding bump. Little did I realize what lay ahead for the rest of the gang and that I would be wearing those snazzy maternity clothes long before Sarah would have the opportunity to enjoy them, but that's a story for her to tell.

Shortly after my therapeutic, rejuvenating week in Spain, I fell pregnant with Ella only one month after my miscarriage. Annette gave birth to her second daughter, Megan, that month, when Emily was just sixteen months old. It was so strange to hear of all the perils and joys of the second child by phone. Annette had moved away from the area by then. Having lived so closely through the experiences of having our first children together, the geographical distance was suddenly painfully evident. Over the next few months, we all gradually started to piece together the different phone conversations we were having with her and realized that Annette was genuinely worried about her health – she told us all of the discomfort she was having in her guts and how she was struggling with tiredness. Annette was definitely not a moaner in life; she was a 'getta onna'. She never complained about anything, even when the rest of us would sit and dissect the walking domestic disaster zones we live with – otherwise known as husbands. She just wasn't prepared to compete for the Who's Got the Biggest Useless Git Award. She would laugh to the point of tears, but would never join in. It was because of this enviable personality trait that I began to become concerned for Annette's health when she kept mentioning it on the phone. For Annette to repeatedly complain of tiredness and pain, even after a baby, was just not something she would do unless it was severe. However, having said that, I am someone who likes to turn a drama into a crisis and always think the worst.

'Having a little knowledge can be a dangerous thing' – I think that's what the phrase is. Well, that sums me up perfectly. My learning disability nurse's training gave me a taster of all sorts of signs and symptoms of life-threatening ailments, but did not provide me with the broader picture of all the minor and easily treatable ailments those same signs and symptoms could also represent. This has pretty much turned me into the bearer of bad tidings when it comes to people's latest complaints. Rather than being the reassuring voice of logic, I turn into the medical equivalent of the Grim Reaper and start producing a mental list of all the possible terminal conditions it may be. So the others took my concerns for Annette's health with a pinch of salt. It was mortifying to discover that for once I was right.

Andrea was the mainstay in keeping close and regular contact with Annette and therefore keeping us updated and close to her, too. But even with their close bond, Annette certainly wouldn't have opened up about any concerns with her bowels. The trouble with those embarrassing body parts is that it usually takes people that bit longer to have them checked out when things aren't right. Not many people would rush to their GP to discuss their pooing habits or the lump in their testicles, in the same way that they would with an ear discharge or a lump in their foot. They are the sort of things we hope are temporary and will just go away on their own. Still, Annette did seem concerned from quite soon after having Megan, but then lethargy, stomach pains and disrupted bowels are hardly unusual symptoms for anyone straight after having a baby, so it did take a few months for the cancer to be detected.

When Annette told us she had bowel cancer, again she was nothing but positive, and this positive state of mind remained throughout her exhausting months of treatment for the next year. If being friends with Annette for this brief spell in my life taught me anything, it was to make the most of whatever is thrown at me and to stop looking for things to moan about. The self-pitying summer I had experienced the year before was suddenly a mere pimple compared to the volcanic boil that was erupting in Annette's life.

Since Annette's death, life has been pretty traumatic for both the Gardeners and the Greens (my maiden name). Last year, when I was five months pregnant with our third child, David's eldest brother, Chris, committed suicide. He had been suffering from depression for a couple of years, but to die in such a way at thirty-eight just seems so pointless. We are all having to come to terms with the fact that for some sufferers of depression it can be as terminal an illness as cancer and absolutely no 'if onlys' are going to help. Chris lived on the same farm as us, with his wife and two young boys, and was part of the farming partnership with David. David didn't just lose his brother, but also one of his business partners who he worked with on a daily basis. If you work for someone else and something like this happens in your family, you take time off. For David, his other brother, Richard, and his father, it meant that they instantly had to take into consideration how they were going to fill the gaps from Chris's working day, as well as face the prospect of doing their own jobs after such a horrendous loss. Livestock can't be put on hold – they need feeding. Emotions are all still so raw that I don't want to and don't think it appropriate to dwell on this, but to have let this chapter pass without so much as mentioning this life-changing, horrendous loss in our families' lives would have been so wrong.

Finally, just as my mother and father were retiring and planning an active and worldly future, my father was diagnosed with multi-system atrophy. This is basically a degenerative disease causing the gradual breakdown of all the body's systems. Over the past couple of years since his diagnosis, he has gone from being a sporting, albeit mainly social, active, outgoing man, to someone who is totally dependent on my mum. He is no longer able to care for himself or get about unaided. The loss for both him and my mum is immeasurable, as not only has his life been completely turned upside down, but so, too, has hers.

For me, the guilt of not being able to help my family more, combined with the raging hormone imbalance of having a third child, did trigger a minor bout of postnatal depression after the birth of Alfie. I didn't recognize the signs at first, as I was so besotted with my boy that I couldn't begin to see how it could be postnatal depression. I say a 'minor' bout because it is definitely something I am managing to fight without medication. Some days I feel as if I am trudging through mud, I can't face getting up, I'm snappy and churlish with the girls, I'm on a short fuse with David – and then the self-loathing kicks in. The guilt of feeling so lousy when I have so much to be happy about is almost palpable. Then the blubbing starts, and once it has started it's set in for the day. Luckily the good days do now far outweigh the bad and, with my resolution to adopt Annette's positive philosophy on life always in the back of my mind, I do feel that I'm winning the battle.

Sarah

* * *

Following on from Hilary makes me feel an exceptionally lucky person when I see in print what she has had to deal with in her life since I have known her. When I was twenty-five and living in Paris, someone I worked with once said to me that I always gave the impression of being happy. My reply was that I had everything to be happy about – I had a fun, well-paid job with BT, a solid and loving relationship with Tim, a wonderful family and large network of friends who often visited us in our flat in the centre of the French capital, so what possibly was there in my life to make me 'unhappy'? With both of us enjoying a healthy, sporty lifestyle, it meant that we were probably at our peak. Almost ten years on, I cannot say that either of us has suffered extraordinary periods of sadness since then, but I think it's certainly true to say that, as we have grown older, and we have seen friends' lives change so dramatically as a result of the passage of time, we have definitely learnt to value the precious things in our lives much more. Having children of our own has inevitably enhanced this, and we don't take life for granted as much as we once did. Learning to appreciate the bonuses in life and to realize the lack of control one has over the sudden pitfalls that may lie ahead is a reality check and one which we have been exposed to on a few occasions over the past five years.

The first 'blip' in our otherwise rosy life came shortly after Hilary and Molly visited us in Spain. As Hilary has already said, I was sixteen weeks pregnant and discovered just how good a friend she was when it came to spending my money for me! She was like a woman possessed in the Spanish maternity boutiques, with a voracious desire to spend, spend and carry on spending.

If it hadn't been for the horror that happened, I'm sure this would have led to one of those marital disputes, arguing the justifiable confiscation of my Visa card! However, only a few days after the frivolous shopping spree, Tim and I returned to England for the sixteen-week dating scan, which coincides with the triple blood test. It was then that we discovered that our baby had died. The scan revealed no foetal heartbeat, and what had begun as a morning of excitement with the anticipation of seeing my baby for the first time had ended in fear and disbelief. I will never forget the sonographer's face as she broke the news to us in the most sympathetic way she could. I had difficulty knowing how to handle her apparent disappointment and discomfort at having to deal with this delicate situation. Tim, with his forever pragmatic approach to life, said something like, 'Well, these things happen,' but I knew that his shock and disappointment were just as great as mine – except I just lay there in stunned silence.

After further examination by the consultant and registrar, it was decided that it would be best for me to be induced in order to deliver the baby and placenta as naturally as possible. I had hoped that I could have a quick 'D&C' under general anaesthetic to sort the problem out instantly, but there was concern over a potential haemorrhage due to the size of the placenta. It was such a surreal experience; it didn't feel as though it was really happening to me at all. The fact that Jack was having a tantrum on the floor beside the couch – because he was tired after our long journey home from Spain the night before – was a problem that Tim was left to manage single-handedly: I had already gone into internal 'mind over matter' mode in order to deal with the situation. I needed to concentrate 100 per cent on what I had to do mentally to get myself through the shock of this missed miscarriage. The first and most embarrassing thing that it meant for my body was the uncontrollable need to empty my bowels . . . immediately. When I look back now, I can laugh, but at the time, despite the mind-numbing shock I was experiencing, I still managed to feel mortally embarrassed to have to run to the toilets, normally reserved for ladies relieving their bladders after their scans, to empty the contents of my entire intestines in a matter of milliseconds. I'm surprised that the hospital didn't cordon off the area in order to identify the cause of the explosion occurring in the antenatal outpatients department.

After our week together in Spain, it was Hilary that I phoned to explain the outcome of the scan. As I calmly and logically told her how I would be going back into hospital later to undergo the unavoidable procedure, my mind was in total overdrive. My emotions were on hold as I dealt with practicalities like doing a quick family food shop, arranging for Jack to be looked after for the weekend and cancelling the girlie get-together I had planned to take place at our house the following day. Hilary sounded decidedly wobbly as she absorbed the grief she knew I was suppressing and quickly undertook the task of phoning all my friends to cancel the get-together. Ironically, this had been the first day I had ventured out in my newly acquired Spanish 'fat lady' clothes. Needless to say, I changed out of them the second I got home from the scan: going to the supermarket and bumping into people I knew whilst wearing obvious maternity clothes would have freaked me out. I suddenly felt like a total fraud. Although the baby was still inside me, knowing it was no longer alive meant that my rights to pleading pregnancy had immediately and abruptly ceased that morning. We had been given the option to take a couple of days to come to terms with our loss, before going through labour, but I found it a completely black-and-white decision to make and didn't want to waste any time in getting it 'sorted'.

It wasn't until after I was through the worst scare of all – a bad haemorrhage after the delivery – that I allowed my emotions to take over. I was reading through the hospital ward's Book of

Remembrance, which I had initially declined to write in, when I spontaneously shed the first tears. Maybe it was reading about other families' losses, or it may simply have been the relief that I wasn't alone in my experience, that prompted the outburst. I instantly felt the need to write something and wrote, 'To my little girl that I'll never know,' and it surprised me how much this small act helped me in my grief. It left me feeling complete in that I had at least acknowledged her existence – however short that existence had been.

Tim and I had wanted to have our children relatively close together: it seemed the most logical path was for us to have our family whilst I wasn't working and we were spending our time between Spain and the UK. Everything had been going according to plan: falling pregnant so easily second time around and reaching an apparently 'safe' sixteen weeks of pregnancy. We suddenly felt as though fate had ripped these best-laid plans straight out of our hands. Those next weeks immediately afterwards saw me hugging Jack regularly very close to my side and wanting to spend a lot more quality time with him, as I appreciated the simple fact of his existence so much more than before.

It was another four months before I felt strong enough, emotionally and physically, to embark on pregnancy for a third time, and thankfully I fell pregnant straight away again. Life was back on track, or so we thought. I then had a second miscarriage, this time whilst in Spain. I was twelve weeks pregnant when I had a slight bleed, and, because of what happened last time, we headed straight to the local Spanish hospital for what we hoped would be a reassuring scan. I think I already knew deep down, even before the gel was applied to my stomach, that once again there would be no heartbeat. As I had already started to bleed, I was sent home to wait for the inevitable. That weekend we also had our friends Emma and Guy to stay. Fortunately they are very close friends who proved to be a huge comfort rather than an added complication. Thankfully, with Ems being a nurse, she was able to allay my fears over the amount of blood I was losing: I wasn't about to peg it as I had suspected.

What was different about this miscarriage was that I had already had time to go through the emotional grieving before the physical bit happened. Although I felt a million miles from people that could help me and sympathize, especially the local Berkhamsted midwives who are always a source of great reassurance, I felt sure that my body could sort it out naturally this time. Thankfully it did. At the time, I felt desperate that we would never be able to relive the joy of having another baby in our lives – I had even reached the point of questioning Tim about his opinions on adoption. Added to this, I felt a real guilt that we might never be able to give Jack the fun of a balanced upbringing with siblings. I always said that I would never fully get over losing the pregnancies until I had had a healthy second child. And how lucky we were with having our darling Eloise almost exactly three years after Jack was born (twenty-one months after my first miscarriage). Her arrival immediately dispelled any concerns that I had about not being able to carry girls. When her little face looked up at me and Tim, as Jo the midwife laid her on my chest, it achieved a massive 'turning of the page' in our lives, which made the birthing moment even more emotionally charged than it would normally have been.

The sadness surrounding a miscarriage still catches me unawares sometimes. Even with the passage of time, I can find myself getting a lump in the throat when the subject comes up of 'losing babies', even though my losses were fortunately quite early in comparison to others. It is also quite surprising to discover just how many women have had miscarriages when you start talking openly about it. I find it is always the lost hopes and dreams for that pregnancy which are difficult to overcome, as well as the frustration of often never knowing *why* it happened at all. In my case, I never had any proof of what had caused the pregnancies to fail, but I certainly curtailed the amount of flying I did in the first three months of my next pregnancy, just in case I was in some way susceptible to problems caused by high altitude. Having flown almost a dozen times during the first lost pregnancy, and a few less during the second, it was more for my peace of mind that I followed this ban on flying than as a result of any medically approved advice.

Throughout all of those months, the other Fat Ladies were a source of strength for lots of reasons – the unspoken understanding from Hilary, who even treated me to a rejuvenating and therapeutic massage at a local salon, as a get-well present after my first miscarriage, and the letters of constant support from Annette, now that she was living away. She always gave the rest of us and our mini-crises in life so much time, and she treated them as though they far outweighed that 'trivial hiccup' in her life known as cancer. It was as though she needed to concentrate her thoughts elsewhere in order to momentarily blank out the severity of her own situation. She tackled the disease with grit determination, endlessly researching every possible angle of treatment. As well as following conventional medicine, she was taking, amongst other things, powdered shark's bone and adopting a more vegetarian lifestyle. True to her usual form, she was also contemplating setting up a website with all the information that she had managed to accumulate. She wanted to help others in her position to have easy access to all the options available, through one comprehensive site, instead of having to trawl the entire Web as she had done. Unfortunately she was never able to accomplish her mission.

I was just pregnant with Eloise when I heard the news that Annette's condition had become terminal; my fears of a third miscarriage paled into insignificance. A couple of weeks later, she brought Emily and Megan over to stay with Andrea, and we all met up for what was to be the last occasion that all the Fat Ladies and their children were to be together. We went to a children's farm where it was packed from fence to fence with mothers and their children running around mauling the extremely tolerant livestock. How she stopped herself from screaming at the top of her voice, 'IT'S JUST NOT FAIR!' I'll never know. She looked so deceptively healthy and even said that she hadn't felt so well in ages – the diet she was following combined with the alternative therapies she was taking were making her feel quite buoyant. I remember her saying how cruel it was that she was feeling so well when inside she knew things were far from right. The thought that she would never live to see her little girls have their first periods, graduate from university or even get married was far too painful for her to dwell on. All this morbid talk didn't seem relevant somehow, as I stood talking to this apparently healthy young mum on this sunny autumn morning. She even managed to laugh about a recent conversation she had had with her husband, Gavin. She explained how she had told him that she didn't want him wasting his life, forever mourning her after she had died, and how he must build himself a new life and find a new woman. But just as I was admiring how pragmatic she was about the whole issue, she added with a big smirk, 'but woe betide him if he goes looking before I die . . . I'll kill him!' I can't imagine how people find the strength to make light of something like this when they must be feeling such despair and desperation inside.

Sadly, Annette was not the only close friend of ours who died young of cancer in the past five years. Our best man and very dear friend, Guy, was also a victim of this indiscriminate disease. Guy had suffered from cancer since his teens and defied all medical expectations of how long he had to live. It still hits hard, even a year on from his death, to realize that he is no longer with us. Annette touched my life for a relatively brief period of time, but during one of those periods where friendship is cemented instantly due to a shared life event. Losing her hit hard because it was my first experience of death within my own age group and because she was someone who was in exactly the same position in her life as myself. Suddenly the reality of mortality was very evident: it could have been any one of my friends . . . it could have been me. Losing Guy, however, was like losing a limb for us. He had been part of my life ever since Tim and I had been together. It was only two years earlier that I had been so grateful that it had been him and Emma staying with us in San Sebastian when I had my second miscarriage. I had really appreciated their strength and understanding at a time when I was feeling particularly vulnerable. He had a wicked sense of humour, driving ambition and a seemingly endless ability to defy death, which left us firmly believing that he was indestructible. And so it was such a massive blow to return from a weekend away to discover that the disease had finally beaten him. Always believing he would bounce back yet again, we were even robbed of the chance to say a proper goodbye. Tim had wanted to visit him in hospital before we went away, but as he had a cold he decided to put it off until our return for fear of passing on any unwelcome germs. If only we had known – but that is a harsh reality we have come to understand over the past few years: life is full of unknowns.

As I have, dare I say, 'matured' with experience over the years, I find that my happy-go-lucky image that I used to portray in my Paris days has certainly mellowed, and I have become a lot more pragmatic about life. If there's one thing I've learnt over the last five years, it is to live for today . . .

Andrea

* * *

Until Annette's illness, I was in the fortunate position of never knowing anybody close who had suffered from cancer, but this also made me particularly naive about it. It sounds awful to write this, but when she first told me that the investigations into her bowels had found a cancerous lump, which had been removed, I wasn't overly concerned. As far as my non-medical mind was concerned, the lump had gone and the chemotherapy treatment she was facing was purely precautionary; my friend was fine.

Throughout the months of treatment that followed, Annette and I developed a routine as to which days of the week we could call each other and when she was wiped out. I am such a phonaholic, though, that, needless to say, I did manage to call her on a couple of occasions, slap bang in the middle of her 'wipe-out' zone. It was then that I realized just what hard work the chemo was; on the good days, she managed to sound so bright and positive, but on the dodgy days she sounded as though she had just woken up with the world's worst hangover. Even then she still managed to feign polite responses to my ramblings, but it was so much better when I did manage to curtail my desire to call whenever I wanted to and fit in with her; after all, my phone does have a listening bit as well as a talking bit, and it was great to catch up on Emily and Megan, too! I don't know what it is with me and phones, but I really am addicted to them. I like to call people the minute I think of something I need to tell them, never mind the time of day that might be cheaper. I couldn't possibly wait until 2 p.m. or, heaven forbid, 6 p.m. just because of reduced rates; if news needs telling, it needs telling now. I also absolutely hate the thought of messages being on my answer machine that I haven't picked up, so even if I'm only out of my house for half a day I find myself calling in to my machine, and if I ever forget my mobile . . . it just doesn't bear thinking about. So for me to train my brain to curtail my calls to Annette really did take some doing, and by the time our weekly chats came around I was absolutely itching to catch up with her.

Annette was told that the cancer was incurable just after I had given birth to Sam. When I heard the news I just sat sobbing, tears dripping onto my tiny new baby, as I thought of all the things my friend would never experience with her two precious children. But after a conversation with Annette a couple of days later, I had adopted her positive philosophy again. Despite being told her condition was terminal, she was determined to beat this disease using whatever means possible, and I was going to support her all the way.

Our routine of weekly catch-up calls carried on for the next few months. With her positive attitude to the pioneering treatment she was trying, I was totally oblivious to how fast the evil disease was, in fact, taking hold of her. In the end Hilary, I think for my own good, had to be quite forthright in telling me that she did not think Annette had long left. Through her own chats with Annette, Hils had realized how serious things were.

It was incredibly fortuitous that a couple of months earlier the four of us had made plans to take a night off from our children and visit Annette at this time. Little had we realized that it would be our last visit, within the last week of her life. We travelled over there in two cars, and it was on this journey that Hilary was hit with the full impact of my unfortunate habit – getting the giggles during times of turmoil. There was absolutely nothing funny about the last ten minutes of our journey and, really, parking the car was a pretty straightforward experience, too, but that didn't stop me. You'd have thought that Ben Elton was in the back of the car doing a stand-up comedy routine by the state

I was in! I was positively whooping with laughter, the tears running down my face, and it was all down to sheer nerves. This is an extremely unfortunate habit in my job, too; the other key moments in my life that these anxiety giggles frequently threaten to take hold are when I am about to give evidence in Crown Court. Thankfully, to date, I have always managed to get a grip of myself just before I take the oath and have not yet done a full-blown impression of the laughing policeman in front of the judge.

Well, this occasion was one of the most nerve-racking moments in my life, but thankfully I managed to get control just before I went in to see Annette. I had left Hilary outside, so I could have a while with Annette alone. I was still giggling as I left her, but, as soon as I rounded the corner into Annette's room, my hysteria immediately subsided and I just hugged my poorly buddy. We all spent the afternoon with her before saying our goodbyes. It was so lovely just being able to spend time with her, catching up, the five of us together again. But every conversation seemed to end abruptly as the painful realization that Annette didn't have a future hit us. It was simple things like telling Annette about taking Max to the cinema for the first time. This sparked off a general conversation about who had and hadn't taken their children to the cinema yet, and Annette joined in by saying that she didn't think Emily would sit through the whole film yet . . . 'Maybe she will this summer.' Silence struck as we all welled up at the painful truth that this was just one of the millions of first experiences she would not have with her girls. Thankfully Annette had a task for us that day: to help her put pen to paper to write letters for Emily and Megan from their mummy. This now sounds like something from a tear-jerking film script, but at the time it was an honour and privilege to help her do this and a relief to have a useful function at a time when we all felt so unbelievably helpless. The real honour for me, though, was that

Annette entrusted these letters to me, to read to her daughters at the right times. She knew that that way I would never lose touch with the girls, and they would always have a memory of their mum from her friends, as well as her family.

It was while I was at work, a few days later, that I received the news that Annette had died. I took some time off and walked straight up to Sarah's house. I felt totally numb as I rang the bell and said the words that really didn't need saying at all. Sarah knew – my face had told her everything. We just stood in her hallway and hugged each other in total silence. It was then that I felt the kick from her bonny six-month bump, objecting to my closeness, and I remember thinking how bizarre life is. We were all friends because we had created life together and yet, so soon afterwards, one of us had already lost hers.

Up until eight months ago, I would have been able to end this chapter here. Apart from a stressful second pregnancy, which I'll cover later, my life was pretty straightforward and stress-free, but now I'm facing the top two stresses in life: moving home and separating from my husband. Thankfully I have had some fantastic support from friends and family, which has so far helped me to keep my sanity.

Bruce first broke the news to me that he was unsure of what he wanted in life two weeks before Christmas. It's amazing how Christmas does this sort of thing to people; apparently a huge percentage of marriages break up during the festive season. I wonder then if the national divorce statistics would dramatically reduce if there was a ban on Christmas? Anyway, having dropped this delightful clanger into the conversation, he then threw me into a four-week limbo by saying that he didn't want to discuss it any further until the New Year.

I needed an ear to bend at this time. As Bruce and I had only just returned from a weekend away in Amsterdam with Hilary and David, it was Hilary I called. She had spotted that Bruce wasn't his usual self with me whilst we were away, and we had only talked about this the day before. Neither of us had even the slightest inkling that my questioning the change in my husband's mood would be the trigger for the end of my marriage. Those next few weeks, which turned into months, while I waited for Bruce to 'work out what he wanted' really dragged. I needed to call in a second sounding board, in the form of a close police friend, Jane, mainly to give Hilary's ears the occasional day off. Jane and Hilary were both adamant that Bruce would realize what a prat he was being and make a decent comeback, but, despite the fact that our marriage was carrying on as normal, I knew in my heart that Bruce had already left home. I didn't dare talk to anyone else during this time, not even my family, who I am very close to, nor Lyns or Sarah. I knew that when they did find out they would be so hurt that I hadn't turned to them, but I needed to keep the number in the know to a bare minimum just in case, by some small miracle, we managed to work things out. It's always embarrassing when you give your friend's partner a decent supportive slating when they're being treated badly and then have to do a dramatic back-pedal when they rekindle their flames of passion! I didn't want to put anyone in this position and also didn't want people thinking what a saddo I was to accept him back after what he had done to damage our seemingly perfect marriage.

It took Bruce four months to reach his final conclusion that we had no future, and we decided straight away to put the house on the market and make a clean break of it. Initially I actually felt an element of relief that at least a decision had been made and I could start planning my future. But the reality that I was facing the future as a single mum, without my best friend, sporting soul mate and lover all rolled into one, was soon smacking me in the face in tidal waves of emotion. The hardest part has been telling people, largely because it is a bolt out of the blue for everyone and always requires a lengthy explanation. If there was someone else involved, I could simply say, 'He's having an affair.' If I didn't want to elaborate that would be enough said, but to say 'He's in love with his career' somehow doesn't have the same effect. You can instantly see their looks of cynical sympathy as they clearly think that I'm a total mug for believing there is no third party. I have had to harden myself to deal with people's disbelief by training myself to realize that, at the end of the day, I know the truth about my marriage and that's all that really matters. Because this has all been so hard, though, there are, in fact, some people who still don't know. As I move in two weeks time, I am going to have a whole new round of explanations to make when people receive my change of address cards with just Andrea, Max and Sam on them. There's something to look forward to!

Over the past eight months I have gone through the full gamut of emotions, from crying myself to sleep night after night, to wanting to shave off Bruce's goatee beard while he slept. Never liked the thing anyway. One day I would be driving home from work listening to a song that would trigger me off. I would be full of thoughts of how much I still loved him and couldn't cope without him and would need windscreen wipers on my eyeballs to make it home. But later that very evening, just one comment about his money-making skills at work and I'd be ready to shove a pair of sweaty socks down his throat if he so much as thought about doing his habitual tickly cough that I used to find endearing. I think it's a good thing that the months before moving dragged on, and we gradually drifted apart. I don't have nearly as many blubby moments, and I think I have accepted things. It also helps that I will be back in Berkhamsted in the heart of Fat Ladies' land again. Don't get me wrong, I have been deeply hurt by these events, but I am not about to mourn his loss for the rest of my life.

My main concerns now are Max and Sam, and how they will come to terms with things. Any tears I have now are usually triggered by thoughts of my boys and their loss, not mine. I also worry about coping with the responsibility of being a single parent. I am very much aware of the fact that I am a complete soft touch when it comes to parenting – Bruce is certainly the stricter of the two of us – and I do worry that they will turn into a pair of wild, rebellious louts over which I have no control. I know I'm overreacting, but since deciding to separate I seem to have had more jobs at work involving the need to arrest tearaway youths from broken homes than I previously had in my entire fourteen-year career. I know there must be as many well-balanced teenagers from broken homes out there, but my career doesn't bring me into contact with them. Both Bruce and I are united in our desire to get it right for the boys, and Bruce, I must stress, still adores them and fully intends to play a very active role in their upbringing. There is no way that I will ever let my children hear anything negative about their father from me, which is going to be tongue-bitingly tricky at times, but there is nothing worse for kids than feeling piggy in the middle of two parents they love equally, so I am determined on this one.

We had a huge decision to make about when we felt it was best to tell the boys. We didn't want to tell them, then have the move delayed for months, which is exactly what has happened, so we decided to wait until contracts were exchanged and we had a definite moving date. As we were still living amicably under the same roof, albeit in separate bedrooms, we were able to get away with this without it affecting the boys. I was dreading telling them. They are so young and innocent, and in their little minds they are safe with Mummy and Daddy. I hated the thought of them having something like this to worry about at such young ages. Sam, who is not yet three, I do not expect to fully understand and I am not overly concerned about him, as he is a mummy's boy anyway. Max, on the other hand, is besotted with his father and has always been quite sensitive to change, so I strongly suspect he may struggle. With the move now booked in for two weeks time, we recently sat them both down and broke the news to them. This is not an experience I would ever like to repeat, although Max did come out with a few corking comments. As I started to tell them, before I'd even finished my first sentence, Max burst into floods of tears and sobbed his heart out. He was desperately trying to talk, but we couldn't understand a word he said through his howling and sobbing. Bruce and I were beside ourselves, our hearts were breaking at what we were doing to our little boy. Then we finally worked out what he was asking . . . 'What about *The Simpsons*?' We were so relieved at the triviality of his concerns it was a job not to smile, but once we had reassured him that he could watch *The Simpsons* in the evening at Mummy's house, even though Daddy wouldn't be there, his pain visibly subsided. We explained that they would have toys in each house, videos in each house and even an Arsenal bedroom in each house. We did the full chat about how this wasn't happening because of anything they had done, it was all Daddy and Mummy's fault and nobody else's, and Max sat taking it all in. Then the heart-rending questions started like, 'What if Daddy gets lonely when he's on his own, or you get sad when you're on your own?' This was when one of my first tongue-biting experiences kicked in, and I managed to smile and assure him that he could ring Daddy or me if that happened.

Sam, in the meantime, had sat smiling throughout this dis-cussion. He had been fascinated by Max's emotional outburst, then became sidetracked into asking for his usual bedtime hot milk. I asked him if he understood what we had been saying. 'Yes,' he said, grinning happily. 'So who will be living in our new house?' I asked. 'Daddy, Mummy, Max and Sam,' he said. He had obviously been totally oblivious to the entire conversation's content and so Bruce and I had to start all over again. He does appear to understand now, but I think we will have to repeat the conversation on a daily basis. Even then, I don't think he will fully understand until he has his first stay at Daddy's new house.

My last remaining fears about life as a single mum are the practical ones. The simple things like not being able to go for a run in the evenings or just pop out somewhere. The logistical things like not being able to use a baby-sitter who can't drive or get themselves home, and the public things like being partnerless at social functions. Attending weddings and christenings won't be a huge change practically because Bruce was always a bit antisocial and avoided any function like this anyway. So the actual attending alone won't be strange, but it's the change in status that I'll find hard. Suddenly I will no longer be Andrea, whose husband is at home or away on business. I will have to boldly wear the 'I've a failed marriage' label, which somehow still doesn't feel like something that could possibly be happening to me.

Lyndsey

***

We thought that the sex chapter was difficult to write in *The Fat Ladies Club*, but I think this one has to be the most challenging one in this book. So where should I start? I suppose at the beginning, once Bethan was born, or even pre-Bethan. Whilst Tim and I decided to leave our child-bearing to fate or in the lap of the gods, we never really discussed how many children we would like. I have an older brother and Tim has seven siblings. When I first met him and we talked about our families, I couldn't believe my ears as the list of brothers and sisters just kept going on and on; suddenly it wasn't a family, it was a school! Thankfully it hadn't rubbed off on Tim, though, and one thing I knew for a fact was that he certainly didn't want to match his parents in this stake. If he had, I would have been hotfooting it out the door before we had even finished our first date. Other than that, though, we hadn't ever discussed the matter. Just achieving the figure of one was about as much as either of us allowed ourselves to think.

Once Bethan was born, as far as the pregnancy and birth bit goes, I really felt that I had been there, done that and was proudly adorned in the T-shirt. I didn't feel inclined to go through the experience again in a hurry, if at all. I knew quite a few only children, and they seemed to have turned out okay and had not felt as though they had missed out on not having a brother or sister. Another factor that deterred me was that Bethan was such a good baby. Why should this deter me? I hear you ask. Surely this is just the sort of baby to have to lure you into a false sense of security to go for it a second time? Well, I had spent many an occasion listening to the agonizing tales of my parents about what a little horror I was in my infant years to the extent that both they and I needed to be drugged in order for any of us to get a good night's sleep. My mum had spent years ready to reap her revenge should I give birth to a nightmare child and was amazed at what an angel Bethan was. I thought if we did go for number two, my chances of the offspring having my infant temperament would be pretty high, and this was enough to deter me. Why rock the boat? As a family of three, we were getting settled into our routine.

The turning point, however, was Annette's illness, diagnosis and eventual death. A huge comfort to me during this time was the fact that at least Emily had not been an only child and she had her sister Megan – they had each other. Increasingly my concerns haunted me – what if something happened to Tim and me, and Bethan was left an only child? I know that her guardians would love and cherish her, but suddenly that wasn't enough. I wanted her to have her own flesh and blood, and so as Bethan's second birthday approached we started to try again for another child. I had fallen pregnant so easily with Bethan that it didn't occur to me that this wouldn't happen again. Little did we know what the next two years had in store for us.

Once again, I fell pregnant pretty quickly – just after Bethan's second birthday – but lost the baby at about six weeks. Although I hadn't done a test to confirm the pregnancy, the fact that my period was so late, heavy and painful held all the signs of a spontaneous rejection. It was after this that the agonizing wait each month and my obsession with my menstrual cycle began. As each month passed and the first day of my period approached, I felt a mixture of excitement and anticipation. Was this going to be it? Was this going to be the month that I had conceived? Was I feeling premenstrual? I tried to keep my emotions on a level pegging, but it was an impossibility. No matter how I tried to tell myself to keep calm and not get too excited, I couldn't help but feel the excitement of anticipation. When my period came I just cried in disbelief, asking myself why it was happening to me, when it had all been so easy with Bethan.

When my period arrived a day or so early the next month, I still felt sick in the pit of my stomach at failing again. The months rolled by and I'm sure I started to lose my sanity. I had hoped it wouldn't take over my life, but once you get yourself on this roller-coaster ride you just can't get off. You either have to wait until it stops or you fall out, hurting yourself, big time. Furthermore, I had never considered myself to be a superstitious person, but I became haunted by magpies and the 'One for sorrow, two for joy, three for a girl, four for a boy' rhyme (I wasn't interested in the silver, gold or story never to be told).

*I became obsessed by magpies, so much so that I nearly burst
into tears every time I saw one*

Each month, as the day that my period was due approached, I
would be driving to work and began to notice the solitary magpie
perched at the side of the motorway or in the staff car park at
work. Sure enough, a couple of days later my period would start.
I became obsessed, so much so that I nearly burst into tears every
time I saw a lone bird, knowing the implication that would have
for me later in the month. The worst occasion was when I finally
did fall pregnant eighteen months later, when Bethan was three
and a half. I can't remember if I had seen two, three or four
magpies prior to my positive pregnancy test, but I can still
remember the single magpie that hopped on to the fence post
next to my car in the car park at work two weeks later. I saluted

it, as the old wives' tale indicates, to try to deflect the bad luck, but I couldn't believe it when, four days later, I started to bleed. There was nothing I could do. I had lost the baby. All I could think was how it had taken me eighteen months to get there and whether I had another eighteen months ahead of me before I could experience the joy of pregnancy again. At that point I felt as though I had fallen off the roller coaster and wasn't sure that I wanted to get back on only to be hurt so badly again. I wasn't sure I could cope with the monthly highs and lows any more. What's more, when you already have a child, the timescale of conceiving or losing a baby is made worse by the presence of your fast-growing first child. Each month that passed was another month to add to the age gap, and I began to reach a point of questioning whether it was in fact too late. The ever-increasing age gap meant that the siblings would no longer be growing up together as I had longed for.

I decided to climb back aboard the roller coaster, though, and go for tests to check my fertility status to see whether there was a medical reason for the length of time it was taking to conceive and for the miscarriages. A barrage of tests began: blood tests, internals and scans. As I waited anxiously for the result, it felt like an eternity. Many of the tests were linked to the menstrual cycle and hence it took several months for all avenues to be checked. The only thing that kept me level-headed throughout it all was the fact that I was a very lucky woman. I had a beautiful, healthy daughter already and, if a second was not to be, I was thankful for Bethan. The results were back and all was well. This was good news, said the gynaecologist, but for me it was difficult to comprehend. If there had been a fault, at least I would have had something to blame and focus on, but being told to go away and relax did not give me the reassurance that I needed. During this time, Tim was feeling the pressure, as he feared that I may be sending him for tests, and he didn't want to think about what that may entail. As I poured my heart out to Hilary, Sarah and Andrea over dinner, I had their sympathetic ear. I, too, was now experiencing the pain and emotion that Sarah and Hilary had been through previously with their miscarriages, and I decided that I was going to be the Fat Ladies' statistic of not being able to have a second. Of course, the others couldn't let the situation pass without adding a few tips, which they found highly amusing. Their best advice was that I buy myself a turkey baster, as they had read that in the olden days this is what women would use if they experienced difficulties conceiving naturally. I don't know what books they read, but I was already having problems enough suggesting Tim went for medical tests, never mind asking him to fill a pot, then help me baste my proverbial turkey. So I put that suggestion on the back burner. Thanks, girls, but no thanks.

So it was back to the monthly nightmare that so many women experience. I, too, was obsessed with planning and confirming my ovulation and acting on it at precisely the right time, followed by the waiting game. I spent a small fortune on ovulation tests and the 'making love' had gone beyond passion to functional and mechanical. I finally managed to fall pregnant and hang on to the baby just before Bethan's fourth birthday, two long and agonizing years after our first attempt and six months after my second miscarriage.

During this time, Annette's death occurred, and the prospect of attending the funeral approached. This was going to be a huge mountain for us to climb and conquer, but at least, as the Fat Ladies Club, we had each other and decided to travel together. Panic struck days before the funeral as Andrea had been asked to do a reading during the service and was just given the reference to locate the passage in the Bible. Not possessing a Bible and being of Greek Orthodox origin, she started her search for the said verses on the Internet, but even being the PC whiz that she is she failed to find it. She then started phoning the whole world and his brother in a desperate bid to get it right. What bigger request can be asked of you than to read at your friend's funeral, and what bigger boo-boo could you make than to get it wrong?! When she phoned me in the vain hope that as an occasional churchgoer I may be able to bail her out, she drew yet another blank. '. . . But don't worry, Andrea, I'll ask my dad,' I heartily reassured her. I had total confidence in him, but not even our family Bible could trace the verses. So, at the last minute, Andrea had to call Annette's mum and ask her to send the text. It was all cut a bit fine, but with hours to go Andrea finally had the reading in her hands so that she would be able to have a quiet practice.

The day of the funeral arrived and I offered to drive, which was a shrewd move on my part as I was forced to concentrate on the 100-mile journey rather than on the event of the day. When the other three arrived at my house, I instructed Andrea to sit in the front next to me as she needed to be separated from Hilary, who may have sent her into emotional turmoil before we had even got ten miles down the road. Sarah and her mohair maternity cardigan were also banished to the back seat to be as far away from me and my allergy to fluffy jumpers as possible. I could then at least arrive at the church without itchy, red, tearful eyes, even though I knew I'd be leaving with them, for entirely different reasons. And so we set off on the journey that we were dreading. Four friends brought closer by circumstance. Next to me, Andrea was dressed uncomfortably in the only skirt she possessed, clutching her piece of paper. She used the journey to practise her reading between her nervous giggling bouts. Her biggest fear was whether she was emotionally up to it; it was going to be a tough one. So, we allocated a 'takeover' chain should she begin to blub. Thankfully I was allocated last position, as I was obviously unable to rehearse the reading whilst driving up the M40.

The whole event, as expected, was a mind-numbing, emotionally draining, tear-jerking trauma which was punctuated by the sound of a noisy, breastfeeding baby, slurping away at the back of the church. This was so painfully reminiscent of the noises Emily had made with Annette only two and a half years earlier. We said our goodbyes to our friend, whom we had known for such a short but extremely intimate time in our lives. When we got into the car to return home, silence struck. We were all drained and exhausted, and no words could even begin to quantify how we felt. Even Hilary was stunned into silence for once in her life. Half an hour into the journey, the constant sound of the rain on the roof and the rhythmic squeak of the wipers on the windscreen became too much. We all needed a release valve, and Andrea found it. Suddenly the silence was shattered by Andrea's opening line of 'Okay everyone, what age did you lose your virginity, who to and was it any good? Sarah, you go first.' Okay, so this may seem a slightly bizarre approach to dealing with the emotions of grief, but it worked for us. We ended up baring our souls and all our inner secrets, which would have sent the proverbial fly on the wall crashing to the floor in stunned shock. Needless to say, the details of that drive will always remain the secret of the Fat Ladies Club.

Braving It Again . . . and Again

Labour . . . gobsmackingly shocking and unrepeatable as we may have found it the first time round, we have all done it at least once more, and some of us have even ventured to a third.

We remember thinking after our firsts how sad it was that, even if we did do it again, we would never be able to experience the exhilaration of discovering we were pregnant for the first time with all the naivety that accompanies it. Nor could we relish in our ever-expanding bumps, knowing the miracle that was occurring on the inside. Why? Because we were now in the know, we were on the inside of that best-kept secret of womanhood: what labour really is like.

But then the wonder of women's hormones kicks in, or is it just the fact that the brain has shrunk so much from the first pregnancy that any 'memories of labours past' are permanently eradicated. Whichever it is, we have found ourselves proudly announcing the conceptions of our second children, without even a thought to the labours that we'd have to face again. Well, not at first anyway!

If you're pregnant for the second time, rather than remind you of just what labour has in store, we thought we'd write about the big differences between our first and second pregnancies, dealing with our first-borns and how we helped them come to terms with the imminent addition to their families. Suddenly the juggling balls all start going up at once. Here's how we attempted to catch them!

Lyndsey

***

By the time I fell pregnant with Caitlin, I was on my fourth pregnancy. After two miscarriages, and nearly two years of trying, I faced each day of this one in fear and trepidation of the anticipated bleed of disappointment, which thankfully never came. In the early weeks, I was permanently preoccupied with every gripe, every twinge and every sensation across my abdomen. So, it was with great concern that I faced my first dilemma having just done the positive pregnancy test. At work I was told that I had to go to the United States the following week to make a presentation at a meeting. I knew that this meant a quick 48-hour trip: flying out one day, presenting the next and flying back home that same evening. It was a gruelling trip for any person, never mind for me with the desperation to hold on to this baby. I was making myself ill just weighing up the possible consequences of this decision. If I did go and lost the baby, would I ever forgive myself? Yet the impact on my job if I refused to go was equally inconceivable. What plausible excuse could I give? None it seemed, so there I sat in business class on the transatlantic flight supping my water rather than the complimentary champagne and wine. Instead of focusing on the presentation that I had to give the next day, I spent the entire flight willing the foetus to cling on. Well, we survived the trip, and I decided that if the baby had managed two transatlantic flights in two days it would be here for the duration. But my paranoia did not subside. If anything it became even more irrational, as I then imagined all the defects that may have resulted following exposure to high-altitude radiation at such an early developmental stage. The next thirty-four weeks were going to be incredibly long.

Given my age (now thirty-seven) and my paranoia, I decided to have the nuchal scan at thirteen weeks for early detection of Down's syndrome or major disabilities. This helped calm my concerns – the results knocked ten years off me, giving me odds of carrying a Down's syndrome baby equivalent to a 27-year-old. This reassurance that the baby was alive and well was fantastic, so I did not have any further tests.

It was at this stage that we decided to tell Bethan of the impending arrival. Having fobbed her off by telling her that my swelling stomach was due to eating too many crisps and chocolates, she was delighted with the news. In fact, from about two and a half years old, she had been asking if her mummy could have a baby in her tummy just like her various friends at nursery. I had worried that at thirteen weeks and with twenty-seven still to go we may have had a daily ritual of 'Is it coming today?' But at the age of four she was able to understand when we explained that she had two other events to focus on before the arrival – Christmas and my birthday – so she knew not to ask until at least Christmas was over. The scan dates had indicated that the baby was due around my birthday, in February, so Bethan could relate to the arrival date and was already planning the baby's party, as well as my own. In fact, I was amazed at how mature she seemed about the whole scenario. She liked to look at the pictures in the pregnancy book, which showed the growing foetus and described its stage of development, and she delighted in feeling the kicks and movements from within. I did wonder how far to go with the educational bit, though, when I found her with the TV controls in her hand. She'd managed to navigate her way through the menus to find a baby channel and was watching live births with her morning cornflakes. 'Look, Mummy, the baby will come out of your bottom,' she explained, pointing at the television as I stood totally horrified in the doorway. I don't know whether it was horror at the thought of

*'Look, Mummy, the baby's going to come out
of your bottom!'*

her watching the graphic scenes or horror that this was a reality
that I would be facing in the not-too-distant future. Needless to
say I tried to be more restrictive in her viewing, especially after
she saw a Caesarean. She was appalled and cried that she didn't
want my tummy to be cut. We stuck to the books after that and,
whilst I found it difficult to look at the birth chapters with all
their intimate photographs, I would have to relent on occasion
just to satisfy Bethan's fascination with the whole subject.

Tim, during all this, was simply thrilled to be providing a
sibling for his daughter, who was acting as though she was on a
promise for the best toy in the toyshop. We soon became caught
up in her excitement. She would delight in announcing, 'My

mummy's got a baby in her tummy,' to friends and visitors who came to the house before even a hello had been uttered, or to supermarket checkout ladies, the postman and indeed anybody who cared to catch her attention. The one element of concern for us that crept into all this was the sex of the baby. It was one thing for Bethan to have a new baby on the way, but under no circumstances was it to be a boy. We toyed with the idea of asking to know the sex at the twenty-week scan so that if it was expected to be a boy we could start brainwashing Bethan. However, I felt that if I knew the sex of the baby it would have more of an identity. My paranoia, which still existed, directed me to self-preservation. Should we lose the baby I felt it would then make it a far greater loss if we had been treating it as a person rather than an unknown entity. However, it's hard to think of the growing foetus as anything but a little person second time round. The first pregnancy had been the complete opposite   I found it difficult to associate my swelling stomach with a life form at all then, never mind a baby. Anyway, the question was never asked and we had to start preparing Bethan for the worst . . . a boy! We explained to her that we couldn't guarantee a sister and that you can't choose to have a boy or a girl; you have to accept what is given. Anyway, a brother would be equally as fun and wouldn't steal your Barbies. No way! Bethan had turned into the girliest girl, liking pink and frills, dolls and babies, and to her boys were the annoying little tykes that she encountered at nursery who ran around doing impressions of aeroplanes and pretending to shoot her. We had an uphill struggle with this one, to the extent that she started telling everyone that she was going to have a sister called Eleanor. I would have to quickly interject or stand behind her mouthing that this wasn't true and that we didn't know what we were having. I'm sure half the time people thought that we did know, but weren't letting on and that Bethan was divulging the big family secret – but this is my chance to say, hand on heart, we truly didn't know the sex.

Christmas came and went with great excitement, of course, and my pregnancy was passing smoothly and progressing into the last few weeks. I felt more nauseous and tired than I ever had whilst carrying Bethan in the first twenty-five weeks. 'That's a good sign,' everyone would say. 'It means the hormone levels are higher and the baby is more tightly bound,' knowing I needed the comfort of a safe pregnancy. But it didn't seem to ease how lousy I was feeling. In the latter weeks I had a bout of high blood pressure. Then, when I had just two weeks to go, I sat aghast at my antenatal appointment as my GP suggested I just pop down to the hospital to double-check that it wasn't breech or transverse. Throughout the previous few checks there had been no doubt that it was head down, albeit heavily lying over to the left side, and I was sure I would have felt it turn, so I couldn't believe what I was hearing. I was suddenly thrown into panic and all those earlier conversations with Bethan about Caesareans came flooding back. Those few hours of waiting were hell as I went through all the scenarios. I knew I was carrying a bigger baby, and suddenly I felt the pressure of its imminent arrival was on. It was with great relief that it was confirmed the baby was head down and ready to go. However, an appointment was booked for inducement three weeks later – just in case.

The next week during my check with the midwife and listening to the foetal heartbeat I asked what her guess would be as to the sex of the baby from the speed of the heartbeat. I had heard that a lot of midwives thought they could tell the sex by listening to the heart rate, but this midwife wasn't one of those. She said that, whilst she didn't believe in the old wives' tale, the way I was carrying the baby seemed to suggest to her that I was carrying a boy. Having told this to Tim, and with days to go before the due date, we went into full battle plan on Bethan to convince her boys were okay and avoid the feared disappointment and rejection. She fell silent and said very little on the subject.

Two days to go to my birthday, and due date, I had a show. Now when this had happened with Bethan, she was born twenty hours later. They say with the second child you could halve the time of labour, so I felt quite excited that the baby could be born in the next ten hours. I called the hospital, but the midwife there explained that a show can occur three to five days prior to the birth and advised me just to sit tight and not to worry. My mum was already with us, and had been for a week, to be on hand to look after Bethan should I go into labour. One of my worst fears of an early delivery wasn't the aspect of the birth, but who should look after Bethan. But with Mum now staying with us I could put all my concentration on my other fear – the birth itself.

The midwife had been right about the three to five days, and my birthday arrived with still no baby. Bethan was doubly excited, first about preparing a heart-themed tea party for me and secondly that the baby would come the next day, so she kept telling us! As I read her a story that night, I felt quite sad that this would be one of the last times there would be just me, Tim and Bethan, as very soon a new person would be living with us. I lay with her on her bed as she drifted off to sleep and began to feel dull aches in my groin. I realized that the baby's arrival was imminent. Then, out of the blue, a little voice said, 'Mummy, if you have a boy baby, will it have a little willy?' I nearly fell off the bed, as it was the last thing I was expecting! 'Yes, darling, it will,' I said quietly, thinking that this was the beginning of her accepting it. 'Then I don't want you to bring a boy baby back from the hospital. I don't want my baby sister to have a willy.' Bethan was now sitting upright in the bed, cross-faced, arms folded and meaning business. I had visions of needing to banish kitchen knives and scissors should we bring a boy into the house for fear that his older sister may take it on herself to do a quick snip or chop in a vain effort to turn him into a girl. It seemed our intensive brainwashing of the past few days had not worked. I fell into bed that night feeling tired, uncomfortable and now worried, even more so, about the sex of this child.

At 1.30 a.m. I awoke with the most awful contractions. This is it, I thought, and by 3 a.m. I had woken Tim saying that I felt we should be on our way to hospital. He didn't seem in too much of a rush and dawdled, sleepily, into the shower to wake himself up. I was at the hospital by 4 a.m. and at 5.13 a.m. our cherub was born. The fast delivery had been a bit traumatic for me and the baby, who had decided to come out face first, and a registrar was called into the room to be on hand. Eventually I was handed a very bruised and swollen nine-pound baby . . . girl. Our relief was a bit deeper than the delivering midwife could imagine, given the previous night's conversation. When Bethan came to the hospital that afternoon, her first words to me were: 'I told you so. I told you that I was having a sister today.' And so Caitlin joined the Lawrence family.

I was certainly worried about Bethan's reaction to the baby, but it has to be said that she has been the best big sister in the short time that Caitlin has been with us. With the age gap of four and a half years, I was concerned that Bethan, who had had all our attention up until Caitlin's arrival, would feel jealous and pushed out. But not so – she has welcomed her into the family and can't do enough for her. Caitlin's birth coincided with Bethan starting full-time school, which has also meant that I have been able to spend great chunks of the day really enjoying my new baby as though she were my first again. So this big age gap, which I had feared so much, has certainly worked in our favour, and I just hope that Caitlin grows to be as loving and generous as her sister.

Sarah

* * *

Having had a couple of miscarriages after Jack, there was a definite feeling of 'braving it again' when we decided to have another shot at getting pregnant. We had learnt that Mother Nature has the ultimate say in whether or not a pregnancy is going to make it, and we had grown pragmatic, if not slightly blasé, about the next time I conceived. The fact that Tim had once expressed a desire of having five children was by this stage quite an unrealistic expectation, considering the way our family plans were going so far. I certainly remember saying to him when I got the result from the 'pee on the stick' test early on in my fourth pregnancy, 'Well, we'll just have to see how this one turns out!' It was easy to joke at such an early stage, but as the pregnancy continued I was noticeably on edge as each milestone loomed, whether it was the first preliminary scan at eight weeks, the nuchal scan at twelve weeks, the triple blood test at sixteen weeks or the scan at twenty weeks to check all the baby's bits and pieces in detail. I was extremely tense before each appointment. Even the regular checks by the midwife for the baby's heartbeat brought me out in a cold sweat. I tried to keep my anxiety at bay by reassuring myself that we already had one healthy baby and that there was no medical reason why we couldn't have another. But somehow, after having had a miscarriage, no pregnancy can ever be relaxed and carefree again. As Hilary so eloquently puts it, 'You've always got your head in your knickers.' With every dribbly sensation you get down below, you're set off into a mad panic that perhaps all is not well. For me, this paranoia is accentuated by the fact that I can't even be reassured that all is well if I'm not bleeding. With my history of hanging onto unviable foetuses, I need to actually hear the heartbeat inside me to have absolute peace of mind.

To put my mind at rest in a big way, we decided that it would be a good idea for me to put the Heathrow–Bilbao commute on hold for the first three months of the pregnancy. As I had conceived whilst in San Sebastian, and discovered that I was pregnant whilst back in the UK, I grounded myself in Berkhamsted as soon as I found out. The timing couldn't have been better because it was a couple of months before Christmas, and it made a lot of sense for me to be back at home, preparing for the festivities and doing all the Christmas shopping, without the need to return to Spain. It also made explanations as to why I was around so much more in England far easier to handle with those people to whom I really didn't want to announce my very early pregnancy. I've learnt that it really serves no purpose avoiding telling close friends early on that I'm pregnant because if things don't work out then they would be the first to know why I'm feeling so miserable. I didn't feel comfortable, however, broadcasting my state to girls I knew only on a superficial level through our weekly excuse for cake and coffee at toddlers. I feared that if I didn't see them for a few weeks, if things had gone pear-shaped again, I'd be having to field very emotionally charged conversations which I really couldn't face. My self-enforced grounding in the UK just meant that no one received delicious Spanish continental chocolates in their Christmas parcels that year!

I did make a return flight to Spain in the New Year, once I had passed the all-important three-month stage, and that was basically an unavoidable necessity because we were moving all our belongings back to the UK, in preparation for Tim's change in job. It was a manic week of packing, running around to see all my old haunts and mad, frenzied shopping before flying home. It was certainly reassuring to see that we still had a discernible heartbeat when I had my twenty-week scan a few weeks later. I have to say that, with every milestone I reached in this fourth pregnancy, I felt a certain achievement at having reached that far; passing the dates of the previous failed pregnancies was a major boost in itself.

We left it a long while, for obvious reasons, before telling Jack the news that he was to be an older brother. We found it relatively easy to avoid the subject with him being only two and a half and so totally accepting of changes around him. Even the metamorphosis of his mother into some whalelike creature didn't seem to perturb him. Plus, I thought, nine months in anyone's life is a long period to have to wait for something to arrive, let alone a toddler waiting for this baby brother or sister. I was prompted into explaining the growing size of my stomach to Jack when I was about twenty weeks pregnant by the fact that my neighbour had already told her daughter that Jack was soon to be a 'big brother'. Holly is the quintessential 'girl next door' for Jack, and they are quite inseparable, so I knew that it wasn't going to be long before the proverbial cat was well and truly released from the bag, and questions would start flying. As it turned out, Jack was quite unexcited by the news, but later told me rather seriously that he didn't mind the idea of having a little brother or sister as long as we called it 'Traffic' or 'Panic'. This concerned me a little at the time, as I hoped it wasn't due to some childish intuition about where or how I would be giving birth that had prompted Jack to choose these names. When the time came, he fortunately didn't object to the choice of Eloise Daisy!

As for my current pregnancy, I wasn't able to leave it nearly as long before telling Jack, simply because he is now older and far more observant; Eloise, at eighteen months old, is still blissfully ignorant of my growing fat state. When we first told Jack that we would be having another baby, he was chuffed to bits and extremely excited at the prospect of at last having his much requested younger brother. I had to let him down gently, explaining that there's a high possibility that it may be another sister for him – if we are to believe the sonographer's estimate. But, for him, the fact that he already has a little sister means that he cannot possibly have another one – it will have to be a boy. We'll just have to hope that she turns out as much of a tomboy as Eloise. A couple of days after I told Jack, his teacher asked me discreetly if congratulations were in order. She had simply wanted to check that Jack's announcement to the school assembly the day before was well founded, as apparently children have been known to invent these things!

But back to Eloise, who was born a fortnight after Jack's third birthday. The week she was due, Tim had a particularly busy time at work and had said to me, 'If there's any way you can hold off for a few more days, that would be superb!' As if I had any way of crossing my legs and putting labour on hold until it suited him, I ask you! As it happened, we got through the week and, on the Friday night, Jack and I walked the ten-minute journey down the road to meet Tim from the station. On the walk back, I noticed the first telltale twinges and the 'undercarriage about to burst' sensation, and I remarked to Tim that I thought I deserved a medal for timing it just right. It wasn't until I briefly nipped round to Holly's Mum next door at eight o'clock that evening to check that they would be around that weekend to look after Jack, 'just in case', that it suddenly dawned on me that our second child might well arrive on its due date, just as Jack had. For someone who is renowned for her appalling punctuality, I do a good job of producing punctual babies!

It was a strange trip down memory lane, as I went into labour for the second time. All those well-stored memories came flooding back with force as I had a warm bath late that evening. I didn't dare stay in the bath too long, though, because I remembered one of Carol the midwife's anecdotes about a lady who had left it too late to get out of the bath during the labour of her second child and ended up delivering the baby on the bathroom floor. The warm bath had apparently masked her labour pains. Seeing that we have old pine floorboards in our bathroom with plenty of gaps, I couldn't contemplate the spectacle of me going through the motions in our bathroom, let alone clearing up the hideous mess afterwards. I would dread having to call the plumber forever after, for fear of what he might find should he have to lift the bathroom floorboards to get to the pipes!

As soon as I was out of the bath, I slapped the TENS machine on and once again went through my pacing of the house routine as I clung nervously to the hand control and that important red pulse button. At this stage, I told Tim that it would probably be wise for him to get some sleep and continued pacing about huffing and puffing. Just before 2 a.m., I woke him to say that we needed to go to hospital, only to be greeted with, 'Oh, so you were really meaning it then – we might have another baby tonight?' I can't imagine what else he was expecting . . . a heavily pregnant woman breathing like a heifer, pain relief pads on, baby-sitter checked in – and all on my due date. I would have thought that these were all sure giveaways that a baby was about to arrive.

Tim had no sooner woken from his slumber than I was ordering him up into the loft to fetch the baby car seat down – I had lost count of the times over the past month I had asked him to get it down in case I went into labour when he wasn't around to fetch it for me. It was with a feeling of well-deserved 'comeuppance' that I watched him shin up the ladder into our loft in the middle of the night! Fortunately, Holly's big sister had just rolled in at 2 a.m. when Tim called to ask if she would mind coming round to sleep at ours, to be there for Jack the next morning. A quick kiss to a sound-asleep Jack before shooting off to the hospital, and I felt sure that I would be well and truly dilated by the time I was examined. I was massively disappointed when the attendant midwife pronounced that I was only five centimetres, having been almost nine centimetres when I arrived at the hospital ready to give birth to Jack. I almost felt ready to turn around and go back home to pace another few circuits of the house before coming back to carry on.

Fortunately, things continued to happen very quickly, and at one stage I wanted to try delivering on all fours, which was something I had learnt was a natural position to deliver in, after attending an excellent course of 'Yoga in Pregnancy' classes. I couldn't bring myself to carry on, though, because something about waving my bottom in the air, pushing for all my might and trying desperately to ignore the natural sensation to clench my buttocks just wasn't for me. So, I opted for the position I knew had worked for me first time round and remained 'seated'. Eloise entered our world as smoothly as Jack had done, weighing in at seven pounds fifteen ounces, and with her hands on the sides of her head, which meant that I needed several stitches. Despite having requested it at each scan, we hadn't been able to have any prior confirmation of the sex of our baby because she had always discreetly hidden herself away, keeping us guessing right up until the end. Somehow the wonder of realizing we had a daughter helped negate the immediate pain and discomfort. Not having had stitches with Jack, the stirrup and stitching-up experience after the birth of Eloise was altogether quite shocking, and all I can say is thank goodness the entinox carried on functioning for as long as I needed it to! So much for having used the perineal massage technique, something else advocated by the midwife running the yoga classes, that is supposed to loosen you up down below and prepare your bits to be stretched. But I suppose you have to expect some damage to be done when arms and head come out simultaneously! I still believe in following this perineal massage technique, if only as a damage-limitation exercise: I keep meaning to buy myself a new bottle of wheat germ oil in preparation for my next due date. You can never be sure of how easy or difficult that last stage of labour is going to be, but I'm one of those people who thinks that, if I have at least done some sort of preparatory work, then it should have some positive effect on the end result.

Soon after Eloise and I had been taken to the postnatal ward, Tim returned home to have breakfast with Jack. When Tim brought him in to see me and his new baby sister, he was positively beaming with excitement. It was a quiet day on the ward, which meant that the midwives and hospital staff paid him a lot of attention and even took him off for biscuits and drinks. This must explain why he is looking forward to coming to see me in hospital so much again, when our third child is born. The lure of such edible treats, as well as the prospect of the baby bringing him a present equivalent to the 'Monster Truck' which Eloise had brought with her for him, is enough to get any child excited about the prospect of going to hospital.

Even after the relatively straightforward arrival of my second child, I still had a certain degree of anxiety about being a mum again. I continually wanted to check on her to make sure she was still breathing, to make sure she was feeding properly, and so on. I remember thinking how awful it would be to let my baby suffocate in her hospital cot beside me because I had wrapped her too warmly or die from cold because I hadn't dressed her in enough clothes. Worse still, I had visions of dropping her as I tried to pick her up to feed her, still feeling so weak after the birth. Being a mum second time round puts a certain pressure on you to get things right straight away. I felt that I should know better than to make an obvious mistake. Hence, for the first few hours, I felt really quite uptight. Maybe it was something to do with not wanting to spoil this chance that we had been given; after all, she had been a long time coming and I did not want to ruin things before they had even had a chance to start. However, as soon as we arrived back in the 'safe haven' of home, everything suddenly seemed so natural – the breastfeeding, the nappy changing and the cradling of our newborn. That sense of *déjà vu* hit me with a wallop, and the real enjoyment of being so totally relaxed with our second child properly began.

Andrea

***

Whether it's my Greek blood or just strong maternal instincts I don't know, but I was brimming with broodiness from somewhere around Max's first birthday. I am a middle child with an older brother and a younger sister, and there is just five years gap from oldest to youngest. I remember how close we all were as children, and that was something I wanted for Max. We also fought like cat and dog, and nearly killed each other on numerous occasions, but we were always there for each other when it mattered, which was a huge childhood security blanket.

Unfortunately, Bruce was not nearly as keen on expanding our family so quickly. Whenever I broached the subject, he would always evade the issue by saying something like, 'Let's just leave it a few more months. No rush.' We would probably still have been waiting when we separated if it hadn't been for my doctor advising me to come off the Pill after I had a few problems. I would like to make it perfectly clear at this point that Bruce knew the situation and I certainly didn't trick him into a second pregnancy. Birth control was down to him and he chose not to bother, so the silent decision to try for a second was made. It did happen incredibly quickly, though, just as it had with Max. I was off the Pill one minute and pregnant the next.

When I was about ten weeks pregnant, I started bleeding quite heavily. After seeing Hilary and Sarah both suffering miscarriages with their second pregnancies, I was convinced that I was heading the same way. Following a telephone call to my GP, Bruce and I found ourselves heading to the hospital for a scan. I was totally convinced that my baby was going to be confirmed as dead and tried desperately to psych myself up for the inevitable. We drove in absolute silence. I couldn't help but think that, after Bruce's lack of excitement at this pregnancy, I might not ever have my second child, and Bruce I think was just feeling guilty.

We were eventually seen by a consultant who I was to get to know very well during the next few months. I had a scan and was desperately trying to see if I could work out anything from the screen. It seemed like forever before she said these exact words, which I will never forget, 'The good news is, we have a baby and we have a heartbeat.' I was so relieved, and I know Bruce was, too. Nothing was said, but he was squeezing my hand so tightly throughout it all. At that point in time, I didn't care if there was anything wrong – my baby was alive and that was all that mattered. They were unable to tell at this stage why I was bleeding, but it was me and not the baby, so I was sent home, with instructions for complete bed rest until the bleeding stopped. I then had to return on a fortnightly basis to have the pregnancy monitored throughout the duration.

The bleeding subsided after about a fortnight, and I relaxed a little as I decided that the baby was making a big effort to stay put. As a result of this early problem, I was really looked after during this pregnancy, which meant having extremely detailed scans on a very regular basis. Because of this my next concern arose. I was having a detailed scan at about fourteen weeks, and I knew something was wrong when my consultant called in a second scan lady. They studied me for ages, then I was told that the scan had revealed something in my baby's bowel that could be one of several things, most of which were completely innocent, such as the baby swallowing some blood. But it could also have been indicative of cystic fibrosis and would need to be looked into further. Having extremely limited medical knowledge, I did not have a clue what cystic fibrosis was. I had heard of it and it sounded serious, but I didn't really know the implications. I was told that Bruce and I would both need to have immediate detailed blood tests to find out whether we were carriers. If neither of us was a carrier, the chances of us producing a baby with the condition were minimal. The tests were done, and we then had to wait three weeks for the results. During this time, we couldn't help but have discussions about 'what if?'. I tried to keep calm and not get worked up when people gave their opinions, but I knew that at the end of the day I would not have been able to have a termination regardless of the outcome. The results revealed that neither of us was a carrier, but there was still a 5 per cent chance that the baby may have the condition and only an amnio would clarify it. Before I decided I had a further scan, and it showed that the problem in the bowel was no longer visible. That was all the information I needed. After all the baby's efforts to hang on in there, I would not have an amnio and put him at any further risk.

It will come as no surprise that because I was banned completely from any form of exercise during this pregnancy I was absolutely HUGE. Despite this, Max, who was approaching two, did not even begin to grasp what was going on. Once all the initial scares were over, I tried to explain to him what was happening, but he wasn't convinced. I could tell by his face that he clearly thought I was mad to expect him to believe that there could possibly be a baby in my tummy. It wasn't until Ella arrived and he saw Hilary's big tummy suddenly shrink that the penny finally dropped. At last he realized that all the talk of baby brothers was for real after all. I say baby brother because, yes, I am someone

'What, Mummy? A baby, in there?'

who finds out and quite happily tells everyone. With both children we even chose names before they were born, and so by the end Max was referring to my bump quite affectionately as 'Baby Sam'. Max was fairly excited about the idea of a baby brother, but I didn't anticipate him being quite so involved in the hospital dash as he was. As Max had been a week overdue, I continued booking Arsenal tickets for matches to week thirty-seven, thinking this would be quite safe. When I was exactly thirty-four weeks pregnant, on a Tuesday night in August, Bruce and I set off on our journey to see Arsenal play Bradford. Unfortunately we couldn't park in our usual spot that night, which resulted in us having to practically jog about a mile to get there in time for kick-off. As we took our seats, I felt distinctly rough.

I was very hot and flushed, my hands were sweaty and tingling, and I just did not feel right. Arsenal got an early penalty, and it was as much as I could do to even stand up and watch, let alone celebrate, which is unheard of for me. We ended up leaving early, which is again unheard of even if we are losing, and on the way home I announced that I probably wouldn't go to the Villa game the following week. I told my baby-sitter, who works at the same police station as me, that I would not be at work the next day and went to bed. Three hours later, at 2 a.m., I got up needing a wee, but as I stood up my waters immediately broke. Boy, did I panic! I was only thirty-four weeks and that was too soon surely? We had absolutely nobody to look after Max, so Bruce rang his mum and she started travelling from Kent, but would not be with us for at least two hours. The hospital was insisting I went straight in because of the early status, so Max was awoken and in we all went. It soon became very apparent that thirty-four weeks was not ideal for the baby's lungs, and I was given injections to boost their development in case I went into labour. I have no idea if Max will have any lasting memory of seeing me on a labour suite bed surrounded by doctors and midwives, but he seemed to take it all in his stride before Nana arrived to take him home.

As with Max, I did not go straight into labour and was therefore sent to an antenatal ward where I ended up staying for another week. It was horrible having to watch lots of other women come and go. As I was on the inducing ward, every morning overdue mums would come in to be induced, we would get chatting then they would visit me the next day showing off their new babies. I became the Queen of the Ward – all the midwives knew me, newcomers asked me where everything was and everyone felt they needed to ask my permission to turn the television over! As for my family, they soon got into a little routine, whereby Max would be at the childminder's until about

4 p.m., then Bruce would bring him in to have dinner with me at the hospital, which he loved. I was relieved, if admittedly a little jealous, at his contentment with this situation, but I also was fearful of what effect it may have on his bonding with the new baby. The focus was now so much on me and the baby I was scared he might be ragingly jealous of Sam when he finally came out.

After a week, my consultant told me that I would be induced at thirty-six weeks. Sam, of course, hadn't done anything to plan so far, so why should he start now? He had no intention of waiting another week. When I started bleeding again that night I was induced, and I knew that whatever happened he would be born that day. After a long and tiring day, we finally reached the stage when his arrival was imminent. The midwife explained to me that because he was premature we had to call paediatricians in for the delivery. All of a sudden there were two midwives and three other people whom I assume were specialists, and Sam literally popped out weighing five pounds, which is actually a great weight for being five weeks early. He was given to me and I could tell straight away that something was wrong, so he was whisked into the care of the specialists, whilst I watched in silence. They worked so quickly and expertly. I kept hearing one of them say, 'Come on, boy. Come on, boy.' Eventually I heard a slight gurgle and a whimper. He needed to go into the special baby care unit immediately, so I was briefly shown him again before he was gone with Bruce in tow.

I can't even begin to explain how this felt, after everything that had happened with the pregnancy. To have him taken away so quickly without even a cuddle was awful. Left lying there on my own, not knowing what was happening was torturous. Within five minutes, a midwife came and told me that Sam was okay, but they were doing tests and Bruce was staying with him. I was happier with this news, but because I had needed an epidural I wasn't allowed out of the delivery room for over an hour and I was then taken in a wheelchair into the baby unit. My tiny baby Sam was in an incubator under lights and seemed to have wires everywhere, but I was happy to just sit with him holding his hand. I was assured by staff that he was fine. He had just been what they term 'flat on delivery', and he would have to stay in there for about a week.

The next day I was discharged and sent home, but Sam had to remain in hospital, which was incredibly difficult. I felt emotionally torn between my two children. I desperately wanted to go home and be with Max again, but also wanted to be with my new, helpless baby. I had to think logically rather than emotionally and accept that Sam was being cared for and, of the two, he needed me least at this time. I don't know if it was down to this extra bit of time I had with Max, but thankfully he never did develop the jealousy I had feared. In fact, Max was delighted with his new brother when we took him into the baby unit and couldn't wait for him to come home. It helped that we had always planned that Sam would bring Max a present when he came into the world, and at the time Max was besotted with *Toy Story*, so Sam brought 'Woody' with him and Max was ecstatic. To this day, whenever Sam plays with Woody, Max tells him the story of how Woody came to our house.

As a result of being separated from Sam and not able even to cuddle him for a couple of days, I didn't bond with him at all until after we left hospital. After a couple of days at home, though, we were very close, and if anything my bond was extra strong because of all that we had both gone through. Bruce definitely did not bond with Sam straight away – he was very wary of how tiny he was and spent more time helping with Max. Sam was also very difficult for about the first ten weeks of his life. I am sure it is something to do with his early arrival, but he just cried all the time. This was so different to how Max had been, and I would regularly cry at 3 a.m. because I was so tired, but somehow I got through those early weeks. It helped that I was able to keep Max at the childminder's for two days a week, so on these days I was able to nap when Sam did. Max also got fed up with Sam's constant crying, and I had to laugh at one point when he announced that he wanted his brother to be taken back to live at the hospital. I think parents do often think that one baby will behave in the same way as another, but this was definitely not the case with my two.

Bruce bonded with Sam once he got to the smiley age and he became a happy, contented baby, but it is still clear that I am Sam's favourite. Max would not be able to choose between us, but Sam is definitely a mummy's boy. I am delighted to have had two boys, and they are great buddies. We rarely have any jealousy issues. In fact, Max goes off to school, knowing that Sam is spending the day with me, going swimming or out to friends, and he always says, 'Have a nice time swimming, Sam.' They really stand up for each other, too. On holiday recently, a young Spanish chap decided to lay into Max for no particular reason and Sam, at half his height, went in for the kill like a pit bull terrier. Nobody was going to hurt his big brother and get away with it. Sam has also been known to blame Molly for things Max has done to keep his big brother out of trouble! It certainly is not all fun and friendship, though. They fight like mad at times, and I mean really punch each other – if I don't get in there quickly there will be injuries. I have visions of them being buddies as they grow up, being each other's best man and that sort of thing – who knows? If I am honest, as I am one of three, I would have liked another child, too. Obviously I think it is safe to say that Bruce will not be the father of any more, and the thought of any other relationship at the moment, well, I can't even go there. But I guess I can't completely rule out the possibility; after all, a year ago I'd never have dreamed I would be where I am now.

Hilary

* * *

As you will already have gathered, I'm the only one so far to have braved labour two more times, but, as I sit here with my ten-week-old son Alfie, I can finally say that I feel our family is complete. I don't think it's a boy thing either, as my life ambition was to have a girl, so, although I'm over the moon to have a mixed bag, it wasn't the be all and end all. It's just that three children feels like a finished family, for me anyway!

My pregnancy with Ella was very precious, having miscarried the previous baby, but also something very personal. With Molly I kept David posted on the baby's progress on a weekly basis and grabbed his hand to feel the kicks. It was all so new and exciting. With Ella, I still had all the same rushes of excitement at the first big kick and hearing the heartbeat, but David didn't seem nearly as interested, and, to be fair, I didn't push him to pay any interest, as I had with Molly. Being a livestock farmer, the miracle of new life is all a bit of a daily occurrence for him, I suppose. My second pregnancy was pretty similar to the first. Ella was due the week of Molly's second birthday, so I was even neck and neck with the time of year for my ever-expanding bulk. Summer saw the expansion of my feet by two sizes again, and my pork-sausage fingers meant that my wedding ring had to be cut off. This was totally gutting, as I had never removed it from the day it was put on. With Molly it was a close call, and I'd hoped to get away with it again, but by thirty-four weeks my finger was turning decidedly blue.

The second pregnancy also introduced a whole new range of deteriorating body parts. I developed carpal tunnel syndrome in my wrist, which basically means you have permanent pins and

needles in your hand and a constant ache in your wrist. So I had
to wear a delightful buff-coloured splint for the second half of
the pregnancy. I developed chronically bleeding gums and my
eyesight deteriorated to the point that I was no longer legal to
drive without specs. Naturally my varicose veins also saw this as
an ideal opportunity to make their presence even more obvious
by developing some attractive bulges to them, too! And I still
wanted to have a third: the power of progesterone or possibly
just blatant insanity . . . who knows? The water retention and
veins weren't quite as bad when I was pregnant with Alfie, but
then it was winter, but my gums were a nightmare. Every time
I brushed my teeth, it looked like a massacre had occurred in the
sink. I flossed and gargled like mad for fear of developing that
overgrown gummy look. For me that was a far greater fear than
flab and veins.

Not only did I not receive the husbandly interest in my later
pregnancies, but also there was a distinct lack of nurturing me
through this physically exhausting ordeal. With Ella, I carried on
working three days a week up to thirty-eight weeks, running
round after Molly four days a week. I even organized a big
barbeque and birthday party for Molly's second birthday the
week I was due. So much for all those lovely, lazy days of lying
around, siestas in the garden hammock, packing and repacking the
hospital bag for four weeks before the birth that I'd experienced
the first time. So much for David preparing bowls of cool water
to bathe my swollen feet this time. I was lucky if he faced up to a
bowl of washing up. After all, surely I could do that. What else
had I been doing all day with our two-year-old daughter anyway?

Two weeks before Ella was due, I managed to fall over whilst
carrying Molly through a gravelly car park. My instincts were all
out to protect Molly, so as I fell forwards I threw my arms with
her in them outstretched in front of me, in a desperate bid to
keep her off the ground and uninjured. I was successful, but the

end result was that I landed flat on my bump. My arms and legs were peppered with imbedded gravel, and I couldn't walk as my bump hurt so much. To top it all, it seemed as if the whole world came to my rescue. I desperately tried to escape their prying, pitying eyes by bouncing back to my feet, laughing off my stupidity and thanking them for their concern as I tried to walk as normally as possible. 'I'm fine honestly. Yes, silly me. Thank you. Honestly. Goodbye, bye, bye!' Once I had shaken off my concerned audience and sought out the sanctuary of my car, I immediately rang David and burst into tears, petrified that I'd killed our unborn child. He came to my rescue at high speed, and thankfully after a quick check-up the baby was confirmed as being fine, but I had torn all the muscles in my lower abdomen and couldn't walk at all for days.

It's funny how with Molly, from starting my maternity leave and being a temporary lady of leisure, I was counting down the weeks, days and almost the hours until our baby would join us. With Ella, there seemed to be hundreds of hurdles to overcome. First, my abdomen repair – I couldn't possibly deal with labour in that amount of pain. This was shortly followed by Molly's birthday. I was so anxious that the baby would arrive on the actual day and spoil her party that I wouldn't tell her when her birthday was until the morning arrived and I felt safely intact. Each day she would ask about it, and I'd say something vague like 'Soon' or 'This weekend', so when she trudged into our room all bleary-eyed one morning and was greeted with a resounding chorus of 'Happy Birthday to You' from David and me, she looked at us as though we'd completely lost the plot. I'm not sure what I would have done if Ella had arrived on her birthday, but I was tempted to just move her birthday by a day or two that year and tell everyone invited to her party to just come the next day instead. It would have been awful for her to have had her party without David or me there.

I thought I'd be ready for labour as soon as the big birthday was out of the way, but that was followed immediately by a horrendous bout of cystitis requiring antibiotics to knock it on the head. Once again the fear of labour whilst unwell took hold and I prayed for a further reprieve. As it goes, Ella's timing couldn't have been more impeccable. My first contractions started at 7 a.m. on her actual due date, exactly one week after Molly's birthday, and I was ready at last. Unfortunately, this timing wasn't quite so ideal for David who was needing to order new carpets for a farm cottage he was renting out. I tried to point out that being a bad landlord who didn't provide new carpets on time compared to missing the birth of his second child was pretty immaterial, but he was convinced that, as Molly had taken thirty-six hours to arrive, he surely could risk a couple of hours absence that morning. After all, he had offered to take Molly with him to give me a break! As this delightful discussion was developing between contractions, my sister-in-law, Sarah, decided to pop by for a cuppa. That was definitely one impromptu visit she regretted for a long time. David seized the moment, asked Sarah if she would mind staying with me for an hour and, before she even had time to ask why or give an affirmative response, he grabbed Molly and hotfooted it out the door and down to Carpet City. Sarah, a high-powered businesswoman who really 'doesn't do children', went ashen when she realized what she had been left with.

During David's absence, my contractions hotted up quite dramatically – the TENS machine was on full power and I was doing the all-fours puffing and bum-wriggling contractions by the time he returned. Between contractions, I was desperately trying to reassure Sarah that I really did have hours to go yet and not to panic, but her eyes were darting around the room like a cornered fox. When David did return, she was out of that door faster than you can say second-stage labour, and I was ripping off my TENS machine and leaping into the bath. David called my mum and asked her to come over to Molly-sit. 'No major hurry, though,' he said. 'Grab her a McDonald's on the way.' This, from the pain-relieving depths of my bath, seemed spot-on advice for timing, but when I got out of the bath I realized that the gaps between contractions were now down to seconds, not minutes, and I was no longer able to stand up through them even if I tried. It was a very long ten minutes on all fours on the doorstep waiting for Mum's arrival, especially with Molly saying, 'Are we playing horsey rides?' and leaping on my back as I wriggled dementedly. I was ready to divorce David by the time we reached the hospital, and every time he touched those brakes it felt like a personal attack. I was sure he was intentionally trying to cause me pain. It didn't cross my mind that maybe he was averting major collisions . . . it was personal! I got my own back by mortally embarrassing him all the way across the car park. Contractions were only thirty seconds apart, and I would do a little wobbly run, then plummet to my knees, wriggling and puffing, then clamber back up the side of his body, make another little dash, then drop to the ground again. It took about eight contractions to reach the sanctuary of the labour ward and my best friend, the entinox mask.

Ella was born within the hour. It would have been sooner, but the midwife refused to break my waters and it took me twenty minutes of entinox before I braved standing up and bouncing until they broke themselves. Poor David really was fairly redundant throughout this labour. With Molly I clung to him, eye to eye constantly, willing him to get me through it. With Ella I felt like a machine. It was a job that needed doing. I knew the routine, so it was eyes down, get on with the job. I didn't want to be touched or talked to; I just wanted someone I could hurl the occasional abuse at.

My biggest fear with having a second child was that I wouldn't have enough love for it, I'm sure this is the case with all parents, but even as I was delivering all I could think was, 'Good, it's only 3 p.m. I should be home in time for Molly's tea.' I just could not get my thoughts on to looking after child number two. When she was born I was totally emotionally numb. It felt as though I hadn't really been there this time. I was just an observer. Anyway, this baby couldn't possibly be mine; it didn't have a willy for a start. I had been *sooo* totally convinced that Ella was going to be a boy, it really hadn't entered my head that I was having a second girl. It wasn't that I didn't want another girl, it was purely down to expectation. If you order vanilla ice cream yet when you take the first mouthful of the pale yellow dessert in front of you it turns out to be banana flavoured, it's a shock. You may love it, but if it's not what you're expecting it takes a while to get used to it. Not only was Ella the same sex, but she also looked exactly the same to start with. Even I have difficulty identifying whose are whose baby photographs if there aren't any distinguishing features in the background to help date them.

Fortunately, despite David's blasé approach to the pregnancy, he bonded instantly with Ella, as he had with Molly; for me, it took a few days. As soon as she was born and confirmed as fit and well, I sent David home to bring Molly. By the time they returned, only three hours after us leaving home in the first place, I had talked the hospital into giving me an early official discharge. Unfortunately, the meptide I had been given in the last twenty minutes of labour decided to really kick in at this time and, while David was desperately trying to pack up our bag, wrap up and car seat our new baby and deal with Molly's continual questions, I kept dozing off. I'd put one shoe on, then fall asleep with my chin on my chest. David woke me saying, 'If you want to get out of here, you'd better look conscious.' I agreed whole-heartedly, bent down to pick up my other shoe and promptly fell asleep again. After a few tame taps around the face and a cold flannel on the neck, I was conscious enough to make it to the car. At home, I flopped on the settee and set in for another good kip, whilst Molly insisted that Daddy carry the new baby around the house, as she gave her a guided tour. While they were gone, David's brother, Richard, turned up and stuck his head around the sitting-room door. It was his wife who had been with me for the morning, so he knew I was in labour. 'All died down again, has it?' he asked as he looked at my still enormous belly. I was gutted – inside I felt positively sylphlike again, and Richard couldn't even tell that I'd given birth! He desperately tried to cover his huge faux pas with lots of embarrassed waffle, but I knew that it was going to take a serious quantity of sit-ups to sort out my jelly belly this time!

Initially, I was so obsessed with making sure that Molly was happy, contented and feeling loved that I really didn't have time to learn to love Ella, too. For the first two or three days, my dealings with Ella were purely practical and functional. I fed, changed, hugged etc., but all with Molly's needs and emotions in mind. It didn't help that Ella didn't sleep at all that first night either. I was fully anticipating a knocked-out baby for the first night, which was what had happened on Molly's first night, so I have to confess to even experiencing a degree of annoyance with my new child for making me too tired to give my best to Molly the next day. David and Molly, however, seemed to accept and adore our new addition with total ease. After a couple of days, David gave me a sharp reality check by pointing out that Molly was absolutely fine and I needed to chill out and enjoy my new baby. That night I prepared myself for another wakeful one, took Ella into her room and spent all her wakeful hours cooing and chatting to her. By the next morning the 'whoosh' had happened. She was my precious, new, totally adorable little bundle of love, and I was smitten. Up until then, I hadn't really spent much time just holding her and taking her in because, every time I held her,

Molly was rushing over. I found I was just talking Molly through the process of how to talk to her sister rather than doing it myself.

We never did experience any of the aggressive jealousy from Molly, but the sharing of attention was something we had to tread very carefully with. Molly would be quite happily playing, but as soon as she heard me chatting to Ella she was there in a shot, zapping her head between mine and Ella's, and cooing in a slightly manic fashion. I ended up finding myself cooing in silence out of Molly's vision! I'd do all the coochy-coo faces to Ella, but would mouth the words, not daring to emit any sound for fear of the tornado of her jealous sister stealing our precious few moments together. To be fair to Molly, though, this really was the only form of jealousy she showed. Toys and baby equipment never proved a problem, but I think that was largely due to my cunning forward thinking. When I first discovered I was pregnant, I took absolutely everything even remotely babyfied and put it into the attic. Then, when the due date drew nearer, I made a big thing with Molly about getting all the baby things out so we could see what we had and what we needed to buy. She thought this was great fun, and I'm sure the fact that these items came from the attic made the difference between them being 'the' baby items and not 'her' baby items. It was a great way of helping her to realize that my fat tummy was not a permanent fixture – the new baby was imminent. I really felt pretty smug about this successful sibling introduction, but when a friend did the same, it was a total disaster. The older child just grabbed everything, screaming, 'Mine, mine, mine!' and hoarded it under their bed! Just goes to show what works for one is a nightmare for the next. It's like the advice all the books seem to give for easing an elder child into accepting their sibling. Make sure that guests make a huge fuss of the elder child and buy them gifts, too. At the age of two, this was sheer hell for Molly. She hated everyone gushing over her and asking hundreds of inane questions. I ended up asking people to act as if it was their second visit to the new baby. In other words, greet Molly as they do normally and greet the baby as though that, too, was something they normally do. The less manic greetings to both children, the easier it was for Molly.

Molly was four and a half when Alfie was born and, unlike when Ella came along, she loved the oodles of attention she received for her part in producing this new child. She pranced around the school playground like a peacock on the pull, puffing out her chest, pushing the pram and demanding that everyone admired her new brother. Ella, on the other hand, was just like Molly had been the first time. She adored her brother at home, but really could not understand why everyone in the playground was suddenly gushing at her.

My fast delivery, speedy return home and lack of repairs with Ella meant that life very quickly returned to relative normality, just with an additional person to juggle into my day. I was doing a full food shop, with both children in the trolley, when Ella was just forty hours old – admittedly with my mum in tow just in case a crisis of tears or tantrums occurred – but it all went incredibly smoothly. I was so chuffed with myself. It had taken me weeks to truly venture out after Molly's birth so this was a huge boost to my self-confidence.

When I fell pregnant with Alfie, which was just before Molly's fourth birthday and Ella's second, I naturally thought it was going to be a breeze again. After all, it's bound to get easier each time, isn't it? This time we went for the nuchal scan for early detection of disabilities. It was a really tough decision for me, when my job is caring for people with learning disabilities. I could not imagine how I would deal with any disability diagnosis. With both Molly and Ella, I had refused to have any tests, other than the twenty-week scan, as I preferred to take the ostrich approach: what I didn't know, I didn't have to worry about. I would happily have taken this line again, but David pointed out that we could no longer be selfish about this. He said that when it was just us, and even when we only had one other child to think about, we knew we could and would deal with whatever life threw at us. When it came to a third child, though, we realized that we had to also think of the impact a child with a severe disability would have on Molly and Ella, and the time and devotion we could give to them. Reluctantly I agreed with his common sense and logic, but I still couldn't imagine facing the consequences of a less-than-positive result. Fortunately we came out with a top result. My likelihood of producing a child with Down's syndrome was something like one in 3,700, which, we were reliably informed, was equivalent to a fifteen-year-old. David, of course, decided to rephrase this and told everyone that his wife had the body of a fifteen-year-old and he felt like a positive cradle snatcher having such a nubile missus!

In my negotiating with David over the pros and cons of going for this scan, I did get him to agree to allow me to ask the sex of the child. We hadn't done this with either of the other two, but, after my shock at Ella's lack of a willy, I really felt that I needed to know, but didn't want to tell anyone else. The doctor informed us that she'd give 70/30 odds on the child being a girl, and we were really pleased we had asked. Mentally I could then draw up a list of all the pluses for same-sex siblings and would not have to deal with the disappointment at the delivery. As much as I felt convinced that I was carrying a girl, I still planned to creep to David again to get total confirmation at the twenty-week scan. Tragically, it was the day before that scan that David's brother died, and so the details of the scan faded into insignificance. We really turned up and were just going through the motions, and it wasn't until the jelly had been applied and the first sign of life was visible on the screen that it even crossed my mind to ask about the sex. I turned to David and mouthed, 'Can I ask the sex?' David came back with a resounding, 'No,' and there was no time or scope for negotiating as the speedy scanning lady whizzed through the essential measurements. I was gutted at the time, but afterwards I was glad. It's a bit like Christmas presents: you have a fair idea what's in them, but it's much nicer to not know exactly what it is until you open them on Christmas Day. If you go peeking beforehand, you only end up disappointed in yourself. I have a theory that the people who do ask the sex of their child are the people who peeked at their presents in childhood. Andrea and Sarah were clearly present-peekers, whereas Lyndsey and I were definitely not.

With the nuchal scan's 70/30 odds in favour of a girl, you can imagine the shock we had when we did finally unwrap our Christmas present and it came out with appendages! Alfie was no girl, but also things were definitely not a 'breeze', as I had anticipated, with the delivery. After my three-hour hospital stay with Ella, I was in for an entire week with Alfie. At ten days late, I went in to be induced, taking the girls to my mum's in the morning and fully anticipating being able to pick them up that night. To cut a very long story as short as possible, I ended up being induced every morning for three days, causing plenty of contractions, but zero on the dilation score sheet! The midwives kept saying, 'Go for a walk, that'll bring it on.' Walk! David and I didn't just walk, we practically did a marathon around Hertfordshire. In real desperation, on day three I jumped down a flight of thirty stairs (one at a time that is, not all at once!).

A three-day stay on the antenatal ward for my third child really did nothing for my nerves either. Seeing all those women in labour brought the memories flooding back. With Molly, I had naively thought that labour couldn't possibly hurt that much and had no fears. With Ella, I had thought, well, the first time it was all new and a bit of a shock, so I probably didn't help myself deal with the pain very well. This time, it'll be fine. With Alfie,

I had done it twice before and knew all too well that it really did hurt like hell, and I was totally petrified.

That night, my waters broke, full-blown contractions started and I finally made it to the long-awaited and dreaded delivery suite. Here we go, I thought, but when four hours later I still was hardly dilated at all I conceded to an epidural. This was something I'd never even considered with the girls, but I had a sixth sense that things weren't going to end up running smoothly. And what a fantastic invention it is! Prior to the epidural I was at the full-blown mooing stage of labour, clawing and clinging to David. Suddenly I smiled, sighed and sat back saying, 'Ah, that's better.' David was totally gobsmacked, then a look of complete confusion came over his face as he said, 'Sorry, love, but why the HELL didn't we do this the other two times?' A question I really couldn't answer. All I know was that I was still glad I had previously done it the painful way, but that watching my contractions on a screen, with no pain at all, was fantastic this time. David was glued to it, saying things like, 'Cor, that was a good one. Imagine how much that one hurt.' Alfie was still determined not to use the usual exit and, a further four hours later, his heartbeat plummeted, so I was stripped and shaved, and Alfie opted for the emergency exit! I had always enjoyed mocking my mates who had Caesareans by saying that they were 'too posh to push'. But by the time the decision was reached with Alfie, we were just relieved that something was being done and done quickly. We just wanted our child safely on the outside. My relief bordered on hysteria when David entered the room in full scrubs. I have to say that even in the state I was in, I couldn't help but notice how gorgeous he looked. George Clooney, eat your heart out. Here comes David Gardener. My camera was immediately called for to capture this Clooney look. Having been so independent through the delivery of Ella, the crisis that enveloped Alfie's arrival really brought David and me close together. The shock of being told from behind the surgical screen that we had, in fact, got a banana ice cream and not the vanilla we'd been expecting was one that saw us both well up with relief and pride. The flavour by then was immaterial, we were just glad to get any ice cream at all!

The strain of a four-day labour really took its toll on the girls, but Molly especially. She spent the whole time leaping at my mum's phone every time it rang, and I could see the strain on her pretty little face when she came to visit. Ella, on the other hand, was pretty oblivious to all the anxieties. She was just a bit impatient for this baby she'd been promised for so long and couldn't understand why we weren't at home. She had told everyone at playgroup that if it was a boy it was going to be called 'Father Christmas', and Santa was just proving too slow for her liking. She now calls him 'Elsie', which is somewhat confusing, but at least it isn't Father Christmas, and Molly brands him around for all to admire as though she made him herself, out of a couple of egg boxes and some sticky-back plastic.

The timing of Alfie's arrival has proved to be pretty perfect. Molly has started full-time school and Ella had just started three mornings a week at playgroup, which means that this time I actually get my precious moments of unadulterated baby cooing with my boy. It all sounds so perfect, doesn't it? The only downside is that, although there is no jealousy towards Alfie's arrival on the family scene, the vying for my attention is now between the girls and has hit fever pitch. My gorgeous girls who have always been best friends are now snarling sisters who are constantly spitting feathers. I suppose I can't complain, though. It would be a miracle or a lie to say a third child has had no denting impact on us, but thankfully there are very few hours in the day after school for them to really frazzle my nerves with their fighting – although they still manage to have a damn good go at it!

Eat, Drink and Will We Ever Be Merry Again?

It's hard to recall now what meal times were like before children. They just seemed to be something that happened relatively easily with limited preparation and no forward planning. Shopping lists were something carried by middle-aged ladies – why would you possibly need a list to choose what you fancied for that week?

With children on the scene, meal times suddenly became an integral part of the day. Battling with fussy eaters, planning meals to encompass variety and vitamins, the do's and don'ts of junk food and treats, and all of this three times a day. It's a wonder that mums manage to fit anything else at all into their existence. The daily dealings with meals are exacerbated by the sudden introduction into life of working to specific times. No longer is lunch an occurrence somewhere between twelve and three, depending on how hungry you are and when you can fit it in. Suddenly lunch is at 12.45 p.m. precisely and your child is in danger of turning into the Incredible Hulk if you are anything more than fifteen minutes late with that plate. But when it is put in front of them, that's when the fun really starts . . .

So here are our tales: do they or don't they eat, do we or don't we do battle and what about chocolate and treats? . . . the dilemmas, the decision, the diets.

Talking of diets, what about us? The battle of avoiding that comfort food of sausages, smiley faces and baked beans is damn near impossible. Why is it that at 5 p.m. a plate of kiddie's food is so much more appealing than the tagliatelle and garlic bread you have planned to eat later? And how well does the booze flow now we're mothers of at least two children? Weaning, feeding, cooking, snacking and not forgetting the all-important drinking . . . we cover the lot.

Lyndsey

***

Bethan has always been an incredibly good eater, so I fear my tales will be a bit limited on this subject. She switched from breast to bottle with total ease, then when she started on solids she roared her way up through all the different levels of lumpiness without even a hint of hassle. She was always a bit of a guzzler when it came to her milk, though, which had its pluses and its drawbacks. I would look at mothers with slow feeders and think how frustrating it must be to have to wait so long for the child to finish its feed. Bethan could drain a bottle like a contestant in a drinking boat race, but the downside was that, also like a drinking contender, the whole lot would often projectile its way out just a couple of minutes later. When we were at home, I would be fully prepared for this with muslin squares spread around ready to catch the offending burp. But her favourite place to do this was just as we strapped her into her car seat. I would be starting the car engine and thanking God for the miracle of punctuality with the unpredictability of a baby then *burrrppp* . . . there in her car seat, the whole flaming lot. As I lifted her out, the rancid, curdled milk would be dripping off her clothes into the pool that had collected in the bottom of the rock-a-tot. It was all I could do to change her, mop out and clean up the car seat, then line it with a towel to reduce the dampness, let alone worry about the fact that she now had an empty stomach. It's a wonder the car seat cover survived to see another child with the amount of burp abuse it received, although admittedly it didn't go through the wash as often as it should have. Sometimes it took the rising aroma as the sun shone through the car window to trigger the 'Must remember to wash the car seat' thoughts. It's amazing how much more pattern a car seat has after a cycle through the washing machine.

Bethan does love her milk and, in fact, to this day still has warm milk as soon as she wakes up and last thing at night as we read a story to her in bed. I used to worry that this is a bit of a baby habit that needed breaking, but then I think of all the calcium and goodness for her and, after all, isn't a warm, milky drink at bedtime to be encouraged to enhance sleep? Anyway, at least it's not out of a baby bottle and she doesn't burp it back up any more.

Bethan was born with an extremely independent streak. She was walking by ten months, and once she had found her feet she also insisted on her hands having control of her cutlery. I don't know who it was more frustrating for, me as the watching mother or her as each quivering spoonful plopped into her lap a millisecond before it would reach her mouth. If I tried to be helpful by offering to take the spoon, the little madam would rapidly snatch it back in temper, catapulting the contents across the room. Being ever persistent, she would then return her mind to the bowl, but this time as the spoon approached her open mouth she'd turn it just a fraction too soon and deposit the contents in the lip of her plastic bib. Once her bowl was empty, she then concentrated her efforts on the remnants sitting in her bib, and so the whole process continued. Sometimes I thought that lunch would merge with tea, as the meals seemed to go on for so long.

As you can imagine, I was incredibly grateful for the arrival of the finger food stage, when once again meals hit a more realistic time zone. Bethan took little encouragement to catch on to the fact that her stomach would be filled a lot quicker by stuffing a fish finger or sausage in her mouth rather than faffing around with a spoon. Unfortunately my preference for speedy 'no cutlery required meals' for Bethan saw the beginning of her only element of food fussiness. Once she had a fix on finger food, I had great trouble getting anything 'saucey' past her lips. Spaghetti Bolognese had to be separated into pasta with Bolognese sauce on the side. Even now she prefers her sauces to be kept on the side and would never dream of eating a bowl of soup. Going round to people's houses also had a cringe factor about it as you never knew if this would be the time that your child would cry out, 'I don't like this,' or 'I don't like that,' or would just leave the food untouched on the plate. I tried to save this embarrassment by quickly asking to leave off the carrots or not to put the sauce on the top to ensure that Bethan would leave a clean plate. Thankfully to date she hasn't drastically let me down in public and has always managed to politely choke down any mixed-up meals, although I still feel myself breaking out into a sweat when someone has gone to the trouble of preparing the meal I fear will be Bethan's first refusal. Recently we went to Andrea's and she had spent a lot of time preparing macaroni cheese for the children. Believe me it is a great feat for Andrea to even enter her own kitchen, let alone find the ingredients to prepare such a meal, yet I knew that this would be a total 'no-no' for Bethan if I served it at home. I politely requested, 'Just a small portion for Bethan,' and willed her to at least attempt a couple of mouthfuls. To my utter amazement she wolfed the lot down and asked for seconds. Why is it that children do that? 'Don't like it' seems to be one of the earliest sentences mastered at home, yet once they are out of the house it rarely rears its ugly head. It's tempting to take it personally, as I know that cooking is not my forte, but I'm just grateful that it is this way round and that no one else meets the food fads of Bethan.

When I say that cooking isn't my thing, what I should say is that I am actually rarely allowed to cook any more. After Bethan was born, Tim took on the role as family chef. This is mainly because the alternative option of bathing and putting to bed our tired baby and toddler obviously is far more exhausting than standing in the kitchen with a beer can in your hand. He also works in pricing strategy for one of the big supermarkets, which he clearly feels makes him an expert on the food purchasing side of things as well, so what he purchases in his research is cooked. As a result of this, I have basically been reduced to underchef with sole responsibility for fish fingers and smiley faces.

As for eating out, I can probably count on one hand the number of times Tim and I have been out for dinner since Bethan was born. Pre-Caitlin, we tended to do more as a threesome at the weekends, rather than on our own. I think this stemmed from guilt on my part, having left Bethan in nursery for four full days a week, so I simply didn't want to then leave her again in the arms of a baby-sitter. To be quite honest, though, I thoroughly enjoyed these outings with her. As she was an only child until the age of four and a half, trips to the pub were actually pleasurable and relaxing, not the endurance test they seem to turn into when the second and third children come along with a smaller age gap. Bethan also enjoys a pub lunch in the child-friendly local. In fact, I'm sure one of her first words was 'pub', as she could spot those swinging signs with remarkable accuracy as we travelled about the country and would be heard shouting, 'Pub,' and pointing frantically from the confines of her car seat. Her favourite tipple is a glass of water (she won't drink anything else) with a pink straw and a bag of red crisps. This gives us enough time to have a couple of drinks before heading for home. On the occasional times when Tim used to pick her up from nursery in the evening, I would arrive home to find no one there. A quick call on the mobile and Tim would say Bethan wanted to go to the pub – how convenient for him – but it's true she does ask to go to the pub. I hasten to add it's the crisps she's after, which she wouldn't otherwise get at home.

Whilst on the subject of crisps, that reminds me of the one thing that has deteriorated quite dramatically since the commencement of my child-rearing years, and that is the state of my car. Before Bethan was born, I could boast a reasonably clean car. Well, at least it wasn't the health hazard that it has become. We do spend a lot of time in the car travelling far and wide most weekends to visit friends and family. Also, for the past four years we have travelled to France for our summer holiday, thinking it to be an easier option. Packing an entire car with all our essential supplies seemed so much less stressful than being restricted to the capacity of a suitcase. Bethan is very tolerant of these long journeys, but then with the snack supplies provided I'm hardly surprised. When it comes to packing the nibbles for the journey, it seems more like I've packed for a nuclear attack than a two-day trip down to the Dordogne, and the car becomes our bunker. But when we arrive at our destination, it always appears as though this nuclear attack has actually occurred *in* our bunker! Breadcrumbs, crushed crisps, bits of sausage, spat-out grapes or cherry stones and the inevitable sticky sweet wrappers littering the back seat – absolutely disgusting I know, but at least she has had fun on the way! Anything for an easy journey, that's my motto.

Generally, I do feel that so far on the children and food front we may have been experiencing the calm before the storm. So if Bethan is our calm, here's praying that Caitlin doesn't turn out to be our storm. The introduction of solids lies just around the corner, so I will be dusting off my Annabel Karmel baby recipe book and requesting permission to access the blender in 'Tim's kitchen' before I know it. By Caitlin's age, Bethan was already on the bottle, but Caitlin is certainly putting up a fight over this one. So maybe I'm destined for some tricky times with my second little girl . . . who knows?

Andrea

* * *

I can start by saying that, when it comes to children's diets, anything frowned upon I have done. When I talk to the others, I realize just how hopeless I am when it comes to grub. I bottle-fed both boys from birth, I used dummies and powdered baby food, and I introduced them to McDonald's including fizzy cola, from the day they could chew a chip.

Having had the horrendous guilt trip of bottle-feeding Max with the 'breast is best' campaign being permanently rammed down my throat, I was dreading the looks of disdain from the health professionals if I failed again with Sam. By then the breastfeeding campaign had stepped up a peg, too, and they'd even removed the option of free ready mixed baby milk from the postnatal ward at our hospital. So when Sam was born six weeks early, I really thought I was going to be in for a grilling if I didn't do my best to supply him with the real stuff, but how wrong I was. After all that hype about not giving your child the best start in life if you don't breastfeed, the midwives looked positively relieved when I opted for formula. This clearly made their lives a lot simpler, as they could keep tabs on exactly what was going in, so why do they have to give us mums such a hard time when we want to do exactly the same? I can safely say that I have no lasting guilt at bottle-feeding. Even the argument of passing on the mother's immunity fell flat for me when Molly went down with chicken pox whilst still being breastfed by Hilary. Despite numerous opportunities to contract it from her, Max on his formula diet managed to remain spotless.

Along with the early diet of formula milk, both my boys also managed to get through the odd gallon of Infacol. When people say, 'Oh, I love that baby smell,' the only smell that springs to my mind is that sickly sweet smell of Infacol, which my boys gave out from every pore and poo. I have absolutely no idea if my boys would have suffered from colic, and if I'm honest I still don't really know what colic is. All I knew was that in an Enid Blyton book some horse had to be walked around the paddock all night because it had colic and if they had let it lie down it may have died. I wasn't taking any risks, so introduced my children to the wonders of Infacol pretty much from day one. If there hadn't been a national shortage of the stuff when Sam was five months old, I fear I'd still be giving him the odd pre-meal squirt of it now.

My next dietary downfall was the introduction of solids. Having used the freebie packet of powdered baby rice from one of the Bounty packs, I never quite ventured beyond that powdered food shelf when it came to introducing new flavours. It has to be said that I have never smelt anything quite so disgusting as powdered Sunday roast, whatever the hell that's meant to be, but Max wolfed it down. It wasn't until the Fat Ladies were all feeding the children together one day that I realized quite how poor my culinary expertise was. It had never even crossed my mind to boil and blend fresh veg, but guilt spurred me into action. The next day I rushed out and bought shedloads of carrots and broccoli, plus of course the essential blender, as I hadn't previously possessed any mixing-type gadgets. I spent the whole afternoon cooking, pureeing and trying to work out what utensils are meant to be sterilized in this process and, more to the point, how. By the end of the afternoon, it was a bit of a case of Delia Smith, eat your heart out, as I stood proudly admiring enough ice cubes to last him at least one hundred meals. Would Max touch it, though? Absolutely no way! His lips were pursed shut, and the lad went on hunger strike until he could smell the delectable aroma of the trusty old packet mix again. As far as I was concerned, that was it for home cooking, and I'm embarrassed to say that it was also pretty much it for cooking fresh vegetables for the boys from then on.

I have some hideous childhood memories of gruesome greens, and being a soft-touch mum I was never going to inflict such vile vegetables on my boys. I can vividly remember having vegetables put on my plate with a Sunday dinner and not being allowed to leave the table until they had all gone. And so there I would still be sitting at teatime with a plate of cold, congealed cabbage in front of me. I can remember gagging as I desperately tried to swallow hideous sprouts, and I had to resort to extreme measures in order to survive. I either had to waste a much-desired roast potato by cutting a hole in it and hiding my one sprout inside it, or I had to persuade my brother to eat it and would then have to be his slave for the week in return. I remember my mum once telling me that if you didn't eat your vegetables you would smell, but despite my obsession with personal hygiene I still couldn't face them. This was never going to happen to my boys, so I admit I have tended to simply avoid vegetables altogether. It was only when we were round at Sarah's for tea recently that I discovered that Max actually has a passion for broccoli. As Sarah dished up the dinner I said, 'Max won't eat broccoli, I'm afraid,' as I thought back to the mound I had pureed four years earlier. At which point Max waltzed through the kitchen cheering, 'Yippee! Broccoli, my favourite. I only usually get this at school.' Time to explore that fresh veg counter again, I thought, as I notched up another nutritional failure. Thank God it was Sarah's house he had said that in. I would have been mortified if he had chosen one of the other school mums to announce my catering limitations to.

Finally, whilst slating myself, I may as well also hold my hands up to an early introduction to fast food, although at least I wasn't alone on this one. Hilary and I started taking Molly and Max for a weekly swim followed by a McDonald's Happy Meal from quite a young age. We can't remember exactly what age they were when they started tucking into nuggets and chips, but it was definitely way before their first birthdays. Bruce was absolutely horrified at this and requested that we alternate our eating venue each week with a healthy little wholemeal café up the road. We humoured him and superficially agreed to this, but basically carried on with our weekly routine. He really didn't have any argument anyway because I frequently found evidence of additional McDonald's trips discreetly hidden in the bin from when he had been on childcare duty. Max finally grassed me up to his dad just before his second birthday, when Bruce was trying to teach him the letters in his name. Having written out a nice big 'M' on a piece of paper, he asked Max, 'What does that say?' 'McDonald's!' cheered Max, so unbelievably proud of himself for recognizing a letter for the first time. Ooops, I thought, as I made a swift exit before the questions started. Having admitted to such an array of dieting disasters, I would like to say that, despite the fact that my children are fed the least healthy diet of all the Fat Ladies' offspring, they are seldom unwell, touch wood. They have never had a day off sick from preschool or school so far. So I must be doing something right.

Moving on to my own eating habits, you will have gathered by now that I am no cook. I would claim to have cooked a meal if I have chucked a frozen chicken Kiev in the oven along with a potato waffle and simultaneously heated a tin of baked beans. You can imagine how nervous I get when Fat Ladies' lunches come to my house then. Everyone has now come to accept that lunch at mine means a pizza thrown in the oven and a bag of salad, but Sarah with all her home baking and home-grown vegetables still manages to frighten me. Last time it was my turn she turned up with a big bag of home-grown rocket saying, 'I thought you might like to pad out the salad with this.' Lovely, I thought, but what the hell do I do with it? I could work out that it needed washing, but had no idea if I was meant to chop or destalk it. As I plonked the washed leaves in a bowl, Lyndsey came into the kitchen, and I seized the opportunity to ask her opinion on my rocket preparation. 'Do I have to do anything else to it?' I whispered, not wanting Sarah to think I was ungrateful for her contribution. 'It might be an idea to pick the slug out!' Lyns replied. Sure enough, there crawling across the top leaf was a dirty great big slug that I must have been blind to miss. Suddenly my oven-ready pizza seemed like heaven compared to the slug salad I was offering on the side.

As for booze, this is where I have to confess that after thirty-three years of being teetotal I have finally found an alcoholic drink I like. My friend Lizzie offered me a sip of her cranberry Bacardi Breezer on a girls' night out and I was pleasantly surprised at how it didn't taste of alcohol at all. For any drink to have a chance of being accepted by me, it really can't have even a hint of alcoholic taste about it. Even a chocolate liqueur would be spat out in disgust, and for me to spit out chocolate is unheard of, so it must be a serious aversion. Once I'd discovered this cranberry drink, I decided to buy a four-pack on my next food shop. When I went football training that week, I came home exhausted, sweating buckets and gasping. Just as I reached for my usual Pepsi Max, I remembered my new Bacardi Breezers and decided to opt for this thirst-quenching drink instead. I know now just how stupid this was, but having never drunk before I managed to neck two bottles of the stuff in the space of a couple of minutes. I then found myself giggling and staggering my way to my muscle-relaxing bath looking remarkably like Eddie from *Ab Fab*. I flopped straight from the bath into my bed and just lay there while the room span around me. I didn't dare even attempt to get out of bed again as the combination of exercise and alcohol had rendered my legs totally unconnected to my brain. I even

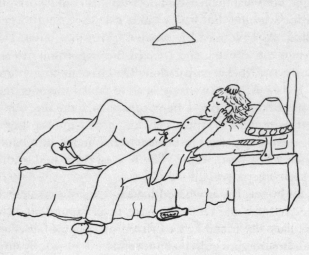

*I even had to call Bruce on his mobile to get him to come
upstairs and switch my light off*

had to call Bruce on his mobile from the phone by the bed to
ask him to come upstairs and switch my light off. God knows
what he thought. He'd been married to me for eight years and I
hadn't ever touched a drop, then a month before we parted ways
I'm blind drunk and drinking alone! I can't see this becoming a
regular occurrence. The truth is I still prefer my Pepsi Max and
having control over my limbs, but at least I have a drink on
stand-by should the urge take me.

I have to end by grassing up Hilary on her alcohol consumption
one New Year's Eve. I have always loved New Year and rau-
cously bellow the words to 'Auld Lang Syne' in my usual tone-
deaf fashion – and this was certainly a New Year to remember.
Bruce and I were invited to Hilary and David's for what was
meant to be a fairly sedate evening with one other couple. The
idea was that all the children stayed up to play, then we had a

late supper once they had all crashed out. What we hadn't anticipated was that Hilary, our host and chef, was going to be plastered before we even sat down to eat. A few glasses of wine on an empty stomach took rapid effect, and her desire to dish up dinner seemed to go out the window. She forgot to put the jacket potatoes in the oven and simultaneously forgot to take the beef in beer casserole out of the oven. The end result was us not sitting down to eat until 10.30 p.m., absolutely starving, only to be served rock-hard jackets with dried black-pan scraping on top. This was one occasion I was sorely tempted to tuck into the accompanying broccoli. Just as Hilary was heading for the kitchen to fetch the much-needed puddings, Sam started coughing and crying from upstairs, so I had to disappear. From their alcoholic haze, Hilary and her nurse friend casually informed me that Sam had croup and packed me off to the bathroom to 'steam him'. This did work and, half an hour later, I had settled Sam again and headed for the puds. Quite sensibly everyone else had gone for the shop-bought profiteroles, which left me the only option of what amounted to a block of charcoal with cream. Apparently this had been an apple strudel in a former life, but I was so hungry I tucked in anyway. I'm sure that the two fillings I needed on my next trip to the dentist were a direct result of Hilary's pudding!

When we retired to the comfort of the lounge, Hilary then spotted Molly's Early Learning Centre microphone, and before we knew it Meatloaf was in the CD player and Hils did a seriously entertaining performance of 'Bat out of Hell'. She not only knew all Meatloaf's lyrics, but also took on his entire persona as she head-banged and leapt around the room seemingly oblivious to the rest of us. Admittedly everyone else was also singing into their beer-bottle microphones. It would have taken a brave man to try to part Hilary from the real microphone, that's for sure.

At half past one, exhausted and hoarse, there was a lull in the singing and the sound of Sam still coughing could be heard yet again. When I brought him down, my two on-site albeit paralytic nurses then casually announced that, if Sam were their son, they'd take him to casualty. Thanks for telling me now, girls! So there I sat in casualty at 3 a.m. on New Year's Day amongst yet another bunch of drunks. Despite all this, I have to say it was an excellent evening and apparently when I did eventually get home at 6 a.m. Hils was just finishing her last bottle of wine and still hadn't released her grip on the microphone.

Hilary

* * *

I have to hold my hands up to being a tad tipsy on the New Year's Eve that Andrea has so eloquently sold my soul on. But if that isolated incident of alcohol consumption makes me the Fat Ladies' lush, it has to be said that we really have turned into a sorry excuse for a cheap date. I could count on two fingers the number of times I've been drunk since having children, but I will admit that, when I do, I do it with all the style and grace of a teenage cider drinker. When I think about it, it's hardly surprising that my drinking capacity has plummeted so dramatically. After all, as Molly now approaches five, I am beginning to realize that really I have had very few windows of opportunity to take on alcohol again. What with three pregnancies adding up to twenty-seven months, plus two and a half lots of breastfeeding adding up to sixteen months so far – and still counting – there really have been only a few months when alcohol has been an option. Even when I can drink I still begrudge the expense of a taxi and so 'lardy ladies taxi services' were formed. But when I'm driving home in the early hours of the morning with matchsticks holding my eyes open, there is nothing more irritating than my drunken husband asleep next to me. David has a frustrating habit of playing the hard-done-by party animal who is being dragged away at his prime by his boring wife. The fact that we are already past our baby-sitting deadline is totally immaterial. Then, no sooner has David slurred his goodbyes than he's snoring and dribbling next to me for the entire journey home. So I don't think it is the alcohol I miss after all. Perhaps it's just that I'd rather not reach the point where I want revenge so badly that I would stuff chillis into my snoring husband's cheeks, if I had some handy.

So, on to one of those causes of my alcohol limitations: breastfeeding. This was something that came extremely naturally for me with both Molly and Ella. They each had gobs on them like the Mersey Tunnel, and I became totally adept at feeding on the move. I could cook an entire meal one-handed whilst breastfeeding. They would cling on for dear life as I sped around the kitchen. Okay, so I didn't quite pull off the sexy Nigella Lawson look when it came to culinary creations, but, hell, meals were made and babies were fed. Then along came Alfie; he was born at nine pounds and was very hungry, so I naturally thought that he, too, would take to breastfeeding like a duck to water. The first pitfall was that I had a Caesarean and what a nightmare that is when it comes to feeding your new baby, even for a professional wet nurse like me. I cannot imagine how daunting it must be for first-time mums to try to get the hang of their new charge in that situation. It is frightening enough trying to handle your precious new baby when you can move, but, when it takes nothing short of the services of Bob the Builder's Scoop and Lofty just to get you into the upright position, it's rendered almost impossible. You feel so useless and totally dependent on others for both your needs and your baby's. Being an old-timer, this wasn't quite as bad for me. Whenever I could, I would avoid that hospital bedside buzzer for assistance and use all sorts of cringeworthy highly unrecommended means of getting by.

Alfie was kept in one of the goldfish bowl cribs that was

latched on to the side of my hospital bed, so my favourite trick would be to lift up my top, grab him firmly by the back of his Babygro, spin him around, then lower his mouth directly onto my boob – a bit like one of those teddy-grabbing machines at the amusement arcade. I could do this without moving my pain-riddled body at all, but I have to admit that his head did slump a bit, so I'm sure I'd have been in a lot of trouble if I'd been spotted by a passing midwife. We muddled through in some very peculiar positions and I thought that everything was going well, until my milk came in. It was then that I realized that my son really was a sipper and not a guzzler. Both the girls would suck a boob dry on each feed. After they had eaten, I was left in no doubt as to which side they had fed from, as I'd have one Melinda Messenger boob and one deflated granny boob. Alfie, on the other hand, just seemed to hang around having a little sip here and a little sip there. He never did get the hang of that full-blown sucking action, which meant he only ever drank the foremilk, never getting to the good stuff at the back. The end result was that he lost weight, I was so painfully engorged that I looked like a victim on 'boob jobs from hell' and for the first time in three children I had to face the ordeal of having a health visitor grappling with my boob.

This was a particular low point in my relationship with my new son; not only had he not found the natural exit route to join us in this world, but also he couldn't even suck a boob properly . . . men! I had always had a hang-up about being assisted in breastfeeding to the point that I'd said I would rather bottle-feed than that. You can imagine how gutted I was then to have reached my third and final child before finding myself in the humiliating position of having to have my boob gripped by another woman and waggled around my son's face in an attempt to tantalize his mouth open. Putting aside this personal indignity, it was Alfie's weight loss that really concerned me, so as soon as the health visitor left I found myself rummaging in the cupboards for my steam sterilizer and bottles, and immediately started topping up his feeds. I had a feeling of total failure as I had so wanted to really enjoy and cherish every moment of feeding this, my last baby, and I knew that top-up bottles for a weak feeder like Alfie would probably be the beginning of the end of breastfeeding. In fact, Alfie took to mixed feeding brilliantly because, as much as the male in him meant he couldn't cope with me multitasking as I breastfed, it also meant he was totally chilled out and really quite happy with any milk whatever the source. Not only is my easygoing little chap happy to bottle or breast it, but he is also perfectly happy to self-feed when it comes to the bottle. My friend gave him a cuddly dog with long legs and beanie paws when he was born, which turned out to be the ideal bottle prop. Again I am sure that this is a highly frowned-upon feeding method, but I lie him down in his baby chair, put the dog across his tummy with a paw up either side of his head, then rest the bottle on the dog's back, creating the perfect angle into his mouth. I then drag his chair from room to room with me, while I manically go about my chores. Bless him, he has now become so used to this feeding method that he stops crying and starts wriggling his legs in anticipation as soon as I put the dog on his lap. I think I'll have to call this new feeding friend of his Pavlov!

As you can imagine, with three children, school runs, playgroup runs, bottoms to wipe, a farming husband to feed a good wholesome meal twice a day to, house to clean and, to top it all, our latest acquisition of a puppy to train, my desire to take time out to breastfeed is being far outweighed by the freedom to 'get on'. I still couldn't bear to give up completely, though, so whenever I can I do still feed him myself, and we always have a long, unadulterated snuggle feed every morning in bed while David takes the girls down for breakfast. I love this precious time, just me with my little lad.

As for solids, all I can say is thank heavens I produced a family of slap-heads! I used to look at babies with beautiful heads of hair with envy, thinking how wonderful it must be to actually have use for that baby hair brush I had so neatly placed on the nursery shelf since long before the birth of Molly. Now when I see such lovely locks my only thoughts are those of sympathy . . . what a nightmare it must be to clean them up after every meal! Molly could take awards for how far she could spread her food – nothing short of a straitjacket could reduce the smear factor. I would watch Sarah feed Jack with total astonishment as his mouth opened wide and neatly accepted each mouthful; he barely even needed a bib. I tried everything. I stripped Molly down to her vest and nappy before each meal and would then pin down her arms with one hand whilst spooning in the goods with the other. This system worked quite well, until I needed two hands to scrape the bowl. As soon as I released my vicelike grip, she'd make a speedy bid for the bowl, grabbing any last remains to squelch through her fingers, rub across her head and into every little crease on her chubby little limbs. If I tried the alternative of keeping the bowl out of reach, but leaving her hands free, she just went for the spit-and-spread approach instead. I decided that Molly could, in fact, manufacture baby food because there was definitely more coming out than going in at times. And just to complete this mental image of parental bliss, she also demanded a drink halfway through each meal and only breast milk would do! So there I would sit, carrot-encrusted child wrapped around my midriff, totally absorbed in the unspoken pleasures of motherhood . . . not!

Despite the smear factor, meals have always been a firm favourite with Molly, and her declaration of her love of food manifested itself in the form of a low, continuous hum whilst eating. If it was something she really loved, the hum became almost impossible to talk over it was so loud. But it did have its pluses, too; first, at least she was eating with her mouth closed and, secondly, she unwittingly dobbed her dad in to me on his Sunday morning habits. I shall explain. When Molly was a couple of months old, David very generously and uncharacteristically thoughtfully offered me a weekly lie-in on Sunday mornings because 'I deserved it'. Naturally I was very grateful for this new caring streak in him and would always treat him in the godlike fashion such a hero deserves for the rest of the day, but then the game was well and truly given away. It was as we sat down to Sunday lunch some months later that I noticed Molly's appreciative humming had actually taken on a bit of a tune . . . it was, in fact, the theme tune to *Match of the Day*! The sod had been being treated like a saint purely because he had been getting up early to watch the football. At the end of the day, I know I was still getting my lie-in, and if I'm honest I was just gutted that I didn't possess the same levels of deviousness and cunning.

I have to say that humming or no humming (the humming just stopped overnight when she was three), I was extremely smug about my achievement with my daughter's appetite and desire to demolish anything edible. And *my* achievement was exactly how I saw this at the time. I had been one of those opinionated pre-parenting people who said ridiculous things like, 'I'll never allow my children to be fussy eaters. If they say they don't like it, keep giving it to them until they do.' What a total bore I must have been. I was horrified when a lady at work told me she was cooking different things for each of her family on Christmas Day, and I'm sure that 'rod' and 'back' were somewhere in my response to this news. Then along came Ella, and I take it all back. When you have a fussy eater to tackle three times a day, it would prove pretty testing even for the likes of archangel Miriam Stoppard. Ella's first two words were 'mama' and 'yuk', and the second of those two words was used continuously throughout those thrice-daily nightmares otherwise known as meals. She would only eat meals if she were distracted by looking at books whilst chasing cheesy puffs around her tray. If she opened her mouth to laugh, chew the book or actually managed to get her little fingers to grip a cheesy puff, then I'd nip in with a swift nutrient-piled spoon! If I was able to get four or five mouthfuls to actually go in and stay in, the meal was deemed a success, but this was quite rare, and generally all meals were substituted an hour later with what seemed like a couple of gallons of milk. The only guaranteed hit with Ella was an organic jar of spinach and potato for four-month-olds, but when she hit her first birthday and this was still her only 'dead cert' meal I became more ruthless about the whole thing. From then on she was given whatever Molly was having and that was it. No force-feeding, no getting angry, no cheesy puffs – just the calm option of dinner or no dinner: the choice is yours.

Here I am nearly two years on, and I can safely say that the stress of meal times vastly reduced as a result of this. It is just all the hours in between meals that are still hell! Ella always goes for the 'no dinner' option, but then spends the whole time between meals saying 'fudda eat'. This is basically a bit like one of those Japanese TV endurance game shows to see who cracks first. 'Fudda eat,' meaning 'I want to eat the entire contents of the chocolate cupboard,' whined in your ear every thirty seconds for three hours is definitely comparable to having your head encased in a Perspex box whilst 200 cockroaches crawl over your eye sockets for the entertainment of the TV viewing public. In a bid to reduce the 'fudda eat' factor between meals, I have had to resort to careful meal planning, with a limited range of menu options, coaxing, threatening and bribing, and I still have to feed her at least half of her meal if I want a 'fudda eat'-free zone afterwards. The nightmare is that I can't even coax her with healthy alternative between-meal snacks if she does successfully break me down in those between-meal battle zones, as she absolutely, categorically will not touch anything that could poss-ibly have come within a fifty-mile radius of fruit. As far as Ella is concerned, to ask her to eat any form of fruit would be second only to eating dog poo. No, in fact I think she'd prefer to give the poo a go! She won't even drink orange squash because it's fruit or eat flavoured ice cream or sweets. I have even tried disguising chopped-up banana by smothering it in chocolate sauce, but as soon as the fruit hits her mouth, she is physically gagging. Ella has to be the only child I know who looks like they are going to vomit on a trip to the pick-your-own strawberry farm, when she's not even touching the produce, let alone sampling it. She still has her Popeye love of spinach, though, so I'm not overly concerned, but when I mentioned it at a clinic appointment and a well-meaning health worker suggested I might try chopping the fruit up to make it look more appealing I did come very close to snapping. For God's sake, what did she think I'd been doing, chucking her an apple, shouting, 'Here you are, Ella. Catch. Get your laughing gear around that if you're hungry!'

The funny thing is, for someone so averse to eating meals, Ella absolutely loves cooking. If ever she discovers I have prepared a meal without her assistance she's gutted. As soon as she sees me head for the kitchen she is there, chair pulled up to the counter, standing there with sleeves rolled up and raring to go. She could even identify all the ingredients in a spaghetti Bolognese by the age of two; maybe she just hates my cooking and is desperately trying to get her hand in to at least make it vaguely palatable, the poor undernourished child!

The other subject that I was definitely an over-opinionated bore on prior to being a parent was childhood chocolate con-sumption. I had a slightly alternative stance on this one, though. I believed that if you deprived children of chocolate treats you just create a long-term lust for that forbidden fruit. At children's parties, I had all too often seen that treat-deprived child making a beeline for the party food. They were prepared to trample anyone in their way for a chocolate mini roll and fight to the death for something as decadent as a Cadbury's Twirl. I was determined to make chocolate something normal and everyday to eat in our house, the theory being that, if they didn't crave it as a treat, it wouldn't be a major love in their lives. This theory worked just fine on Molly, who chooses between chocolate and chopped fruit after each meal, both being firm favourites. Ella, however, is up there with the best of them at the parties, ready to take on even the biggest boys in the battle for a finger of fudge. So once again the frightening realization that my children really do have minds of their own kicks in. I have done exactly the same with both children, yet one will only drink orange juice, hates milk, loves fruit and eats for England, whilst the other will only drink water, loves milk, hates fruit and only eats under duress. So what the hell Alfie's going to do, only time will tell.

Sarah

* * *

From the first day I fell pregnant, I became semi-obsessed with the nutritional value of everything that passed my lips. When I am pregnant, I am extremely attentive to what I eat and have probably become more so with each pregnancy, mainly to avoid any food that could harm my unborn child. I have no trouble consuming all the right vitamins and minerals in a balanced, healthy diet with plenty of fruit and vegetables, and I still enjoy the regular glass of wine or bottle of beer. But it's when we're in France that I have the most problems identifying what I can and cannot eat, mainly in terms of dairy and meat produce. I am reliably informed that French women are not specifically advised to avoid eating their much-cherished French cheeses, unlike us pregnant women in the UK. So, when faced with a stinking cheese trolley in a French restaurant, neither can I bring myself to try requesting a *fromage pasteurisé*, knowing the pained and quizzical expression I will undoubtedly receive in response, nor can I enjoy eating those deliciously runny and evil-smelling soft cheeses that I normally love. It's the same with a peppered steak, which by my reckoning has to be eaten at least a little bit pink. The thought of tucking into a lump of leathery overdone steak just doesn't appeal to me. I prefer simply to abstain rather than order something that will have me worrying for the next few days about a possible bout of foetus-threatening listeria. It's more difficult when eating with friends, whether here or across the Channel, because I do not want to offend anyone or, worse still, appear a pregnant bore by analysing absolutely everything that I eat. However, I cannot help but squirm as I watch the cooked meat being dished out from the same dish that I swear I saw the raw meat sitting on just a few minutes before it was thrown on to the barbecue. As I know what a late miscarriage is all about, this probably makes me even more edgy than most and certainly more restrictive than I really need be. But, in order to sleep with an easy conscience, I prefer to endure nine months abstention from anything I'm not sure about, happy in the knowledge that I can stuff myself stupid with rich blue cheeses, pink steaks and copious amounts of red wine afterwards!

Having said that, even after my babies are born, I still find myself watching what I eat. After Eloise was born, I gorged myself on mammoth breakfasts of cereals piled high with summer fruits in order to make sure things moved easily through my digestive system, so concerned was I not to have to push too hard on the occasion of my first postnatal visit to the toilet! I was to discover only a few days later that all fruit and vegetables with pips in have a tendency to cause bad wind in newborns that are breastfed. I was sure nobody had told me this before. I expect it might have been mentioned in the antenatal classes I attended with Jack, but that was more than three years earlier. With your second baby, it seems as though you are treated a bit like an expert and so miss out on all those wise and essential pearls of wisdom. Well this, albeit late, pearl of wisdom helped explain the colicky bouts that Eloise tended to experience in the evenings, so straight away I scaled down my daily intake of strawberries and raspberries to just half a punnet and substituted them with a monkey's portion of bananas!

I thoroughly enjoyed doing the breastfeeding bit again and found it far more relaxing the second time round. I really wanted to make the most of it in case Eloise was to be our last child. It seems as though there is an abundance of advice available when it comes to feeding your second child, particularly in regard to simultaneously entertaining your older child so as to avoid jealousy of the baby. I decided to take up the excellent advice of 'making this a special time for the elder child by reading to him as you feed the baby', so I would sit breastfeeding Eloise at the same time as reading Jack stories on the sofa. The epitome of perfect parenting, or so I thought, until these reading sessions quickly declined into a chance for me to catch up on the sleep I was missing out on during the night. All too often they ended up with me being woken from a deep slumber by a little voice saying, 'Have you finished this page yet, Mummy?' I felt virtuous that my intentions were good, even though I didn't always succeed!

Now the Fat Ladies have always enjoyed a decent mickey-take at my expense for the enthusiasm I have for fresh garden produce, and I rapidly acquired the nickname of 'the female Monty Don'. With Tim doing most of the hard work in our modest vegetable plot, I have no shame in admitting that I take the fun in reaping the crop and cooking and eating it. For anyone who has ever grown so much as a tomato in a grow bag, I'm sure you'll be able to empathize with the simple pleasure in tasting the difference between what you grow yourself in your own soil, totally free from all pesticides, chemicals and GM tampering, and what you can buy in the shops. I can honestly say that the more time and space I had, the more our fruit and vegetable plot would expand, and things which I once regarded as slightly 'crusty' and old-fashioned such as making jams and fruit compotes I find I really enjoy. Maybe the ageing process is striking me even more rapidly than I realized. Who knows? Maybe I'll be taking up bridge next year!

My fascination with fresh food, and the cooking of it, has inevitably had an effect on how I try to feed the children. As soon as Jack reached that sixteen-week stage, I began doing the puree thing to excess. In fact, I often found myself trying out Annabel Karmel dishes on Tim, which I was pleased to see he thoroughly enjoyed and which made my life easier because it meant I also had a freezer full of kiddie-sized meals to last me months! I actually found it incredibly satisfying pureeing a whole range of different fruit and vegetables in one go, freezing and bagging them, and knowing that I didn't have to repeat the process for another couple of weeks. This was 'cooking' made easy. It also made it easier to leave the children with Tim during that stage because lunch would consist of 'two orange ice cubes and a green one', and tea would be 'three yellow ones'! What makes me smile now is that, at the tender age of four months, both my children were eating things like butternut squash, mango and papaya, primarily because they were easily pureed or mashed; however, ever since they went on to proper solids, they have never tasted these exotic goods again. I'm quite sure Jack would not be able to distinguish one from the other now.

Moving on to proper solids was in fact a tricky transition in Jack's eating career, as he developed a desire to choke on anything at all lumpy. It might have stemmed from the time when he was only a few months old and a well-meaning friend introduced him to his first ever biscuit. So taken was he by the sweet taste that he did his best to demolish it in record time, half suffocating himself in the process. Having been unsure whether it was a good idea to begin with, especially as I was only just in the process of introducing him to baby rice, I put my reticence down to 'overprotective first-time mother syndrome' and didn't air my concerns. Suddenly I found myself flying across the room as I realized that Jack was in fact no longer breathing and had turned decidedly blue. I whisked him out of my friend's arms, who incidentally remained blissfully ignorant of the effect the biscuit was having on my baby, and slapped madly on his back whilst holding him upside down. My friend was mortified that she had done something that necessitated my reacting like a paramedic. I was just mad with myself for not trusting my instincts in the first place. From that point on, Jack had a tendency to choke on any of the lumpier foods I tried to introduce to him and I would regularly catapult him out of his highchair, put him across my knee and slap his back, much to the horror of any unsuspecting onlookers. So, what with Jack's propensity to choke, coupled with my frozen carrot puree mountain – which I certainly wasn't going to waste – I'm actually quite impressed that I ever got around to introducing my son to finger foods. It's now impossible to recall in detail, but I'm sure Andrea probably had something to do with helping Jack through to this stage with her secret outings with the boys to McDonald's. She would have got away with it if it hadn't been for the fact that Jack always returned from tea at Max's with a small toy bearing the telltale initial 'M' on it!

My interest in the nutritional value of the food Jack and Eloise eat, as well as my abhorrence for wastage, certainly does have its drawbacks sometimes and has often raised my stress levels to fever

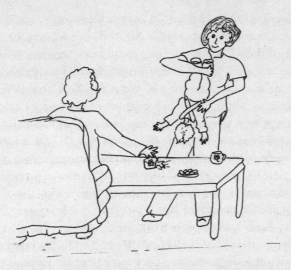

*Jack's tendency to choke regularly had me catapulting him
out of his highchair and slapping his back, much to the horror
of unsuspecting onlookers*

pitch. I forget the amount of times I've lost the plot over an
unfinished fish pie or rhubarb crumble. It's not just because they
are wasting perfectly good food, but, more to the point, it's food
that I have spent precious time baking for them. Generally they
are both good eaters, so you would think that by now I would
have learnt my lesson and would not bother battling on these
rare occasions: after all, life is just too short to get irate too often
over a bit of cod. However, when I feel Jack's refusal approaching,
as he folds his arms and adopts that determined stance not to
finish his plate, I cannot help but feel the steam rising as I know
that all other coaxing options have been exhausted, and once
again we are facing a battle of wills. I find myself changing from
the calm of Mary Poppins to the mean demeanour of the 'Child
Catcher' as I glare into his tiny face nose to nose and spit threats

through gritted teeth. I frighten myself sometimes, but my children are obviously either just far too headstrong or simply immune to their mother's bizarre mealtime outbursts. 'Fine, you can have it for tea then!' is my final line, and sometimes I can achieve satisfaction at seeing the plate finished later in the day. But I have to admit, there are only so many times I can allow myself to reheat a meal in the microwave, and all too often I have had to swallow my pride and throw good food straight into the bin because there is absolutely no nutritional value at all left on the plate. Any more 'nuking' would render it positively *bad* for them! Sometimes I wonder why I bother with this battle of principle and, at times like this, I resort to the emergency rations of Smiley Faces and nuggets from the freezer.

Finally, to meals out. I have always believed that children will behave better in restaurants if they have been accustomed to the experience from a young age. This was something that we managed to achieve with Jack simply because we would eat out a lot at weekends when we lived in Spain. He rapidly acquired the taste for Spanish tapas, hams of any description and calamari (because the battered squid resembled chips, I'm sure). As a toddler, he once swallowed a garlic clove by accident and reeked of garlic for days afterwards: maybe that helped to give him a taste for Continental cooking from early on! Eating out for Jack now is always a grown-up treat which he knows requires good behaviour and proper table manners, especially as it usually involves having a glass of Coke as a special exception! For Eloise, however, who has not had so much early exposure to eating in restaurants because we have less reason to do so now that we're back in the UK, I can see that the learning curve is going to be a colourful one. We were eating out at lunchtime recently and I could see that she wasn't going to be happy sitting at the table any longer than it took her to demolish a lump of bread and a glass of orange juice. It doesn't help either that she has developed a desire to clear her highchair tray with one sweep of her tiny arm, jettisoning everything to the ground below. So, in a moment of inspiration, I decided to go for the threat of the 'monster' that would come up from downstairs and 'get the naughty children who mucked around at the lunch table'. This had the desired effect in persuading her to put her bib on and to stop her clearing her tray just long enough for Tim, Jack and I to enjoy a relatively trouble-free first course. I was feeling quite happy with my slightly unorthodox discipline regime until Jack declared he needed the toilet, halfway through dessert. As Jack and Tim disappeared downstairs to the gents, Eloise suddenly dissolved into a distraught, screaming toddler, clambering out of her highchair and throwing everything aside in her wake. She was wholly convinced that Daddy and 'Jack-Jack' were going to be eaten by the monster. The entire restaurant turned to watch this spectacle and took on that irritating expression of 'For goodness sake, can't you control your child?', which served no purpose other than to turn me as puce as the table napkins. By the time Tim and Jack returned, I had escaped to comparative safety outside the restaurant, with a writhing and yelling toddler in my arms, as I wondered whether the monster was such a good idea after all. Despite residual fears that I may have been creating an unreasonable phobia in my daughter's imagination, I do find that the threat of this 'monster' is very useful whenever I find myself in a social situation where her behaviour needs to be kept under control. I shall just need to be more careful next time about not positioning the dreaded monster next to the toilets!

I do believe in 'grinning and bearing it' when it comes to eating out, as I'm determined to have my children learn the fun of food and, by that, I don't mean in using it to throw as missiles across the room or in spreading it across each other's faces! Even if it does mean the odd boycotted meal, or meals when Tim and I have to take it in turns to stand outside a restaurant with a screaming child whilst the other gets indigestion by rushing down a main course at breakneck speed, I hope we will eventually succeed in our aim. However, perhaps I'm more of a glutton for punishment than a glutton for the food I'm trying to encourage my children to appreciate!

Certainly when it comes to eating out, or 'drinking out' should I say, now that I am a mum, I am a total lightweight. Like Hilary, I, too, have lost my student capacity for imbibing; it takes little more than a couple of glasses of wine to start my head spinning. I guess it must be a combination of three pregnancies, periods of breastfeeding and the knowledge that I won't be able to sleep off a hangover the following morning that has had the general effect of keeping me on the straight and narrow. The idea of dealing with children when I'm tired and crotchety is bad enough, let alone having a hideous hangover and bad stomach necessitating emergency rushes to the bathroom! This paints a sorry picture, particularly when the Fat Ladies regularly meet up with another group of local mums. These other mums generally meet for a bottle or two of wine between them at somebody's house before heading to the restaurant to meet up with us. They then knock back copious amounts of alcohol between them and finish by staggering their way to their taxis home in the early hours. This leaves us feeling drastically lacking in stamina and decidedly feeble when it comes to excuses, as they, too, all have children the same ages as ours. So, in comparison, we do look like a pathetic bunch of prudes, which is something we will have to rectify. Perhaps when babes in arms (and in tummies) have become toddlers who can switch the television on themselves in the morning, we will make it our next Fat Ladies' mission to better ourselves in the consumption stakes!

Sleep and Sex

Sleep and sex — they just had to be coupled together for this chapter. To even attempt to tackle an entire chapter dedicated solely to the subject of our sex lives was just too much for us to endure. Not to mention the limitation of the material available. Sadly our sex lives are comparable to our ability to consume alcohol, but we would like to emphasize that with one of us pregnant, two with new babies and one recently separated, the sorry state of our sex lives we describe is hopefully not reflective of our futures.

The subject of sleep, or, more importantly, the lack of it, is one that is somehow far more emotive at this point in our married lives. It's something that most mums could waffle on about for hours. I don't know if it's a national thing or a worldwide issue, but all women seem to be obsessed with how well a child sleeps. It's always up there in the first three questions, even from total strangers, as they admire your new offspring: 'Ah, how sweet, how old is he?' and 'What's his name?' And, wait for it . . . 'Does he sleep well?' It's guaranteed; all women will ask it, without fail. It's as though a child's sleep pattern from birth will in some way be indicative of their future success. If they wake every couple of hours through the night, then surely they'll never progress in life beyond supermarket trolley attendant, but if you've got an 'all night through' baby, well surely you can anticipate at the very least a career in politics! The sad thing is that we're all guilty of it. We may mock, but then we spark up a conversation with the mother of a young child and, before we know it, we are party to every detail of its sleep routine. The Fat Ladies are no exception, as will become embarrassingly apparent as the subject of our sex lives pales into the occasional paragraph in comparison to the subject of sleep.

Andrea

* * *

I think I am completely justified in only talking about sleep in this chapter, as I am the only one of us who has a genuine excuse to keep the sex side of things to a minimum. First, I said far too much in the first book and have had to live it down with police banter ever since and, more importantly, it's been more than six months since I last had the pleasure (not that I'm counting or anything), so I don't really have any up-to-date news on the subject. However, the others have insisted that I can't leave it out altogether, so I shall be brief.

One thing that has amazed me since Bruce and I decided to separate is how quickly everyone is keen to line me up with someone else. 'Don't worry, we'll find you a new man in no time' seems to be a standard phrase from friends, as the Cilla Black in them comes roaring to the surface. Discussions occur as if I wasn't there, as couples work their way through lists of single male friends, then write them off as inappropriate before even giving me the basic outline of the poor chap. 'What about Jim, he's nice . . . No, too old. Oh, I know, Patrick. He's perfect, although perhaps a little short and isn't he planning on moving back to Ireland? That's right, he's no good . . .' And so the conversations go on. All I can say is thankfully, to date, everyone has exhausted their options for me without finding any suitable candidates, which is a huge relief as the mere thought of dating again totally horrifies me. Sarah, it has to be said, is up there with the best of them on excitement levels at the prospect of me meeting someone else, but I don't think she wants me to settle down at all. I get the impression she'd prefer to see me with a string of lovers, as she keeps referring to my new home as the 'shag pad'. I can barely get my head around the fact that I am about to embark on a new life on my own with the boys, let alone entertain the thought of introducing a new man into the equation. But, then again, I also can't accept that my sex life is over at thirty-three! How do you go about introducing a bloke to your children? Do you wait until you are attached to the chap and think it will last, only to discover they hate him, or do you introduce them early on, then have to explain his absence when he dumps you after the first date? The thought of my boys having a string of short-lived 'uncles' is inconceivable, and what if these 'uncles' didn't support Arsenal? What then? Anyway, forget the introductions to the boys, more importantly how the hell do I introduce a man to the monstrosity of stretch marks otherwise known as my body? At least Bruce went through it all with me, and knew my body at its best when I was fit, healthy and sporty. Some poor, unsuspecting soul wouldn't know what was going on if he clapped eyes on my vast array of stretch marks, which incidentally have barely faded at all in the past couple of years, not to mention my rapidly expanding hips, thighs and bum. I console myself with a glimmer of hope that any prospective chap would not only have to be an Arsenal fan, but would also have to be a boob man, as my boobs never did reduce completely back to their original size. I might then not be a total no-go zone.

But, for the time being, the only person that sleeps in the same bed as me on a regular basis, unfortunately, is Sam, but at least he doesn't care what my body looks like. Without fail he arrives between five and six each morning, and at the moment I just let him crawl into my huge bed, snuggle up with him and we sleep till Max wakes us around seven. This is clearly not a good habit to get into, but it all stems from my desperate attempts to get him off the dummy last Christmas. Both of my boys had dummies from birth, and I was keen to stop them using them once they hit their second birthdays. With Max this was not an issue. He just had such a good understanding of vocabulary that when I said to him before his second birthday that dummies can harm your teeth, within a day or two he had thrown them all in the bin and that was it, job done. When Sam was born three months later and started using them, I thought that Max might want one back, but being born with the desire for perfection does have some advantages, as there was no way he was going to risk dodgy teeth for the desire for a dummy. Sam was a dummy addict, though, and together with his 'friend girl' Ella was not about to give them up without a fight. Both families were on holiday in Spain last year when Ella and Sam were rapidly approaching their second birthdays. It was only then that we realized just how much the pair of them relied on their dummies, as they played on the beach stark naked, but with plugs in place. They were both complete addicts who screamed to high heaven if Hilary and I tried to do battle. They were even connoisseurs of the various types available and were incredibly picky. Ella would only touch Piglet, Pooh Bear and Tigger ones, whilst Sam would only have Tommee Tippee cherry-teated ones. Hils and I agreed on holiday that ugly and embarrassing as they were, it was not worth spoiling the holiday. The day we got back, we both went cold turkey on them and simply removed them during the day, but they could still have them at night. It was bloody hard work, but we both persevered using the 'Ella/Sam doesn't have them' angle whenever the battle got tough. By the end of the week they were over the DTs, and the daytime addiction was cured.

I should have left it at that, as Sam had always been a great night-time sleeper after he got over his early arrival into this world. If he ever did stir in the night, it was because he had lost his dummy, but as soon as it was popped back in he would go straight back to sleep. I was concerned about any long-term effects on his teeth, as he was now well past my two-year cut-off. I planned a strategy in mid-December and started telling him that, on Christmas Day, Father Christmas would bring him lots of presents, but would take all of his dummies away because he was a big boy now. I was off work for two weeks at Christmas and decided I would be able to commit to my plan. It went brilliantly on the day itself, and I threw all the dummies away, so that I couldn't get hold of any no matter how desperate times got. Basically, the actual going to sleep wasn't a problem at all, which had been my biggest fear, but when he woke in the night and I didn't have a dummy to settle him, then the nightmare really began. He would scream for about an hour before he went back off, and this happened every night for nearly three months. By now Bruce and I were in separate rooms. One night I realized that if I brought him in with me he just went straight back to sleep, so I became his new dummy, and that is where we are now. I'm not sure how long my new role as the human dummy will go on and, to be quite honest, I really couldn't give a damn. I have far too much else to worry about and, at the end of the day, I'm sure he won't want to be sharing my bed when he's eighteen. After my nightmare, though, Hilary is certainly holding back on tackling the same battle with Ella, so she may well be packing her plug for her honeymoon!

Another thing I hope will reduce before my boys reach the age of sleeping with anyone other than their mother is the desire to wear their latest fetish to bed. Both boys get hooked, wholeheartedly, on whatever is the latest 'in' thing, and live it on a 24-hour-a-day basis. The first big one was Buzz Lightyear, followed by Action Man, Harry Potter and now Peter Pan. They take on each fad with great enthusiasm, then ditch them as soon as the next big hit comes along. However, they don't just settle for getting the video and buying the outfit, they actually have to become that person. Max was Buzz for nearly a year and would snap the head off anyone who dared to call him anything else. Poor Molly would be most confused and ask Hilary who Max was being today before they came for fear of getting off on the wrong foot and missing out on half the playing time while Max decided whether to forgive her or not. She has always quite willingly become Max's female counterparts and so far has played Jessie the cowgirl, Action Man's girlfriend, Hermione and now Wendy, despite the fact that she has never sat through any of the films.

When Max was in his Buzz phase, he would wear his Buzz spacesuit all day, every day, and the big battle was prising the thing off him each night. On a couple of occasions, the row was just not worth it, so I would tuck Buzz up, kiss him goodnight, then turn him back into Max when he was asleep. Thankfully a pair of Buzz pyjamas was soon purchased and a compromise was found . . . phew! Although he has now grown out of Buzz, he still has sleeping fad companions, with the latest favourite being Peter Pan. He sleeps with Captain Hook's hook next to him, but it has to be covered with a sock to keep it warm. Sam is no better. He also did the *Toy Story* thing last year and now definitely believes that he is Harry Potter. We have to call him Harry, and either Eloise or Ella, depending on who we are with, has to be Hermione. He carries his wand and has the proper velvet Harry cape. This, like Max's Buzz outfit, is a permanent feature on Sam's back, and I have to prise it off him once a week to decrust the week's food offerings. I'm just hoping this phase wears off before the cape deteriorates to rag status, as it is already looking decidedly shabby. Sam has taken this overactive imagination just that one step further, though, by also introducing an imaginary friend called 'Ron'. I have to say that it's becoming a bit of a pain, as I keep getting told off for sitting on Ron during Sam's bedtime story. I also have to sing to Ron, hold Ron's hand and put Ron's seatbelt on in the car. Now that really is frustrating when you're running late for school! If it wasn't for the fact that I'm trying to be extra sensitive to my boys' emotional needs as our lives head into these new horizons, I'd be packing Ron's bags and chucking him out the door . . . bloody nuisance!

One bonus of these fads is the fact that it gains me an extra hour's snooze each morning. Once they have woken me up I come downstairs with them, make their breakfast and then put on their latest video, knowing that I am safe for at least an hour to pop back to bed for a little snooze. This overuse of television for kids is clearly frowned upon, but it gets me much-needed extra sleep and, as Lyns will explain, it did her and Tim a favour, too. Sarah lays down quite rigid restrictions on her children's TV viewing times, as I found out when Jack came for his first sleepover with Max a couple of months ago. Everything was running smoothly until Sam asked to watch television because the big boys weren't letting him play. Well, Jack's ears pricked up because it was clearly an extra treat for him, so he sat with Sam, eyes glued to the telly, totally oblivious to Max's devastation as he howled the house down. The disappointment at losing his big sleepover assistant midway through the puppet show rehearsal was all too much for him. Jack was determined to make the most of this unexpected perk, though, and eventually Max gave up and joined them on the couch for his usual bedtime *Simpsons*.

Max had been so excited about sharing his room with Jack that I didn't think I had a hope in hell of getting them to sleep at any reasonable hour. But this was one occasion that I realized that it really wasn't worth laying down the big hand of the law. Once I had settled them into bed, and they thought I was safely out of earshot, I snuck back upstairs and sat eavesdropping outside their door as they whispered and giggled about all those things four-year-olds find so fascinating. But less than ten minutes after hearing their planned antics to the wee small hours, I became aware that it was now only Jack's voice I could hear. I peeped around the corner to find Jack chatting away to a snoring Max. The midnight feasts, I fear, will have to be put on hold until Max can at least keep his eyes open past eight o'clock. After all, a late supper doesn't sound nearly as exciting. Here's hoping he has a few more sleepovers in him before the midnight feasts commence and all hell breaks loose!

Hilary

***

Nearly five years after having my first child, I am finally in the smug position of being able to say that I have three children who sleep brilliantly. Okay, admittedly the middle one still has a dummy, but Alfie, who is just ten weeks old, has slept dummy-less for twelve hours a night for the past six weeks – and in his own room! Thank God he is such a great sleeper because I seriously do not think I would qualify as a member of the human race if he had given me even half the grief over sleep that his sisters had. For a start, night feeds lying in bed were a definite no-no, so that certainly helped to speed up the process of early persuasion to sleeping through the night. With the girls I had barely become conscious at night. I literally zombied my way to their crib, plonked them in bed next to me and dozed while they fed. Quite often they'd still be latched on when I woke the next morning. With Alfie, this just became too frightening. I had complete faith in myself that I would always remain aware of the girls being with me in the bed, even in my deepest sleep, but, with Alfie, I was just out like a light and totally oblivious to the helpless little addition next to me. He miraculously survived one night like this, but I had to force myself to sit up on a hard chair to do the night feeds after that for fear of waking with him not next to me, but completely flattened under me. This upright at night bit was a new experience and one I absolutely loathed. I could not even contemplate keeping my eyes open, and every so often I'd lose control of my head, slumping forwards, then catapulting upright and awake for at least thirty seconds before I'd be off again. Thankfully my little hero only ever had one feed during the night and that stopped just before he was four weeks old. To actually put that down on paper gives me such extreme pleasure. I thought children that slept were just things you read about or that people made up. In the past, if anyone ever had the nerve to tell me that their child slept through, I had a burning desire to slap them. I do feel as if I have total justification for being smug on this one because I have been to hell and back on the subject of sleep deprivation, so I did deserve at least one good one.

When it comes to my desire to get a decent night's kip, every bit of professional advice on settling your child into a good sleep pattern was totally ignored. But if you could make a list of all the head-shaking, teeth-sucking never-ever-do's that are bandied about, I have done the lot!

Molly's major problem in life has been the actual process of getting to sleep. From birth she was one of those babies that needed breastfeeding in order to sleep. When this stopped at seven months, we then endured months of trial and error of every other means. We tried rocking, pacing, rubbing her tummy, rubbing her back, swinging her in her car seat, stroking her head, loud music, quiet music, no music. You name it, we did it, and all our evenings had to be dedicated to the cause. Needless to say, we didn't even contemplate the cot battle by day, but just strategically planned pushes in the pram or trips in the car to coincide with her morning and afternoon naps. It became highly tempting to do the same at night, but I was determined this minute little thing was not going to get the better of me. At eleven months, I tried the infamous controlled crying.

Excellent in theory, but I don't think it took into account quite how headstrong and determined our eldest daughter was. The idea behind it is that you leave the child to cry and return to them at set time intervals, lie them back down, cover them back up and calmly repeat a set reassuring phrase such as 'No, go to sleep now. It's bed time. Night, night.' During the time that she was left, Molly would build herself up into such a frenzy that the whole thing was rendered impossible. She would hold her breath, vomit, fill her nappy and descend into uncontrollable inconsolable sobs with absolutely no let-up. So instead of simply lying her back down and covering her up, I'd also have to change her vomit-covered sheet and stinky nappy, and wipe her snot-streaked face with a tepid flannel. Even after all that she would still be screaming and impossible to make lie down, as she'd ping back into the upright position and manically clamber at the cot bars. To repeat the set reassuring phrase involved bellowing it over her screams, which somehow didn't quite fulfil the instruction of 'Calmly, repeat reassuring phrase.' It is meant to take five nights to cure your child, but by night three I was a gibbering wreck and Molly had developed a phobia about her entire bedroom. She would scream and start shaking all over if you just went in there to change her nappy. We never did manage to recover from the hatred of the cot, and it wasn't until we turned her cot into a bed at fourteen months that we started to win the war. We took a far more softly, softly line of approach this time and went initially for the totally frowned-upon approach of lying next to her. This progressed to sitting on the floor next to her, to sitting on the floor near the door, to sitting on the floor outside the door, but still in view, reading a book. The next stage after that was a huge step forward – sitting on the floor reading a book, but just out of her field of vision. By then I'd had nearly a year's worth of practice at sneaking out of her room without so much as breathing for fear of those eyes pinging open again, and so this new out-of-sight zone became the perfect venue for my early escapes from the bedtime ritual. By the time Ella was born, when Molly was two, we had progressed to watching television in our room as long as we didn't go downstairs until she was definitely asleep, and that is where the war ended. This was the final compromise. Weapons were put down and treaties were signed which remain in place to this day. I'm sure that she could be coaxed into allowing us to descend the stairs by now, but David has been allocated the role of bed waiter and the appeal of a nag-free hour watching television without being allocated any domestic tasks by me is far too great for him to consider progressing a stage further.

Although the going-to-bed battle was sorted, Molly still didn't like staying in bed all night. I was pregnant and, after fighting her to go to bed for hours on end, I really did not have the energy or inclination to conduct the same fight again in the middle of the night, so from about 1 a.m. the bloodcurdling cries of 'Can I come in your bed yet?' would start, and she'd come hurtling across the landing as soon as she was given the green light. Once again, my anxieties about this were mainly to do with the fact that I knew this was a total no-no in the bibles of child rearing and not because I didn't want her in with us. We debated dragging her kicking and screaming back to her bedroom in order to get it sorted before the baby arrived, but went instead for the alternative approach to sleep management and purchased a super king-size bed – plenty of room for four! I also introduced a sticker chart where she received a sticker for every time she spent a whole night in her bed, and five stickers bought her a new Topsy and Tim book. Molly's always up for a bit of bribery, so this did work quite well, until the next problem arose. We discovered that, when she slept on her own, she scratched her eczema raw. We hadn't realized how much we stopped her scratching in her sleep until we were faced with the bloodstained

We went for the alternative approach to sleep management
and purchased a super king-size bed

sheets and self-mutilated mess of a daughter each morning. It may not have bothered her, but this level of self-injury didn't seem to justify the material gain of a poxy storybook, and so we let her sneak back in. In the end, in true appalling parenting style, we even gave her stickers for managing to sneak into our bed without waking us rather than screaming out from her bedroom. Nothing like a decent reward system to truly cement those bad habits.

Then Ella was born, and I discovered the full meaning of sleep deprivation. She did not let go of my boob for more than an hour at a time at night and even less if I tried to remove her from my bed. Even in our huge bed, Molly wriggling, Ella feeding and David having the audacity to sleep facing me were just too much for me. Ella and I moved on to the futon in her room, and for eight weeks I accepted that, to give my boobs any reprieve at night, Ella needed to sleep face-down on top of me. During this time I gradually turned into a zombie with back ache from the rock-hard futon mattress, and Molly took ownership of my dreamy, comfy bed, calling it 'mine and Daddy's bed'.

Something needed to be done. From here on in, I am every health visitor's worst nightmare, and all my parental approaches are definitely not ones to be adhered to. As an experiment, I popped Ella in her cot one night, but this time I tried her face-down. Nine hours later, she first stirred; I had experienced eight weeks of hell and all because my daughter didn't want to sleep on her back. The problem was that now I had a baby that slept, I of course couldn't. I was adamant that as soon as she slept on her front she was bound to die of cot death, so I was up checking her breathing on average three times an hour. Two days later, we invested in my dream machine . . . a baby monitor that registers the baby's breathing and sets off an alarm if no breathing is detected. This was the best £100 I have ever spent. At that point, I'd have paid more than that for one night's sleep, let alone a whole new future of night and day being separate entities again. What the hell we'd do if the alarm ever went off is a whole channel of thought I barely let myself consider. I dutifully watched the resuscitation video provided and hoped that my nursey brain would kick in if needs must.

This monitor opened my Pandora's box of bad bed practice. After I had the sanctuary of monitoring the presence of life from another room, I did everything in my power to get a full night's sleep. If she woke in the night, no matter what the time, she got a bottle angled across a teddy, which we aptly named Milky Bear, into her mouth as she lay face-down in the bed. I then left her to it – when she finished, she just spat it out, and I'd retrieve the empties in the morning. By eighteen months, she had managed to wangle her way back up to three bottle-feeds a night, plus at least two other call-outs to retrieve lost dummies from under the cot. It was no good; the battle of the bed had to begin again! I had really hoped that if I pretended I wasn't doing such an awful job of handling the nights that maybe they would cure themselves, but Ella was just taking the mickey. I managed to wean her off the night-time milks in just three nights by gradually reducing the quantity and diluting it more until, by night four, she just had a bottle of water in the corner of her cot to help herself to. I was so chuffed that it had been so easy, but also very ashamed that I had let it drag on for so long. She clearly hadn't needed it, and it was no wonder I couldn't get her to eat when each night she was necking enough milk to supply a whole nursery at snack time.

By Molly's fourth birthday and Ella's second, we were getting up a mere three or four times a night to one or other of them, and invariably there were at least three of us in our bed by the morning. But I was pregnant with Alfie and, despite this bed-hopping nightmare, we needed to set the mission for the girls to share a room before the birth. The whole idea of two poor sleepers sharing a room and disturbing each other was my worst nightmare, but bunk beds were bought and the bullet was bitten. Strangely this turned out to be the best move ever. Both girls have gone to bed like angels and don't come in to us until their rabbit alarm clock's ears ping up and its eyes open. Admittedly we'd be pushing it to get the rabbit to wake any later than half past six, but in our house we call that a lie-in!

After all our bedtime antics with the girls, you can see why Alfie has so rapidly earned himself the title of angel child in our house. The only change he has made to our family's bedtime routine is the introduction of military precision timing. With one child, bedtime was in a vague time zone of around half past seven give or take an hour or so. With two, that zone drastically reduced, but still a good hour's discrepancy could easily occur. With three, the countdown to bedtime starts shortly after tea, and I prepare to 'run the gauntlet'. The routine is laid down on tablets of stone, with no deviation. It's five-thirty tea followed by Molly's homework, *Tweenies*, bath, stories, bed, with lights out for all three no later than quarter past seven, and woe betide anyone who dares to call round or phone during this manic zone of the day. Bedtime used to be such a cosy time, but now it's become an existence of survival, as I am so knackered by then and my fuse is so short it barely exists. I hate my new sergeant major approach, and each day after I've tucked them in I sit on my bed and with a huge pang of guilt think how I will try to tackle it with a bit of affection as well as punctuality tomorrow. Even tucking them in, when there are three of them, takes on a slightly less idyllic image than *The Waltons* conjures up. I have made up a little song about each of them, which I sing to them in bed. Now I have three songs to get through, so, when I'm running late and my patience has been tested to the limit by squabbling, overtired children, I find that even my individually written 'Mummy loves you' songs are sung in sergeant major style and at fast-forward speed. 'Could do better,' my parenting school report says. 'A lot better!'

Thinking back over the past four years of bed-hopping, it is a miracle really that we have a second child, let alone a third. Sex is definitely something we now have to remind ourselves to fit in. I find that our love life now tends to happen in sporadic bursts. Sometimes weeks, bordering on months, can pass with no nookie, then something like a night out where we actually talk to each other again will trigger off the memory of who it is we're married to and get us all amorous again. Once we have remembered that this is actually something we enjoy and not just something that infiltrates into valuable sleeping time, we'll have a bit of a run of nocturnal activity for a few days before we forget again. Fortunately we both seem to have the memory of goldfish when it comes to sex, so we seem to remain libido-compatible. What is not compatible to a decent, uninhibited sex life is the need to always have one ear out for the door. The thought of discovering we had uninvited mini-spectators when we reached the finale is totally petrifying. We did once have a pretty close call with Molly, but fortunately, living in an old farm house, we discovered the advantage of a ten-second warning system in the form of a strategically located squeaky floorboard. The funny thing was the greeting we both gave her at midnight. Usually she would be frogmarched back to her room, firmly being told that it was not morning and to go back to sleep. Her little face was a complete picture as we both gave her a rapturous welcome in a demented attempt to cover what she had no idea had been occurring anyway! 'Hello, darling. Look, David, it's Molly!' I gushed as if greeting a long-lost friend. Then we plummeted her back to reality by informing her she actually still had nearly seven hours left in bed. I have to say that this interruption killed the moment stone dead, and it was a fair few months before I could completely relax during nookie without the assistance of a couple of glasses of wine.

It's not just the sex life we have found tricky to keep up; it's also just the bog-standard, everyday conversational relationship. When it was just us, we'd come in from work, and, even if it was while we watched television, we still managed to catch up with what was going on, any gossip, who called, what they had to say etc. With the arrival of each child, this conversation has diminished. I have had to split myself further and further emotionally between all the members of my family, and David being the least needy now gets the smallest part. I used to be so shocked to hear of marriages splitting up when the children were so young. I couldn't understand how two people could do something as magical as produce a family together and so quickly not be able to stand being together. Now I just think what a dozy mare I was to be so romantic. Of course this is going to be the prime time to split up. Even the strongest relationships have to go to hell and back through this humungous change, and our Andrea is living proof. I do think the thing that has helped David and me through these tricky years is our pact to have at least two weekends a year away without the children. These really do rejuvenate our marital batteries, not to mention the sex memory box. I'm just hoping we'll still be able to have these now we have three children to farm out. I also think the fact that David and I had been together for so long before having children has helped us. After eleven years together, we were hardly in the first rush of all-enveloping romanticism when our first child infiltrated our lives. In fact, if anything children have reduced our volatility. We've always enjoyed a decent abuse-hurling row, but having to curtail my foul language when I'm trying to be insulting is totally unsatisfying. Calling David a 'fool' who is talking 'utter rubbish' somehow doesn't have the same effect.

Sarah

* * *

Considering Tim and I have two children who generally sleep very well, and in their own beds, we could easily be expected to be the couple with the very active sex life. But then, I am pregnant again. However, even out of pregnancy, I am sorry to say that we would not exactly qualify as Mr and Mrs Rampant, largely because we are both such active individuals in other things that we hardly ever hit the sack before midnight. After the normal evening meal, household chores, sports, work on business ventures and DIY projects – all things which are best achieved when the children are safely tucked up in bed – the evening is well and truly spent. I am generally climbing into bed at the point my body is so exhausted I can barely contemplate turning over, let alone the idea of any nookie. By the time Tim comes to bed, I'm generally to be found half propped up on my pillow, chin on my chest, still holding my book open at the same page at which I opened it. My ability to crash straight to sleep, added to the fact that I usually cover myself with face and body creams (in my crusade to preserve what youthful skin I may still possess) before I go to bed, is not the best turn-on, that's for sure. Tim ironically refers to my nightly ritual of applying creams after my bath as being 'all creamed up', which is probably not the same way some people would understand the remark! In our case, when I'm 'all creamed up', I'm apparently as appealing to cuddle as a Channel swimmer and make the whole house smell like the Body Shop. So, what we have learnt since having had the children is that we really do have to act spontaneously if the need to sleep and body creams are not going to rule our physical relationship – this has actually added a far more adventurous element to our 'out-of-pregnancy' sex life! When we do visit the nookie scene, we're like children who have just discovered the joy of sweets and simply can't get enough of it for several days. It's certainly so much nicer being able to embark on sex as an enjoyable act rather than as a means to becoming pregnant, but I suspect that those frisky times when we're raiding that proverbial sweet shop and stuffing our faces with sherbet lemons and humbugs have a direct correlation with the time of the month that I am most fertile. I am much keener to get my kit off then, whether I'm wanting to make babies or not!

Shortly after I stopped breastfeeding Eloise, and my first period was just about due, I suffered a strange string of migraines and was advised not to go back on the pill straight away. We were therefore back to using condoms, which made us feel like twenty-year-old students again, but we also played a little Russian roulette during the times I felt sure we were 'safe'. We knew that at some point we'd like to try for a third child, so it didn't matter too much if my calculations had been slightly awry. Once we've finished having children, though, I'm not at all sure which avenue of birth control we'll take. The snip – for either of us – seems such a definitive step to take, but we'll cross that bridge when we come to it.

However, for now the word 'contraception' hardly seems worth bothering about. Admittedly, it was nice to be able to benefit from the larger boob status for the first few months of this pregnancy again, and Tim was certainly very appreciative of the expansion; however, now that my stomach has well and truly taken over, sex has once again taken a back seat in our relationship. Call me old-fashioned, but I find that there's nothing quite like a large and *gyrating* stomach coupled with bulging thighs to kill any spontaneity in a sexual relationship. Plus the fact that my cream application ritual before bed has now increased to include the anti-stretch mark cream that smells positively clinical and is applied to every possible area of my body that I can reach. At bedtimes I am now fearful that even the cross-Channel swimmer is looking appealing in comparison to me, so I'm looking forward to the baby being born and us once again enjoying that sweet shop frenzy.

Now the other three have requested that I put up my hand in this chapter to be counted as the owner of a black vibrator. My admission came when we were driving back from Annette's funeral and baring our souls to each other as a way to lighten the very sombre mood. It almost made Lyndsey swerve off the M40 in shock and certainly left Hilary open-mouthed for a second or two. The way I came by it, however, is far from self-revelatory, as it was a present I got, complete with batteries, at a raucous Millennium New Year's Eve party. Each couple had to wrap a risqué present for a man in black tissue paper and one for a woman in white, and at midnight we all had to delve into the basket and select a gift. Needless to say, my present created the most interest and entertainment, as it was passed around the room on full speed. I was almost four months pregnant with Eloise at the time and felt decidedly embarrassed at the thought of having to take my gift home with me in my evening bag! This was bound to be the one occasion we were stopped and searched on our way home: pregnant woman driving car full of drunken revellers, with a mighty black dildo in her black velvet evening bag wedged down the seat beside her! I can honestly say, hand on heart, that I don't know to this day where we put it when we did get home, but perhaps I should try looking it out, if only as a house warming for Andrea's 'shag pad'! I'm not sure she would necessarily appreciate me offloading my unwanted presents on to her, though, especially as a second-hand vibrator, even with the assurance that it's unused, doesn't sound terribly appealing.

Smut aside and back to reality, I have to say that Tim and I are both people who see the ten o'clock watershed as the possibility of getting another job done before bedtime, instead of the time to start getting ready for bed. I half admire the way friends like Lyndsey don't start anything new after nine at night and are hence in bed well before the clock strikes ten, let alone midnight. Being someone who would love to be up with the lark, to make the most of the early morning hours, I have occasionally tried to get to bed earlier in order to wake earlier. But, I regret that as long as Tim remains a night owl, I'm sure I'll never change. The fact that both Jack and Eloise are good sleepers and don't generally wake before seven in the morning means that I don't have to make it to bed massively early in order to field an early morning wake-up call, as some parents do.

Eloise did go through a patch when she was nine months old, however, when she began waking at midnight and screaming for all her worth from her cot. To begin with, I gave her the benefit of the doubt, assuming it 'must be teeth' or bad dreams, but when the pattern continued and she even began to scream her head off as soon as we put her in her cot in the evening to go to sleep, I realized that this was a behavioural thing that we needed to stamp out as soon as possible. Either that, or she needed to learn how to get herself back off into a deep sleep by herself. Whatever the cause, I felt that we needed to find a solution quickly in order to re-establish the full nights of sleep that I had become used to again. I had heard friends talk about this 'controlled crying' treatment which, although proving a disaster for Hilary, had worked brilliantly for another good friend. She had to try it after she found herself sitting night after night, falling asleep beside her son's cot, just so that he could hold her finger in order to drift off to sleep. As she was heavily pregnant with her second child at the time, she decided that she needed to kick her son's habit before the second baby arrived. It took just four nights and, despite the fact she, too, cried her eyes out in the adjacent room for those four nights, it did work for her, and she soon had a contentedly sleeping – non-finger-gripping – baby.

I decided to try the same with Eloise, except Tim's take on this technique was not so much 'controlled crying' but more 'cold turkey'. He decided that we should instantly shut her bedroom door tight and leave her to scream herself to sleep: this, of course, drove both her and me to distraction. Dads can perhaps be harsher in their methods, but I felt that, although our resolve was exactly the same, I needed to take a more humane approach. I couldn't cope with the sound of my poor little girl sobbing and spluttering in the room next door, having been plunged into pitch darkness right from the start, without reassuring her that we hadn't simply abandoned her to the black hole. So, contrary to Tim's extreme measures, and turning a deaf ear to his 'tuts' and 'humphs', I did adopt the 'leave it five minutes, ten minutes etc. before going back to calm her down' approach, and it did eventually work. There was the odd night when I was so tired I shut her door and went back to bed and fell asleep, only to awake a few hours later in a panic that she had somehow stifled herself with hysterical screaming. I would creep out of bed in the early hours, push open her bedroom door as quietly as possible and be enormously relieved to find her still breathing, but asleep sitting up with her head squashed against the bars of her cot, with her arms and legs dangling out the gaps like a rag doll. Concern for our daughter's sleeping position, and a potential back problem later in life, was a small price to pay for the battle won!

*Concern for my daughter's sleeping position was a small price
to pay for the battle won*

Another subject altogether is discussing the anatomy, let alone the birds and the bees, with children. I never expected their interest in body parts to start so early. As much as Jack and Eloise see Tim and me naked in the mornings, and we never hide ourselves away from them, they still seem to have a giggly fascination about the parts of the body that I suppose even we adults still occasionally 'giggle' about. I remember Hilary having us in stitches over her concern for her daughters' anatomy obsessions. Ella apparently went through a phase of taking positive delight in groping David from behind, shouting 'Bot bot!' as he bent down to pull on his boxers, and Molly even put in a request on her third birthday list for a 'willy like Daddy's'. I pity poor Alfie, having two sisters with such strong cases of penis envy: he'll need protection from an early age, poor little chap. Now I don't know whether it was Molly passing on this obsession to Jack or whether she just simply found a willing ally in him, but between them they became insatiable when it came to their favourite after-tea pastime of 'check bottoms'. This generally involved them skulk- ing under the dining room table – or, worse still, locking them- selves in the bathroom – and removing their lower clothing so they could give each other a thorough examination. How thorough, we never really knew, but hoped it wasn't too detailed consider- ing they were only three years old. Thankfully 'check bottoms' soon became a less appealing option than riding bikes and pre- tending to shoot each other with sticks, and I was relieved that this natural inquisitive learning curve had died a natural death!

It was a good year later that Jack threw me one day by asking me why I didn't have a willy: it was as if it were a vital part missing on my anatomy. I knew I had to come up with an explanation quickly, and a good one at that, because, whatever I said now, it was going to stick. I thought carefully and gave him a brief explanation of the gender differences, using the expression 'girlie bits' to describe the female body parts, and felt relieved that his questioning had finished there. Knowing that Hilary and David always have a range of colourful alternatives to express bodily functions, I thought I'd ask her what terminology she used. After all, babies in their house don't just 'fill their nappies', they 'fudge their jocks', and the children never have a 'snotty nose', they only ever have 'kanga alerts'! So why I was shocked to hear that Hilary's expression for 'girlie bits' was a 'toushdilala', I really can't imagine. Molly had always known her bottom to be called a 'toush', so Hilary just added a bit to make it an extension of something that Molly already knew and understood. All I can say is I am glad I didn't adopt this phrase because, with Jack now approaching five, I can only guess at the taunts he would get in the playground if he started referring to 'toushdilalas' or, perish the thought, 'flossies', 'fairies' or 'ginas'! I fear a boy's street cred, even at this young age, could take a serious nosedive if he got the terminology wrong on such a subject. At least 'girlie bits' is not a description that I would be embarrassed putting my name to if ever Jack truly let me down by blurting it out at school assembly. I just wish my memory went back far enough for me to gauge whether this fascination is perfectly natural or is something that should be sending early warning signs of sex-mad adolescents in the making!

Lyndsey

* * *

Sleep and sex. Well, I'm glad that sleep comes first as, with a new baby, this definitely is higher on my list of priorities at the moment, too. So that's where I'll begin. Bethan was very similar to Molly in that from birth she always seemed to need rocking or cuddling to sleep before I transferred her to her cot. Perhaps it's these headstrong girls, or maybe it's a first baby thing, because there is definitely a far stronger element of pampering to this precious new bundle's needs, not to mention a far greater fear of tears. A mere whimper was enough for me to rush over and scoop up my child for fear the situation would turn nasty and I would find myself with a screaming, out-of-control baby which

I had neither the ability nor the confidence to calm down. As a result of this, she soon mastered the art of not allowing us to place her in her cot without her causing some sort of commotion. Whilst I would let her cry for a few minutes, I felt that when a child becomes so distressed (which she certainly became) she needs to be comforted, and I still to this day do not believe in letting a child cry uncontrollably for any length of time. And so she would be picked out of the cot once more, and eventually with a lot of rocking and patting her back she would drop off into slumber. The back patting had started from day one when it was suggested by a midwife as an aid to help get the babe to sleep. Apparently it resembled the beating of the heart that the baby had heard in the womb. Whether this is true or not I haven't a clue, but it certainly worked for Bethan. I just wished they'd also told me that once she was addicted to this sleep inducement method I would possibly be doing it forever and a day. Once asleep, she would invariably last through to at least six in the morning, at which point a feed and a cuddle in our bed would gain us another hour of much-needed sleep.

All our troubles lay in getting her to sleep, and, as she grew older, and heavier, the cradling and rocking approach was no longer an option without the risk of permanent back injury. We then took it in turns to hang over her cot to gently pat her back. This soon had the required effect, but the hours spent bent double over her cot certainly did test my patience at times, not to mention putting a strain on my lower back. As she became older, she still expected us to stay with her until she was asleep, and once she was talking she even started putting down demands of 'Pat my back.' There was no getting away from it. It was clear who was in control in our house. Despite my dead arm from endless hours leaning over the cot side, I still didn't want to rush into the transfer to a bed. The safe confinements of a cot seemed much less stressful with far fewer variables for the bedtime routine. Unfortunately, somewhere around her second birthday we discovered that the restriction of her cot was, in fact, no longer safe. I had wondered when the right time to move her to a bed would be, then I discovered the answer. I had heard her calling out from her room one night, but by the time I dragged myself to the surface of consciousness she had gone quiet again. I was tempted to just go back to sleep, but something drove me to find my feet and have a quick check. As I opened her bedroom door, the light from the landing caught her like a rabbit in headlights. She was straddling the bars of her cot in an effort to escape. I now truly understood the meaning of the phrase 'staring danger in the face'. What if I hadn't got up? She could have landed on her head, broken her neck in the fall, anything! And so the bed, with all its freedom to wander as and when she liked, was introduced.

Her favourite perambulating activity was into our bed in the middle of the night, and the novelty of this was lovely, but we should have nipped it in the bud the first time her cute little face appeared at the bedside willing us to let her in for a little cuddle. Too tired to battle with her and not thinking about the long-term effects, we let her in rather than fight it out in the middle of the night. But soon something had to be done about it, as it became a nightly ritual. Sticker charts worked for a while – I took a leaf out of Hilary's book for this idea, as there is nothing more rewarding for a three-year-old than to see a chart acknowledging their good behaviour. Also, as Christmas came round, this offered a good bribe – after all, Santa Claus doesn't leave presents for children who don't sleep in their own bed, as he wouldn't know where to find them. So at long last I thought we had broken the habit. Not likely, and still I find myself inventing different bribes to ensure we have the occasional Bethan-free night. On the whole, these work for about five nights a week, but she certainly isn't cured. I have used different tactics with Caitlin, whereby once fed she is placed immediately in her cot, awake or not, and so far she has drifted off to sleep without all the messing around that we had with Bethan. Whether this remains the case we'll have to see, but I hope it's a good omen for the future.

Bethan has never had a comforter or pacifier such as a dummy or cloth, or even a thumb, but she does suck an imaginary dummy using the back of her arm. I had never seen this in a child before, nor have I seen it since, but a sure sign of when she is tired is when her arm goes to her mouth and the big sucking, slurping noises begin. Now this is all well and good when she is in her own bed, but when she's lying next to me at five in the morning, that sucking noise is about as irritating as sitting next to someone sucking up the dregs of a milkshake through a straw. The peace and tranquillity of the darkness are broken and, unless you resort to the extreme measures of wearing earplugs, as I have had to on occasion, you don't sleep another wink until the noise subsides about an hour later. She seems to do it most, and loudest, when she is in a doze or light sleep, and, of course, she is totally oblivious to the disruption she is causing. Just as I finally feel myself dropping back off, then 'Bbrrriiinnnggg', the alarm goes off and I'm up on autopilot, staggering to the bathroom like a zombie. All I can think about is how many hours it is before I can get back into the bed that Bethan is happily still sleeping in. Isn't it funny that we spend our lives creeping around our sleeping children in fear that even breathing too loudly will ping those little eyes open. Yet the earth-shattering decibels of the alarm clock which fires us to the land of the living doesn't so much as cause a twitch from them. When the clocks changed, it became a bonus when they went forward, as this meant that Bethan's early arrival advanced a whole hour to six o'clock, which felt so much better, even if this was only a psychological improvement. Before children, I always loved it when the clocks went back so we got the extra hour in bed; after children, this became hell, as the early morning arrival was then practically the middle of the night. Suddenly losing an hour's sleep but gaining a more sociable waking hour on the clock is far more appealing.

Prior to children I was, like Sarah, quite a late bird, but as the need for sleep grew I found myself going to bed earlier and earlier, which means that by nine-thirty you can usually find me tucked up with a good book. On the weekends that we are staying at friends, or have them staying with us, I do find it a struggle to stifle the yawns as we sit down to eat the starter at my usual lights-out time. My manners always get the better of me, the yawns are swallowed and soon I find myself in a new time zone that is reminiscent of the student days of clubbing it until two in the morning. These occasions are usually accompanied by a similar student hangover the next morning, too. I find once I get over the 11 p.m. threshold I can just keep going, but then I have terrible trouble dropping off to sleep when I do hit the sack. I remember when I first met Tim and we would go out on Friday evenings after work. I found momentum kept me going, and I had good staying power no matter how tired I was at the end of a busy week. Tim, on the other hand, was usually to be found fast asleep in a corner whilst I danced the night away with friends, and I would tap him on the shoulder when it was time to leave. I should have read the warning signals then as his favourite trick now is to disappear upstairs to 'check on Bethan', only never to return and to be found zonked out next to her bed. In some sneaky instances, he would even creep into his own bed, under the false pretence that he was checking on Bethan, and lie fully clothed, sleeping, under the duvet. Boy, do I get angry, not so much as to how rude he is for deserting our guests or hosts, but more because he is already sleeping, which has become a bit of a luxury. After all, if I can manage to stay up, why should he steal the bonus card for extra sleep? Fortunately, our friends are the forgiving type and, now when Tim disappears, even if it is genuinely just to go for a wee, he usually gets a chorus reminiscent of a scene from *The Waltons* of 'Goodnight, Tim,' knowing that's him gone until morning. If he does manage to make it back from the loo, he is rewarded with a well-earned round of applause.

And so to sex. As I said earlier, with a bed hopping Bethan, a breastfeeding Caitlin and an insatiable appetite for sleep, this subject is currently a little scant on material. When I go to bed, I go to sleep and would really rather that nookie didn't encroach on this luxury. So when we were starting to try for our second baby, it had to be morning bonks or nothing. Now, the problem with this, of course, was Bethan's bed-swapping activities. Invariably as we awoke in the morning there was our little cherub lying between us. It has to be said children are a good contraceptive from this point of view, so we had to think up a Plan B of what to do with her once she was awake (Plan A of doing it while she was still sleeping in the bed was never going to work). Her favourite morning routine was to wake in our bed, then rush to her bedroom to bring back her dolls and teddies to play games with; however, if there is one thing she liked better than this, it was the extra special treat of being allowed to watch her favourite video. And so Plan B was born. Bethan was persuaded to come downstairs to choose a video while Daddy got the warm milk for her; he'd then say he was taking Mummy a cup of tea in bed and he'd be back down in a minute. Fortunately, her attention span was about half an hour before she started to shout for Daddy, so this bought us a bit of time for our baby-making 'cup of tea'. We hadn't expected the 'Bethan in our bed' business to go on for quite so long, or indeed our failure to conceive, so by the time Caitlin was conceived Bethan was well established in this morning ritual and has ended up with a fantastic video collection. Don't get me wrong. This wasn't happening every day, or even every weekend, but just around my ovulation where the circled dates were on the calendar. Initially Tim would look forward to the circled dates, but soon the pressure took its toll, and sentiment and emotion went out the window as the months, and years, rolled by. But we got there in the end, and now, with Caitlin in the equation and the desperate desire for sleep, I can't ever imagine an early morning 'cup of tea' again.

Flab and Fashion

Having children and hitting the ageing hurdle of being over thirty have definitely taken their toll on our bodies. Some of us may still be skinny, but the skin is also a bit slacker. Some of us have the old metabolic clock ticking that bit slower, making weight maintenance an impossible and endless task.

What's happened to our bodies, how do we diet, what exercise do we do and does it work? It's all so different for each of us. If we weren't such good friends, there would certainly be room for some envious animosity, with the bonny bump gang remaining perfectly petite despite the tests of time and term.

Fashion, or lack of it, somehow immediately ties in with the worries of the changing self-image. When you're fractionally less than happy with the body, you have two choices: either give in and go with comfort rather than cool or, alternatively, overcompensate by dive-bombing back through the years to the fashion of the local teenagers. It's all so tricky – get it wrong and you look like either your gran or the oldest swingers in town. So here's to our fashion flops and our fat and flab.

Lyndsey

***

I wasn't sure why the others wanted me to go first in this chapter, but I am fast beginning to realize that this was a ploy to give them ammunition against me. I am one of those people that manages to stay thin pre-, during and post-pregnancy, and I don't really have to do exercise for it to happen. As you can imagine, this irritates the others no end, as all three of them seem to be permanently focused on their latest fitness regimes.

The company I work for does have a gym and runs aerobic classes at lunch times and after work. When I worked full time, before Bethan, I would regularly attend these, but, when I returned on a three-day and then a four-day week, my hours at work were just too packed. However, without this token effort at exercise, and with my stomach muscles remaining a bit on the slack side, I soon found that all those chocolate biscuits were finding their way to that saggy skin called my stomach which was just waiting for the fat to fall into it. When I started trying to fall pregnant with Caitlin, I decided to organize my manic working day a bit better and slotted in at least two lunch-time aerobic sessions a week. My thinking was that, if I were fit and healthy, surely this would help me to conceive. But after the second miscarriage I decided perhaps all that pelvic thrusting, tummy toning and bobbing about over a step may be having a negative effect and jiggling the foetus out (I wasn't being completely rational by this stage), so once again I put a stop to the exercise. It was then that I started to put a few more pounds on, not necessarily from missing out on the aerobics sessions, but more from comfort eating.

I have always wished that I had been one of those people who stop eating when they're down, but I am, in fact, quite the opposite. If I'm low, I find that a good slab of cake with a milky coffee goes a long way to help, but doing this on a long-term basis was not conducive to keeping the weight down. I didn't care. By the time I fell pregnant with Caitlin, I could honestly say that my body was in a sorry state, and my size-ten jeans were growing uncomfortably tight. I know how irritating that must sound to so many people as they fight with weight gain, but it's all relative. If you find you've gone up a size and have to consider the need to purchase new clothes to accommodate this, it's depressing no matter what size you started at. Being at my largest when I did fall pregnant with Caitlin worried me before I even started carrying any 'baby weight'. I was anxious about my rapidly increasing waistline, as I feared this could be the beginning of the end of my speedy metabolism. I had got away with being able to eat anything all my life, and I thought that my time had finally come when I, too, would have to battle the bulge. But as the pregnancy hit the third trimester, my body grew smaller as the baby got bigger. Hilary always paints a colourful picture by referring to my babies as eating my backside from the inside. She swears that, as my beach ball bump grew, so my bottom disappeared. I can't exactly see for myself, so I'll take her word for it. What I do know – and please don't hate me for saying this – is that within two weeks of Caitlin being born I was back into my size-ten jeans, even though my breastfeeding bust couldn't contend with my size-twelve tops. Breastfeeding certainly did the trick for me in terms of helping to shrink the beach ball belly, but there is a touch of guilt as I look at the rolls of flesh on my chubby baby and wonder whether the calorie intake from the cake and chocolate that I tend to indulge in is going directly to Caitlin. I dread the day the breastfeeding stops, as I'm sure my metabolism will give up the ghost one of these days. I feel that as the years progress my time might soon be up and I will balloon if I don't curb my chocolate intake or start to do some proper exercise. But I am feeding for two at the moment, I tell myself, as I swallow another chocolate biscuit.

In terms of fashion, for me this is very brief, as with my clothes size not changing, neither has my wardrobe. Tim occasionally comes home bearing gifts of trendy jackets or tops just to make sure my 'wrong side of thirty-five' status doesn't appear too evident in my outfits, but other than that clothing really isn't a major issue for me. For Bethan, though, this is the start of an epic. I remember for our wedding asking our niece, then three years old, to be a bridesmaid. My sister-in-law was in grave doubt as to whether her daughter would agree to wearing a dress at that point. I couldn't understand it. Just put the child in what she's told to wear and take control of the situation. In the end, the three-year-old agreed to wear the pretty dress if, and only if, she could wear her favourite cycling shorts underneath! And so I find myself looking back on my cynical view very apologetically. I've been there and through it, but to the opposite extreme. I had a two-year-old that would only wear dresses or skirts. As she turned three, this became restricted to only pink dresses or skirts, and, by the time she was four, they had to be pink dresses or skirts, but with flowers or butterflies on them. Nothing else would do. I ask myself how this happened to me, as I remember thinking when I saw my sister-in-law struggle with her wilful child that I could do better and that if I had a child it would be told what to wear and that's that. Well, at eight in the morning when I needed a cooperative Bethan to get into the car to take to nursery, I'd have done anything for an easy life; if she insisted on wearing a particular dress on a particular day, then so be it. Even if it were midwinter with snow outside or rain lashing down, I relented and prayed that they would have indoor play that day. Occasionally we might get her into a pair of leggings or trousers, but only with some bizarre explanation or bribery such as taking her to the pub after nursery for a pint and a bag of crisps.

As for the pink theme, I blame our friends' four-year-old daughter for this one. We went on holiday with them when Bethan was two and their daughter was Barbie mad. After two weeks of Bethan following her around like a lapdog she, too, was hooked. I thought we would get away with it for at least another year or so, but it was not to be. Soon her bedroom was changed from 'soothing lemon' to 'in-your-face pink'. The friends we had been on holiday with then thought it an excellent idea to send Bethan some Barbie wall stickers for Christmas, so they, too, are scattered around her bedroom. We've now got a box full of Barbies, each with a different pink plastic gimmick just waiting to get lost or broken. I can't count the hours spent searching for that blasted Barbie shoe which is no bigger than a fingernail. Sometimes I think a needle in a haystack would actually be incredibly easy to find in comparison to those oh-so-essential Barbie bits.

I have to say, though, that even at such a young age Bethan has always had good dress sense and will always be coordinated, which, thinking about it, is not too difficult with an all-pink wardrobe. But sometimes despite the excellent coordination the appropriateness for the occasion is questionable. Last summer we were having a celebratory Fat Ladies barbecue over at Hilary's farm. I had left Bethan with Tim to come over later, as I was going early to help set things up. My parting words were: 'Put one of your lovely party dresses on.' I thought this would please her no end. After all, she loved nothing better than to dress up and put on a frilly party frock. You can imagine my horror when Tim rolled up in the car and Bethan stepped out looking like the sugar plum fairy. There she was in her skimpy, sticky-out fairy outfit, complete with wings, clip-clop shoes that she couldn't walk in, wand and, to top it all off, her pink and pearl tiara. Tim shrugged his shoulders and just said, 'That's what she wanted to wear!' and I knew he'd had a battle to get there on time without tackling the clothing aspect. Wholly inappropriate as this outfit was at this wet August day, outdoor event, she thought she was the cat's whiskers, or is it the bee's knees?

During this fairy phase, Bethan had started ballet and was looking forward to her first show. She dreamt of nothing else but being a shimmering fairy and spent hours dancing around the house and practising her made-up routine. Then, as the date of the show came closer, her enthusiasm seemed to diminish, and she was reluctant to show us her dancing. Then the blow came when the dance teacher gave us an outline of the costume we needed to prepare – a dwarf. Not only was Bethan going to be a dwarf, but she was asked to dress in sombre colours of blues, browns, blacks and dark greens as well – a far cry from the fluffy pinks and glitter of which she had dreamed. Bethan was mortified. There wasn't even a hint of pink to be seen, and she was not prepared to show any interest in the costume preparation, let alone try it on before the dress rehearsal. I tried every tactic I could muster up to sell the pluses of being a dwarf to her, but really the scope for this sales pitch was very limited. Ice to Eskimos has got to be easier than dull dwarves to pink fairies! In the end I found the niche by focusing on the excitement of being on stage in front of all those mummies and daddies, grandmas and granddads. She was soon caught up in the pre-show excitement and even dressed enthusiastically in her dwarf costume before we left home on the big night. I then took her to the school where the show was to take place and, by the time we found the dressing room for her make-up to be applied, she was skipping happily along and singing her 'hi-ho' tune. Then we opened the dressing-room door only to discover that it was filled not only with fellow sombre dwarves, but also with a whole array of shimmering tooth fairies who were in the next ballet class up. My heart went out to Bethan as her face crumpled and her eyes welled up with sheer disappointment. Despite my equally strong disappointment for her, I managed the age-old trick of just keep talking enthusiastically. So I found myself in full pelt of 'Come on, let's get your make-up on. What colour lipstick would you like? A nice bright pink? . . .' We muddled through somehow, and I left her in the capable hands of the make-up artist, who promised to add some glitter to her cheeks. Somehow she managed to hold back her tooth fairy devastation, and I for one

*Not only did she have to be a dull dwarf, but she also had to
share a dressing room with the shimmering tooth fairies*

thought she looked the most loveable dwarf. As she came on to
the stage, I could hardly see the performance for the well of tears
in my eyes. Needless to say, the dwarf costume is sat at the
bottom of her dressing-up box and hasn't been worn since.

Since starting school, the Barbie pink image has started to
wane, and I have recently been told, 'When I'm five, lilac will
be my favourite colour and, when I'm six, I will like yellow.'
True to form, as her fifth birthday is now approaching, she is
gradually reducing her pink wardrobe and selecting lilac tops,
skirts and dresses. She is wearing more jeans and trousers, and
asking to wear black trousers for school like some of the older
girls. Despite this gradual transformation to colour variation, I
have to accept that she is a stubborn girl with her own mind
when it comes to fashion, and I still would not dare purchase her
clothes without her being with me. It's the only way to avoid

wasting money on something that will just end up hanging in the wardrobe never to be worn without first experiencing a major war. My mum has learnt this lesson, too, after purchasing two dresses for Bethan last Christmas. One was the most beautiful party dress and seemed to have everything about it that fitted Bethan's current selection criteria (swirling skirt, lilac and pink, sparkles etc.) and the other was a Sleeping Beauty dress. The second she laid eyes on the Sleeping Beauty dress, it was on her, and it didn't come off her back for the next two weeks, other than for a very quick wash. She wore it everywhere, even to church, much to my embarrassment. As for the party dress, she told my mum very honestly that she didn't like it, wouldn't wear it and perhaps it was best for it to go back to the shop. Even with a 50 per cent success rate, I think my mum now realizes why I don't shop without the little fashion queen present.

Tim and I are already dreading the teenage years and what the fashion statements might be then. Whatever it is, we have no doubt that Bethan will be a follower, and I know Tim is secretly praying that it won't be micro miniskirts and pierced tummy buttons. I just fear that they would merely be the tip of the iceberg.

Andrea

***

If Lyndsey thought that talk of her skinny status would provide me with ammunition, nothing could be more accurate! As she fears the possible progression into a size twelve, I can only long for such a sizing zone. I can safely say that I will never be a size twelve and possibly haven't been one since I was about that age! And as for weight gain all being relative, yes, I couldn't agree more; from where I'm looking in the mirror, it's all relatively huge! I think I can realistically admit that I am the only true, long-lasting member of the 'Fat' Ladies Club. Hilary admittedly joins me on the bloater scales for a fair while after each baby, but Lyndsey and Sarah are about as cumbersome as Kylie Minogue! My top half, I'm pleased to say, does manage to stay pretty slim, bar the big boobs, but my bottom half really is a law unto itself. Being 50 per cent English and 50 per cent Greek, I can safely say that my huge, all-eclipsing backside was definitely given all the Greek genes. I would now look frighteningly authentic waddling around in the traditional Greek black dress!

If you think this means I've given up on myself, then nothing could be further from the truth. I am on a permanent crusade for that quick-fix, thigh-reducing miracle cure that takes minimal effort and does not interfere with my love of food. I haven't yet resorted to liposuction or medication, but am pretty much a connoisseur of every diet on the market. Diets are not really my thing, as my willpower levels are pretty nonexistent. Hilary usually 'buddies up' with me on these diets, the idea being that this gives us both the incentive to carry on. What, in fact, happens is that Hilary, who has more willpower than sense, loses stacks more weight than me, which leaves me totally depressed and seeking sympathy from the biscuit barrel. What takes two weeks to shake off I can put back on in about an hour and a half if I really put my mind to it. Diets we have endured are generally those fast-acting ones that promise pounds of loss in no time at all. We did the cabbage soup one, which we rapidly renamed the 'fart soup diet'. The guffs produced on this were phenomenal, but unfortunately totally unbearable even to the nose of the bum that produced them, so that put a rapid end to that one. Next we tried a three-day diet Hilary found which assured ten pounds' loss in three days. This one was hell, as it involved things like a plate of broccoli and beetroot for supper, which, for an anti-veg woman like me, was vomit-worthy. By day two I was weak and nauseous, and by day three I felt positively faint. So when I got on the scales and had only lost a measly three pounds, I wanted to ram my remaining broccoli up Hilary's nose for even suggesting this diet. The fact that she had lost seven pounds didn't help either! In fact, the only diet that worked for me is the Slim Fast one. For some reason, when the mood takes me and my pannier bags have expanded even beyond my level of acceptability, I find the willpower to stick to this. Last year I lost a stone on it in a fortnight and actually came to quite enjoy my 'shake for breakfast, shake for lunch and sensible evening meal'. I've carried on having the strawberry ready-made shake for breakfast ever since. Sadly, the rest of the diet gradually reduced, so the weight gradually increased again. Once I've moved house, my plan is to have another go at this diet, but there always seems to be a good excuse to wait just one more week before starting again.

If I could still keep my weight down by exercise alone, which I could before children, then I would be in heaven. I remain fairly sporty and still play football, but unfortunately, like my work, this has had to reduce to a part-time activity – mainly due to childcare considerations – and so all my other get-fit schemes have come into play. Basically I have gone from one fitness fad to another and am always on a mission for the quick-fix exercise to go with the quick-fix diets. Yes, I am the mug who falls for the 'You can look like this in just seven days' sales pitch in the Sunday supplements small ads. So far I have bought the sit-up abdominal cruncher thing, the electrical pad things that you stick on your tummy and 'without effort the effects are amazing' and finally a wheelie-type thing that you do a forward press-up on. All of these items have been delivered, been used for a week, then found their way on to my discarded exercise fad corner, otherwise known as the garage. I have to say that I found the electrical pad things extremely painful and, where a couple were placed over stretch marks, they made them go all red and blotchy, so they hit the garage in record time.

By far the best idea I had was investing in ten sessions with a personal trainer who lived opposite me. She would come to my house, and we would work out in the back garden, where she really put me through my paces. The best part was the boxing. She would hold up large pads and I would get to wear boxing gloves and punch away to my heart's content. I found this very satisfying, especially after Bruce announced that he was leaving me! Having someone to motivate me made all the difference, and we would go on three-mile runs round the villages near to my house or sprint training at a local track. I loved it, but sadly have had to call a stop for now due to the cost. I couldn't quite justify the expense as I now face the penny-pinching process of being a single parent.

I invited Hilary along to one of the boxing sessions with my personal trainer, and she loved it, too. And so we bought our own gloves and block pads, and we meet three times a week in Hilary's front room to beat the hell out of each other. We even start with a bit of step aerobics using the stools that the children step on to reach the loo. We then finish with 200 sit-ups. It's not just a decent work-out, it's free and without childcare issues. Alfie has his bottle propped on his cuddly dog, and the others enjoy the uninterrupted opportunity to wreck the house and then join us for the sit-ups! So I'm keen to see if I can make this latest fad last a bit longer than the others, although I must admit that I'm getting a bit bored with just hitting the pads and would like to invest in another pair of gloves so that we can have a real fight – for some reason, Hils is proving to be a bit reluctant to take up this idea.

I would love for Max and Sam to take an interest in sport like myself, but at the same time would hate to force them and become one of the mad parents on the sideline cheering for their kids as they shuffle around the pitch on the verge of tears. Max is so keen on football that I am considering letting him go to a Saturday morning session for over fives to see how he gets on. The only regular exercise that both my boys have had from a young age is swimming. We started taking Max and Molly together when they were about six months old and would take them without fail week after week.

There was one occasion when Hilary was not able to attend Max and Molly's weekly lesson a few years back, and I still haven't forgiven her for it. It was when she was having her tonsils out and I was heavily pregnant with Sam. I was sure that Molly would not be attending as I changed into my maternity cossie and waddled out to the pool. Then I spied a blonde curly head and thought for a minute it could be Molly, but quickly dismissed the idea because Hils was in hospital. It didn't cross my mind that David would come to a pool full of mums singing nursery rhymes with both Molly and brand-new baby Ella in tow. To my horror, I had completely misjudged him, and there he was all ready for a quick round of 'Here We Go round the Mulberry Bush'. Now I am not usually a self-conscious person, but my bum, at this stage in the pregnancy, was bigger than all of the other Fat Ladies' put together, so I found myself scooping up Max, sprinting to the pool and jumping in before my friend's husband rounded the corner to see my all-eclipsing arse in its maternity cossie glory. Poor Max was used to a far more gradual introduction to the water, and he burst into tears just as David and Molly got in. I feigned surprise at seeing them as I waved to greet him, satisfied that all was concealed in the watery depths. But then Max decided to do a total boycott and leapt out of the pool in a bid for freedom. This turned out to be the first of many Max exits from that lesson, and there was no other option but to haul my fat rear end over the poolside to chase after him each time. And so I rapidly gave up all hope of hiding my hefty behind.

We took the kids for the customary McDonald's afterwards and, despite the fact that David supports Chelsea, we have now become firm friends. Firm friends or not, though, I'd still feel more comfortable in his company fully clothed rather than cossied up.

Whilst on the subject of being fully clothed, I, like Lyns, have very little to say on the subject of fashion. Regardless how large or small I've been over the past five years, my wardrobe has not changed in the slightest. Jeans and sweatshirts, or shorts and T-shirts with baseball caps have remained my staple requirements, and that's pretty much all my clothing supply consists of. I do have one confession, and that is due to the influence of the other Fat Ladies: I now own two fashion items that previously would never have been allowed in my house. These items are make-up and nail varnish, but let me just clarify that just because I own them it doesn't mean that I have any intention of using them on a regular basis.

First, the nail varnish: I hold Sarah responsible for that. Last summer we were all invited to quite a posh do in London, and so a Fat Ladies' shopping trip was called for to deck me out in a suitable outfit. This not only resulted in me purchasing a wraparound skirt, which I needed lessons in tying, but also some open-toed sandals. When Sarah saw my new footwear, she stated matter of factly that I simply had to wear nail varnish on my toes and that you just don't wear open-toed sandals without it. I was tempted to take the sandals back, but in the end I dutifully bought and wore some varnish for the function.

As for make-up, that one I blame Hilary for. I am someone who never wears the slightest bit of make-up, the only exception being on my wedding day. Just before this function, Hilary hosted a Body Shop party which I agreed to attend. My motive for attending was clearly the food and company, as I had no intention of buying anything. But, unbeknownst to me, the other Fat Ladies had decided that I should be the 'model' for the Body Shop lady to demonstrate her products on. In the end, the whole party was offering suggestions of what would suit me best, as copious amounts of make-up were slapped on and wiped off until all present were satisfied with my face. The result of this was that everyone insisted that I looked really good, and I ended up buying one of everything. I spent a small fortune and even had to buy a little make-up bag to put it all in. The Body Shop lady must have been rubbing her hands in glee, not to mention Hilary, who as the host was given a whole load of freebies because of how much I'd spent. Now I've just got to get around to using the stuff, before it goes off – that's if make-up does go off, I wouldn't have a clue!

Sarah

***

Andrea may be obsessed with the size of her backside, but all I can say is that at least she has the chest to counteract it. My postnatal problem zone is also my bum and thighs, but I have absolutely no cleavage to speak of. Somehow the hourglass figure sounds so much more appealing than the 'pear'! I have always been someone with a reasonably petite frame and a bust that also met with that description, but two lots of breastfeeding have really taken their toll on my less than ample boobs. They reduced after Jack, deflated significantly after Eloise and I fear that they may completely disappear after my third. I just hope that M&S will have invented the padded plunge 'extraordinaire' by then because, without any doubt at all, I'll be a ready customer! If I were less of a chicken, I would even consider a boob job, but I'm scared of the consequences that it might have. It's one thing having cotton wool sneaking out from the top of a sexy décolleté, it must be quite another suddenly having your silicone implant bursting on you. I think I will probably just remain grateful for small mercies! I cannot even enjoy the benefits of the bulging breastfeeding bust, like Lyndsey, because I do not have the sort of metabolism that means the fat drops off me as I feed: instead, it prefers to remain in milk store pouches all over my lower body. After having Eloise, I knew that I had to put up with the plumper version of myself for as long as I wanted to carry on breastfeeding, and this is something that I really wanted to persevere with this time. It's just as well, then, that the only full-length mirror we have in the house is concealed behind a wardrobe door, so I could easily put off really giving my body the once-over simply by avoiding opening the door too far.

As well as keeping my body nicely rounded, I think that breastfeeding must also play horrible tricks on my fashion sense. I usually stick pretty rigidly to M&S and Gap for my clothing, but, when Eloise was about two months old, I made one massive fashion faux pas by buying a hideous pair of elastic-waisted, floral baggy trousers off the market. I was at that stage where I couldn't bear to wear my maternity trousers any longer, yet my normal trousers were barely making it up over my hips, let alone fastening. Looking back now I realize what a mistake it was: I can still see Tim's horrified face as I tried to persuade him that the raspberry-coloured, floral motif on the navy background actually made for quite a smart pair of trousers, not only because it resembled a William Morris design, but also because it matched a pair of raspberry-coloured shoes I could wear with them. I wore those trousers into the ground for the next couple of months, but thankfully I then gave up breastfeeding and returned to my normal size and far more conservative style. If I had been one of those mums who feed her children until they're walking, I dread to think what state my wardrobe might have ended up in, but I'm certain that Hyacinth Bucket would have been keen on a loan!

When Eloise was just six weeks old, I joined a new gym that had opened in town. They took babies from six weeks in the crèche, and so I swapped my floral trousers for my old leggings once again and thoroughly enjoyed working myself to a sweat, knowing that my little girl was being well looked after in the room next door. I very soon got into the routine of getting dressed first thing in the morning in my gym things, walking Jack to school and heading straight into town for the 9.30 a.m. aerobics class. This often meant that Eloise was still dressed in her pyjamas and finishing her breakfast bottle of milk, in her pram, as I arrived at the gym, so keen was my resolve not to miss any opportunity to 'work out'. The only drawback to this place was that it had full-length mirrors on every wall in the open-plan changing rooms, which meant that I couldn't help but get a full appreciation of my oversized postnatal body each time I took a shower there after my class. To strip off amidst the fit and very toned bodies all around me was too much to bear, so I took on that embarrassing undressing approach created by people on beaches. I would hold my towel around myself with my teeth, whilst trying to peel off my sweaty gym gear underneath: I must have looked like some kind of contortionist and definitely drew far more attention to myself by taking twice as long wriggling around in my cocoon. If I had just stripped off and changed in two seconds flat, no one would have batted an eyelid. I have to admit that I did end up taking the easier option and, having exercised, I would go home for a shower in the peace of my own private bathroom.

I really enjoy my gym sessions and find it relatively easy to maintain the self-discipline to 'keep at it'. As I head into the plumper stages of this pregnancy, however, I find I'm fast approaching that point where the only exercise I am doing, despite a little bit of swimming, is my pelvic floors. I don't even do these as vigilantly as I did during my first two pregnancies – I just don't seem to find the time to remember. Although, as I write, I am now actively 'lift-lifting' and 'down-downing', and hope to goodness that they will remain as intact and leakproof as they were before. After Eloise, I did embark on my pelvic floor exercises rather overenthusiastically, starting when she was just two weeks old, with a half-hour session in all sorts of positions – lying down, sitting up, standing etc. Before embarking on this initial round of pelvic exercise, I was more or less convinced that I had finished bleeding and so was aghast to suddenly feel that telltale sensation of a flood down below. The panty liner in situ was nowhere near equipped for the job, so I had to resort back to the mini-mattress variety of sanitary protection. The same happened a few days later when I walked Jack to school and then pushed a lot of heavy shopping back home under the pram. On this occasion, I went into a mad panic that I was haemorrhaging, and that I had done myself some dreadful injury by wanting to get too active too quickly after the birth. I was on the phone to the midwife straight away, desperately seeking reassurance, and she calmly told me that it was my body's natural way of letting me know that I was overexerting myself: the solution was to take things a bit easier. Frustrating as this was, because I felt loaded with energy I couldn't expend, it was a relief to know that there was a simple explanation.

Not wishing to sound a hypochondriac, I then worried myself stupid when I started having some very strange giddy, nauseous spells. These were compounded by blurred vision and numbness down one side, which meant I wasn't able to stay upright. At the time I lost a lot of weight just simply worrying about what the long-term diagnosis might be. The first time it happened, I thought I was having a stroke, then I was convinced I had diabetes, and then 'nurse' Hilary scared me even further by suggesting I might be getting epilepsy! Luckily, it was nothing more sinister than a string of hormonal migraines triggered by my first post-breastfeeding period. But there's nothing quite like a shocking experience to ruin your appetite for several days and help shed those excess pounds of flesh! That certainly helped to shake off my breastfeeding fat stores, and I ended up being the slimmest I have ever been. Trips to the gym afterwards became more a case of 'toning' than burning the fat, which in some ways I was quite grateful for. In truth, though, I would probably have preferred to do it the hard way, rather than be freaked out about the state of my brain in order to achieve slimness again!

Having refound my figure, it was so nice to wear tight jeans again, and thank goodness for the invention of the padded bra because at least I could feel confident wearing tight T-shirts, knowing that I'd got a bit of extra 'help' underneath! Contrary to what the other Fat Ladies may think, and despite my nickname of 'Posh', I do in fact buy the majority of my clothes from bog-standard high-street stores. The chief reason for this has become more and more important as my family expands and that is so that I don't have to try any of the clothes on: I know that by picking up a pair of trousers in a size twelve, standard length, they will fit. Similarly, I don't need to try on the tops for size, nor do I have to take a flying guess at what size bra or knickers I should pick up. After years of practice in buying M&S clothing, I have learnt that as long as I keep to the classical and understated lines, I can mix and match them easily with other brands to hopefully make them look far more expensive and trendy. So I would like to think anyway. I'm not sure what Trinny and Susannah would have to say about that, though.

Once I became a mother of preschool children, I found that those moments of enjoyable retail therapy that I used to indulge in when I was younger were most definitely a thing of the past. I do find myself quite envious of friends who are working mothers and manage to get out to the shops during their lunch break . . . without pushing a toddler in a buggy. There is something about the fun of shopping which, with children, is totally lost: it becomes something of a necessity that you aim to do in the shortest time possible. Gone are the days of idly browsing the endless racks of clothes, in the hope that something might take your fancy. Gone are the days of taking armfuls of clothes into a changing cubicle and spending half an hour trying on a variety of garments. It's now more a case of dive in, grab your size off the rack, pay and go.

The last time I was forced to try something on when I had the children with me was when shopping for a swimming costume, the size of which I simply couldn't just guess at. Jack spent the entire time crawling around my feet and all over my clothes on the floor, sticking his head under the partitions to gaze up at the women in the neighbouring cubicles. The worst came when he said in a loud voice, 'Mummy, why is that lady so fat?' Not knowing which cubicle he was actually referring to, nor, indeed, the lady in question, I tried to hush him up with whispered explanations such as 'Everyone's different, sweetheart.' But he wouldn't accept that for an answer: he wanted to know, '*Why* the lady was sooooooo *fat*?' That was it, I couldn't bear to face the poor, soul-destroyed woman from the cubicle next door, so hurriedly dressed, scooped up all eight swimming costumes, none of which I had yet tried on, and practically threw them at the bemused sales assistant as I ran out looking very flustered, dragging Jack and Eloise behind me. I really couldn't face staying any longer next door to someone who my son had probably made feel utterly wretched; me trying to splutter an apology for my rude child would have only exacerbated the situation. Jack's antics had made for a very stressful trying-on session, so I avoided a repeat performance until the memory had faded.

More recently, I needed to try on some maternity garments and the memory came flooding back. Once again I had Jack in the cubicle with me, but this time he declared in a very loud voice, for all to hear, 'Mummy, you have got *huge* knickers on!' as he viewed my oversized parachute pants. I think his father has been training him on how to get out of shopping with women and, if this is the case, it's certainly working. I will be restricting my trying-on trips to school term-time from now on!

Andrea, with her two boys, has now given up all hope of clothes shopping, though I doubt she was ever into it in the first place. She has now resorted to mail order and Internet shopping instead. Inspired by these apparently easy and stress-free forms of shopping, I decided to give them a shot myself, but soon learnt that neither really worked for me. The Internet was a complete nightmare: it took me more than two frustrating hours to download and flick through all the pages on-line, and, by the time I had filled my 'shopping basket' to the brim with two different sizes of everything, the whole thing jammed. I think, in all honesty, I would prefer to endure taking Jack and five of his friends into a changing cubicle with me than ever waste another valuable childfree evening on that again. As I was about ready to kick the computer, Tim just looked relieved that the machine had taken control of our finances before I had had the chance to type in the credit card number! The idea of mail order is equally unappealing, and I've reached the conclusion that it's because I like touching and feeling what I am buying first, plus the whole experience of walking out of the shop with bags in my hands. Tim would shake his head in disgust at my last comment because, for him, that's all superficial girlie nonsense and a display of materialism that should not be encouraged. But as this is coming from someone who is still proudly wearing shirts that he bought back in the 1980s, I'm not about to start taking his fashion comments too seriously!

As for the fashion of my children, I tend to stick to the conservative basics for them. I had never made a specific decision to buy only certain colours of clothes for Jack, and it wasn't until he was about six months old and Hilary commented one day on Jack's navy and red wardrobe that I realized that he had very little else in his drawers beyond these two colours. When Eloise was born, I proudly but naively proclaimed to one of my friends that she would be dressed in all of Jack's hand-me-downs bar the occasional purchase of a pair of tights and dress. But as soon as I discovered the world of colours and patterns available for little girls, I was very quickly eating humble pie. She does wear Jack's old jeans and sweatshirts, but my love of retail therapy has resulted in me regularly succumbing to some of the gorgeous girlie clothes on the market – but I hasten to add, no 'Barbie'. I'm dreading the day Eloise insists on buying some revolting candy-pink outfit, which I would never want to accept as a present, let alone part money for. However, seeing how Molly and Bethan have both managed to persuade their mothers to buy pink and lilac clothes for them, I guess I'll very soon be fighting a losing battle. I can already see it now: I will be that embarrassing mother saying to my daughter in the middle of Top Shop, in ten years time, 'But what is wrong with a nice classical navy skirt and red jumper, dear?'

I have to admit to having lots of fun with girls' accessories, as well as clothes, and Eloise is already quite particular about what hair slides or bands she wants to use. One day we were having fun together with a bunch of new hair grips, and for a laugh I had clipped a whole load of multicoloured ones into my hair. About half an hour later, well after our little game had finished, the doorbell rang and it was the postman delivering a package too big for the letterbox. I chatted with him for a good few minutes on the doorstep, and he did have an unusual smirk on his face as his eyes kept gazing upwards. It wasn't until I shut the door that I caught a glimpse of myself in the hall mirror and almost died with embarrassment when I realized that our poor postman must have thought that I had lost the plot big time, or else started taking fashion advice from Bubbles in *Ab Fab*. Mind you, after my raspberry floral trousers deviation from my usual fashion sense, I'm sure nothing would have come as a surprise. To him, I was yet another sad housewife trying to regain her youth!

Hilary

***

After three children, flab – or should I say, sag – certainly is a subject close to my heart. After Molly, I never did get back into shape, but at least the stretch marks were pretty well hidden in my pants, as long as they were big pants. After Ella, I was back in shape after four months, but the stretch marks had hit belly-button height, which put an end to any aspirations I had for belly-button piercing. After Alfie, it is all proving a bit of a struggle. It's not so much the weight, although I do admit to having half a stone to lose off each buttock and thigh, it's more the state of my flesh that mortifies me! 'Don't worry about stretch marks, they turn to little silvery lines,' I was told reassuringly by so many people. What they failed to mention was that those silvery lines are on paper-thin granny skin. The thinner you get, the more wrinkled the flesh looks. With my 200 sit-ups a day obsession, I do get decent tummy muscles back quite quickly, but what's the point when I've got a dirty great, sagging, crinkled pouch of flesh dangling over the top. My boobs, too, although not stretch-marked, have developed that thinner skin feel, and without the uplifting support of a decent bra they immediately plummet about six inches and take on that ski-slope angle. When I see those 'Slimmer of the Year' shots, where a grinning made-over woman is proudly standing in an enormous pair of trousers, with a foot of spare room either side of her waistband, I always wonder what happened to the flesh once the fat had gone. Now I know: it just hangs around in saggy sacks of skin and is strategically tucked in to various corners of your clothing.

Talking of clothing, now there is a depressing subject, too! I'm not sure if it's because I am now in my mid-thirties or because I'm an overweight mum, but suddenly I get in a panic about looking frumpy. When images of my mum flash before my eyes as I stand in front of the mirror, it's enough to give me palpitations. Maybe it's something to do with reaching an age that I can actually recall my mum being that frightens me because that really puts into perspective how short life is. That's all a bit too heavy a subject, though, so back to vanity! When I was in my mid-twenties, I was thin and young, so I pretty much got away with whatever I wore and didn't really pay much attention to fashion. Suddenly at thirty-four I have to be so much more careful. When I'm a stone overweight, that 'classic timeless' outfit I have got away with for so long suddenly looks mumsy and frumpy, and adds at least ten years. I even started wearing thongs under trousers once I was told that the thing takes two pounds off each buttock. I never did understand how shoving a piece of string up your bum could make it look smaller, and I'm not even convinced that it does, but I've got quite used to this previously alien form of underwear now, and it is nice not having that bulge of VPL showing through your trousers. I just wish they'd invent a thong version of the tummy-tucking pants! I have also tried all sorts of fashion phases to avoid the ageing process from dyeing my hair red to chunky leather jewellery, hippy cheesecloth to sporty hoods and bomber jackets. I'm now just dreading the day that Molly makes her first comment on her mum's fashion sense. Here's hoping I have a few more years before that starts, although I have to admit that I've already had the first hint of it. I made a huge mistake last year with my choice of winter coat. I opted for the functional, to fend off the winter weather in the playground, and purchased a particularly nice wind- and waterproof walking coat – or should I say anorak! Andrea immediately christened this my 'sad coat', which Molly rapidly caught on to. You really know you've cocked up when your four-year-old daughter says, 'You're not wearing your sad coat are you, Mummy?' as you get out of the car to deliver her to nursery. I like to comfort myself with the thought that she didn't fully understand why my coat was particularly 'sad', but it still gave me a terrifying taster of things to come.

Fashion for four-year-olds is enough of a nightmare in itself. I have a complete hang-up about girls looking and dressing like ragingly hormonal sixteen-year-olds before they even hit reception class. Once you reach the four- to five-year-old range of clothes, suddenly all the little girls' clothes come to an abrupt halt and boob tubes and miniskirts take over. If Sarah is anxious about Eloise reaching the Barbie phase, she's going to be in for a shock; the girlie-pink Barbie phase feels like a bonus once you start seeing the alternative 'hooker look' looming. Thankfully Molly is still into looking like the princess of pink rather than a slapper, but I know it won't be long before peer group pressure kicks in. Oh, the delights of little girls!

Boys just seem to be a different species altogether. We went on holiday with friends and their four-year-old son, George. The biggest fashion dilemma they were faced with was how to prise off the Burger King crown he insisted on wearing for the entire fortnight. In the end, in a desperate attempt to coax him out of his fast-food crown, his mum got him to make a dragon hat out of a Tetley tea-bag box. This basically amounted to him cutting a hole in the side of the box and putting it on his head – not even a hint of a dragon about it, but with a little imagination it worked for him. His mum seemed much happier with her son striding along the promenade in Spain adorned in a cardboard tea-bag box than she had his Burger King crown. Personally, I couldn't really see much in it. I don't think the tea-bag box, with its corners, was nearly as comfortable in bed, though, so at least he took that one off to sleep.

Finally, to exercise. I've tried all sorts of approaches to keeping fit and fighting the flab between each of my pregnancies, mostly under the influence of Andrea who approaches her get-fit schemes with such enthusiasm you can't help but be drawn in. One brief fad she had, which she brushed over a bit, was swimming. I'm not sure why we did this one because neither of us actually likes swimming at all. The embarrassing discovery I made during this brief phase was the water storage capacity of a postnatal toushdilala (otherwise known as vagina). I have always been so proud of my pelvic floor on the grounds that I have never wet myself since having children, but I have since been told that it is my pelvic floor that is responsible for my embarrassing pool experience. After swimming our statutory number of lengths, which incidentally barely made it into double figures as we were so useless, I got out of the swimming pool and headed for the changing room. As I was retrieving my belongings from the locker and chatting to the lady next to me, suddenly the floodgates opened and, without any warning or control, my toushdi deposited half a pool's worth of water on the floor in one great gush. The lady stopped her social chitchat pretty abruptly and made a speedy retreat to the showers to wash off what she clearly thought was my urine. I just didn't know what to do with myself. There really is no explanation to cover your newfound capacity to store such vast quantities of fluid up your girlie bits. I'm not sure if she would have found that knowledge a relief or worse than the thought that I had lost all bladder control. This unpleasant 'skill' has not improved either. I have to make a concerted effort to try to empty myself every night after my bath, and you can guarantee that the time I forget is when we are going out and suddenly, just as we are leaving, a huge wet patch will appear in my crotch, requiring a quick blast of the hair dryer before we can face anyone else. God, I do hope I'm not alone in this postnatal nightmare. Otherwise I'm going to be incredibly embarrassed when everyone reads this!

The one exercise regime that worked for me was affording myself the luxury of joining the same private gym that Sarah talked about, although admittedly we went with completely different agendas. After having Ella, I became a bit fed up at the lack of time I had to myself. Days were filled with the needs of two children and one hungry husband, whilst evenings became the time to tackle all those domestic tasks I could not do during the day. Even my bath was something I shared with two children. Joining the gym was just the job. On three evenings a week, I would duck out of the house the second the girls were in bed, bomb down to the gym, getting there just in time to whip on my headphones and tune into *EastEnders* whilst on the cross-trainer. No torturous attempts to coordinate the limbs through an aerobics session for me − the opportunity for indulging uninterrupted in an entire episode of a soap opera was sheer heaven, and to be burning calories simultaneously was totally satisfying. I'd then spend another twenty minutes doing the various weight machines and sit-ups, but that was all a bit boring because I couldn't watch the box during those.

Then came the grand finale to my self-indulgence session. The bit Sarah hated most about the gym was my highlight: the changing rooms. I'd have ten minutes in the steam room, just to bring all those zits out, followed by a skin-dentingly powerful shower, smellie girlie products provided, and all with the added bonus of being all by myself. Even once the novelty of the gym wore off, my tightfisted attitude to life ensured I kept going. It cost about £10 a week for membership, which meant it cost less than £3.50 a visit if I went three times a week, which was an absolute bargain. I'd have paid that just to use the shower and steam room. However, if I only visited once, the thought that it was costing me £10 to be there somehow made the whole experience that bit less pleasurable. When I fell pregnant with

Alfie, the early-stage exhaustion meant that sometimes it was, in fact, costing me £20 or £30 a visit, which was totally soul destroying, so I put my membership on hold for a year. That year is now fast coming to an end, and I have to make the decision as to whether I want and can justify the expense of starting up again. As much as I loved it, the thought of trying to find time to go three times a week no longer seems a possibility. So I'm hoping Andrea's latest boxing fad is one that will stick. Not only is it free and achievable, even with five children in the house, it's also extremely satisfying. Mike Tyson, eat your heart out. I'm a woman on a mission once I've got those gloves on.

Mike Tyson, eat your heart out. I'm a woman with a mission once I've got those boxing gloves on!

Toilets and Tantrums

From wees to whining, poos to paddies, this has to be the chapter of all parental nightmares. These are the situations which really test your parenting skills and make you question what you did wrong. There's nothing quite like the guilt trip of losing the plot with your child during a particularly tricky negotiation over whether or not you are going to purchase that toy they have a firm grip on. Nor can you measure up to the magical moment when your seemingly potty-trained child decides to wee down the slide in the public park. There is so much excellent advice on the market on how best to deal with these testing times. This all serves its purpose extremely well, but it also does a grand job of making you feel extra guilty and incompetent when, once again, you discover you're human and get it completely wrong. The fearful thoughts of whether you are unwittingly creating a monster by not tackling those tricky times as the textbooks tell you to are ever present. All you can do is your best and not beat yourself up when you get it wrong. We all openly admit to getting it wrong on numerous occasions when it comes to toilet training and tackling tantrums. If you, too, are not that perfect picture of Mary Poppins that we all aspire to be, then sit back and hear how we mere mortals manage.

Sarah

* * *

Being the mother of a child like Jack has equipped me with enough material on these two subjects to write an entire book. Jack was born with strong opinions about exactly what he wanted to do in life, and he certainly isn't going to let a minor detail like a mother with differing opinions get in his way. This has left me in the position of being both proud of him and his strength of character, but also an irate, hair-wrenching wreck. However, I will endeavour to reduce this *War and Peace* epic to a mere handful of frustrating tales.

First, to potty training: this was something that everyone else did, but as far as Jack was concerned was not something that applied to him. Someone once tried to console me by saying, 'No child ever starts school wearing nappies.' But I had serious concerns that our son was going to prove the exception to the rule. I'm afraid that I may have contributed to his late acceptance of the toilet, despite the fact that everyone says boys take longer, by trying to force him to use the potty too early. I thought that it would be a good idea to try to get him trained when I fell pregnant for the second time, but Jack was, in fact, only just over a year old. This didn't perturb me, though. After all, I had heard stories from my mother's generation about how babies were trained from as young as six months to sit on the potty to poo. But then, I suppose there was more incentive in those days to spend time waiting for that all-important bowel movement in order to avoid the laundry horror of having to scrub out a soiled terry nappy. I would have opted to Superglue the potty to Jack's bottom to be free of that daily pleasure. Thankfully we do have it a lot easier with disposables these days, and I would have been less inclined to rush at the potty training as a route to making life easier for myself had it not been for wanting Jack to be clean before our second child arrived. As it happened, although Jack took a long time before he was 'good and ready', he was in fact potty trained by the time our second child arrived: fortuitously for him, time was on his side, and it took more than a year longer than we had expected for Eloise to arrive!

It was the summer that Eloise was born, and Jack turned three, that he decided that he couldn't put off using the toilet forever. What sparked his interest to eventually take leave of his nappies was Tim's suggestion that he could do a wee in the garden instead of going inside each time to use the toilet. This option immediately appealed to his nonconformist nature and, to begin with, didn't worry me because at least it meant that he was expressing an interest in doing a wee other than in his nappy. However, it was when he started to adopt catlike characteristics by wanting to pee in every corner of the garden and drive, as if to stake his territory, that I started to become a bit concerned. My main worry was our neighbour's drive, which we only have legal right of access to drive down, and it was when I saw Jack, from our kitchen window, drop his pants and relieve himself all over the wall of their house one day that I decided we had to put a stop to this rather liberal approach to toilet training. Thankfully Jack's friend Holly and her parents thought it was all rather amusing and were not about to call the local council to complain about Jack's antisocial behaviour, but, had they been less understanding people, we could have had problems on our hands. For Jack, of course, it was all a great game to be chased around the garden with his pants around his ankles, knowing that he was pushing the limits of social acceptability. We didn't even have that all-powerful weapon that all other parents seem to have: the removal of privileges. Ultimatums and threats simply did not, and still generally do not, work with Jack. 'If you wee on the garden, Jack, you will not get the gingerbread man we just bought' simply didn't work: he would just shrug his shoulders and drop his pants without a second thought for the lost treat. And I am not the sort of parent who gives in to the situation – if I issue an ultimatum, I stick to it. However, I have learnt to check my threats before firing them where Jack is concerned. Having to leave Fat Ladies' get-togethers because I've threatened, 'Do that one more time, Jack, and we're going home!' then having to carry it out, just means I end up punishing myself as well!

With my wilful son and his newfound urination shock factor, his public displays did not stop at the relative safety and anonymity of our back garden. Oh, no, my little darling was determined to show me up in all manner of places. When I was heavily pregnant with Eloise, Andrea and I decided to take the boys out for lunch in town. The meal went relatively smoothly, considering that it wasn't exactly a child-friendly venue and we had three lively lads all under the age of three with us. Having done our best to clear up some of the debris around our table, repack our rucksacks with all our child entertainment and food paraphernalia (whatever happened to handbags?) and negotiate our way past all the other diners with our buggies and brood, I eventually turned to thank the assisting waiter. It was at this moment that Jack decided to push straight past me in great haste and position himself beside one of the two plant pots in the entrance to the restaurant. Before I could shout, 'Jack . . . don't you dare!' he had dropped his trousers and pants, and was weeing directly onto the lovely topiary bay tree. I didn't dare look back into the restaurant for fear of the looks I was getting from horrified diners, let alone the waiter; all I wanted to do was grab my son by the scruff of his neck and quick-march him straight home before bursting into a purple-faced rage of embarrassment. But, of course, being in a real 'fat lady' state by then, Jack knew I couldn't easily react and

*I didn't dare look back for fear of the looks we were getting
from horrified diners*

took pleasure at taunting me with a twinkly smile before he
calmly bent down, pulled up his trousers in a rather skewiff
fashion and casually continued his way out of the restaurant.

And he didn't stop there. He was obviously having far too
much fun in pushing the social limits in terms of places to 'pee'.
The next embarrassing episode came when Andrea and I had
taken the boys swimming at the local sports centre. No sooner
were we in the pool than Jack declared that he needed the toilet.
He shot up the steps, which I naturally assumed meant that he
was desperate to return to the changing room toilets . . . I should
have known better. As I hauled my very pregnant form out of
the pool behind him, I was suddenly aware of a sound next to
me like a fountain. I turned to see Jack standing on the side of

this large, municipal swimming pool, hands on forward-thrusted hips, with trunks down around his ankles, weeing like a mini-fireman's hose in a perfect arc, straight into the water. He then started gyrating his hips and giggling with sheer pleasure as he watched the patterns his projectile was creating on the surface of the water. As he positively revelled in the sheer audacity of what he was doing, I remained rooted to the pool steps desperately trying to decide what my reaction should be. I could hear Andrea's sniggers and have to admit that I wanted to giggle, too. After all, if I'd seen anyone else's child do this, I would have been in hysterics, but when it's your own child somehow giggling at them just isn't acceptable. Anyway, despite the fact that I hadn't yet turned to see the reactions of the rest of the pool's occupants, I could feel the eyes of the immaculate lady swimmers burning into the back of my head. They'd have tutted enough if one of the children had dared to splash water near their make-up and bone-dry hair, let alone wee in the shallow end. Having finished, Jack hoisted up his trunks and jumped back into the pool as if nothing out of the ordinary had happened. I opted for the low-key response of curtailing the swimming session a few minutes later and keeping my head down as I left the pool, avoiding eye contact with anyone. I felt absolutely mortified that Jack had succeeded in showing me up in public twice in one week and swore that I would make Tim take him swimming in future. Thank goodness Andrea was there to commiserate with me and point out that at least he hadn't targeted anyone in particular.

Training in the number-two arena was also an adventure for Jack. As he neared the age of three, I began to lose patience with his unpredictable toilet habits. The lack of wee control, I could more easily understand, but it was the wanton pooing in clothes that drove me spare. There is something quite revolting about having to dunk a pair of pants up and down in the toilet in order to get them clean enough to bear putting them in the washing machine with the rest of your washing; many a time I came close to just binning the offending pair of pants. This says a lot because I am not prone to unnecessary waste, but the £1.99 expense of a new packet of pants compared to the unsavoury scrubbing of a pair of pants which will always bear the stained evidence of past misdemeanours somehow seems totally justifiable. It is bad enough desoiling pants for your own child, but quite another when you have to do it for somebody else's. A friend offered to look after Jack for less than half an hour so that I could go for my antenatal check-up with Eloise. I gratefully accepted, knowing that it would make my trip much easier, but when I returned to pick him up she had to explain that Jack was now wearing a pair of her son's underpants because he had messed his own. I was horrified and could only splutter a stream of apologies, before returning home to clean yet *another* pair of pants. I felt so bad, I decided it necessitated leaving a bottle of hand cream on her doorstep the next morning to thank her for rising above and beyond the call of duty!

In comparison, Eloise has been a dream in potty training herself. She is almost two and already requests the toilet when she wants to do a poo. Weeing may take longer, but at least she is already expressing an interest in what it's all about, even if it is worrying me slightly that she has already started wanting to 'wee on the stinging nettles'. Judging by the interest she is displaying in not only her own toilet habits, but also those of everyone else, she may well prove to be as obsessed by bowel movements as her brother was distinctly uninterested.

Jack mastered tantrums to a fine art as well. He has managed to ensure that they are always either very public or else occur when I am trying to have a serious telephone conversation. Eloise has now caught on to this one, too. It's as though my children see me with that white bit of plastic against my head and read it as 'Come pester me as much as you like and as loudly as you possibly can'. There was one occasion, before Eloise was born, when I was making a long and important phone call. It was the sort of call in which I needed to sound extremely efficient and businesslike, as though I was calling from 'the London office', and Jack suddenly began demanding my attention for something to eat. I mistakenly thought I had placated him with a couple of biscuits, but he then proceeded to scream at me hysterically, so much so that I had to start moving at high speed from room to room in an attempt to outwit him by staying one room away from the ever-increasing volume of hysteria. My continued calm business tone and high-speed escapes from Jack only served to inflame his anger, so I had to resort to barricading myself in the dining room. As I continued the call now slightly less out of breath from running, I watched in dismay as the wooden door physically bowed inwards as Jack threw his angry, screaming, troll-like little body against it from the other side. It then all went blissfully quiet, and I sat back and put my feet up on the dining room table, relieved at the silence to be able to fully concentrate on the rest of the conversation. Then I heard a 'drip, drip, drip' . . . Before I even had time to locate the 'drip', down came the torrent. Water was pouring through the dining room ceiling, hitting the table and waterfalling off on to the carpet. At this, I gave up all pretence of being sat in an office and hurriedly finished the telephone call with, 'Sorry, got to go – there's water pouring through my ceiling!' I ran upstairs to find Jack playing in the bathroom sink – plug in and tap running – and having great fun watching the water as it cascaded over the side and splashed through the gaps in the floorboards. The smug look of satisfaction on his face at not only successfully making me abandon my call, but also finding a fantastically entertaining way to do so, was enough to make me commit a crime of passion. How could I be beaten by a three-year-old child? My mind was racing, I was so livid, but I couldn't decide what should come first: turning off the electrics, buckets in the dining room or throttling my son. I had to opt for the domestic tasks first and ran around the house in true headless-chicken fashion, but this 'chicken' was squawking at Jack the whole time. Needless to say, once damage limitations were in place, a decidedly nervous-looking Jack was silently fast-tracked through the bath-and-bed routine, and safely tucked up by 5.30 p.m.! He didn't object at all – I think he was just grateful to be able to take refuge in his bed and escape the company of his fire-breathing dragon mother. By the time Tim arrived home from work I was on the phone again, recounting the story to Lyndsey. Once again my feet were up on the dining room table, but now the ceiling was displaying a large, damp circle in the plaster, soggy towels and buckets surrounded me and the carpet was rolled up against the wall. Tim's reaction of, 'What the hell has been going on here, and more to the point, what the hell are you doing sitting back and chatting on the phone, with such a mess all around you?' was greeted with my evilest 'Don't you even start' glare. And so the other man in my life quickly opted for the escape route and headed out for a forty-minute burst on his mountain bike in preference to facing the wrath of a hormonally highly charged, pregnant woman.

And so to public tantrums. What is it about these that entitle you to all the undesired attention possible from onlookers? The tutters and headshakers are not even worth a mention they are so painfully irritating, but I also struggle with the sympathetic 'I've been there, too' onlooker. I now try to look the other way when I hear somebody's child screaming and yelling in a shop: no amount of sympathetic onlooking is going to make the poor mother feel any better or make the child miraculously calm down. I was recently doing a big supermarket shop with Eloise and was pleased that she had remained composed, sitting in the trolley most of the way round. It suddenly all went pear-shaped as she saw me try to surreptitiously squeeze a sneaky bag of jelly babies into the trolley. All hell broke loose, and she began to try to climb out of the seat and over the mound of shopping in the trolley, in a vain attempt to reach this packet of 'weeties'. It was as I was desperately trying to manoeuvre my heavily laden trolley down the last couple of aisles that a well-meaning young mother with an angelic-looking child sitting neatly in her trolley seat rolled up to me to commiserate with me for my screaming toddler. I smiled politely and carried on, as only a woman with a mission to get out of a shop as quickly as possible can do, but each corner I turned I kept bumping into this same sympathetically smiling woman who was intent on relaying *all* her personal experiences of tantrums to me. In the end, I just sped off towards the checkout like a contender for the final of *Supermarket Sweep*, with a bellowing Eloise hanging over the side of the trolley, leaving the woman embarrassingly alone as she began the tale of her son having a tantrum on the post office floor. I know she was only trying to make me feel better, but, if she thought that prolonging the process of handling this humdinger being displayed by my daughter was helping me out, how wrong she was. All she actually succeeded in doing was to fuel my frustration to fever pitch. There was practically steam coming out of the checkout girl's barcode beeper as she read the 'Scan, woman, scan!' signals I was clearly emitting. By the time I left, Eloise was still screaming, her eyes bloodshot and her face red and blotchy, I was sweating and the checkout girl's adrenaline was still pumping at a ridiculous speed. And it was then that I wished I could be more like Andrea, who is a total soft touch. If I had just given in to the first request for the jelly babies, I would have had a far more pleasurable supermarket trip with my daughter. Life might be much simpler if I took a more relaxed approach, but I just hope there will be some future benefit to be had from the strict discipline I am so insistent on imposing on my children now!

Hilary

* * *

At last I've found a subject that I can say I got off more lightly on: potty training. Both Molly and Ella hit their second birthdays, took their nappies off and there was no looking back. I can't imagine what I did to make it such a breeze; I think that they just did it themselves. I didn't have to do any of the gradual introduction to knickers, carrying a potty in a bag and letting them walk around nude from the waist down. They seemed to both automatically master holding on until we next found a loo from about day three of being nappiless, even night-times were a breeze. With both girls, as soon as they were dry by day, I noticed that they started waking at about 6 a.m., nappy soaked. I worked out that this was because they were dry all night and had just done a huge all-nighter, which beat even the flashiest brand of nappies' absorbability! So I whipped off night-time nappies, put a potty by the bed and told them to get out the second they woke up and sit on it. Hey, presto! Two wet beds later . . . dry. So either I've cracked it or I've been very lucky twice and Alfie's on stand-by to wipe that smug look off my face when I try the same approach again with him; I fear it's the latter!

Well, that was wee training, so now on to bowels and bottoms. Molly has always suffered from dodgy bowels, so poo talk has been a firm favourite in our house for some years. As a baby she suffered from chronic constipation; I spent hours massaging her tummy while she turned beetroot and bore down like a woman in the delivery suite. It made me quite emotional at times, thinking how she, too, one day would go through that experience of childbirth and there would be nothing as her mum that I could do to help her. The satisfaction when she did finally deliver the poo was fantastic. I finally worked out that the best way to get it out was to massage her actual bum hole – through a baby wipe, I hasten to add. This is brilliant; it's like pressing the go button at the sausage factory, and I found that I actually became quite riveted to watching this less-than-pleasant bodily function. Once again I find myself writing this and thinking, I do hope I'm not alone in this discovery; perhaps it's a nursing thing. This constipation phase of her life was fast followed by a phase of the most revolting sludgy, mucusy, evil-smelling cowpat poos. This turned out to be due to a parasitic bug called *Giardia*, which somehow had come to live in her guts, but it smelt as though she'd lived on a diet of Newcastle Brown ale and vindaloo. I had to carry spare outfits because they were guaranteed to be up-the-back jobs and a box of matches because they could linger in the air for days. The phosphorous-from-matches theory of aroma removal was really put to the test with her poos. It has to be said that matches are so much better than covering bowel stenches with floral sprays; the merging of roses and faeces is enough to make even an iron-stomached nurse like me gag. I did fear for my eyebrows and fringe at times, though. The methane levels would hit such heights that I thought there would be one big whoof as I struck the match, and I'd be left with my face char-grilled.

Teaching Molly to wipe her own bottom was a bit of a challenge, too. The poor child wasn't exactly coming from a straightforward starting point with the skiddiest buttocks in the country, then we found out that she was also getting mixed advice on this new skill. David and I discovered that we had totally different approaches to our own post-poo paperwork. I'm not wanting to divulge too much detail, but one of us was a scruncher and the other was a folder. I shan't tell you who was which, but the upshot of this discovery was that poor Molly was totally confused. One of us had to agree to differ, and the skill was taught incredibly quickly once all confusion was removed, although she still likes to make sure we truly appreciate her new skill by talking us through the process from the next room. If it's a skiddy one she waddles into the sitting room, trousers around her ankles, and touches her toes for us to double-check. Very pleasant when you've got guests – anyone for another chocolate biscuit?

Whilst I'm on pants talk, I may as well reveal my own fascinating discoveries. Having a Caesarean for Alfie added a whole new dimension to postnatal pants. Prior to delivery I had bought in the statutory requirement of a small shedload of sanitary towels for the anticipated 'massacre'. But when they took Alfie out of the sunroof, they also took all the gunk that usually has to make its own exit. I had never even given this aspect of Caesareans any thought before, but the end result was that I barely got through one pack of big pads and a couple of packs of panty liners. Brilliant bonus that this was, it has still left me with such a mass of unused outsized sanitary towels that I'm tempted to donate them to Tracey Emin for her next inspirational example of modern art. It has all sorts of unsavoury possibilities, which have to be on par with her grubby bed piece.

My second fascinating post-Caesarean discovery was the new experience of weeing after being catheterized. The first time I went for a wee I nearly leapt off the toilet in shock as the equivalent of Niagara Falls descended from my bladder. The catheter tube must have turned the exit path into a wide bore route and, boy, can that bladder empty fast! I thought this was brilliant. There's something immensely satisfying about having a wee at twice the usual speed. I was actually a bit disappointed when it all returned to normal after a few weeks.

Well, that's enough from below the belt. Now to the tortures of tantrums. Molly could speak clearly from a very early age, which also meant that she could vocalize exactly what she was thinking. This is all a bit unfortunate for her, as the end result was that I was pretty tough on her and her behaviour from a very young age. Ella, on the other hand, has very poor speech. She is fast approaching the age of three, but still can barely be understood, so she gets away with murder compared to poor 'honest Mol'. From fourteen months old, I had to introduce to Molly the concept of a naughty mat because she was already clearly answering me back. It was things like snatching toys off friends and smacking them with them that got to me. When I'd stop her and tell her to say sorry, she'd stare at me with total defiance and say, 'No, not.' I couldn't believe it all started so young, but basically she really hated being isolated, so the mat worked a treat. I'd put her on the hallway rug, and she couldn't come back until she was ready to say sorry. This sometimes took a good handful of return visits, but I, like Sarah, am not one for giving in and always won in the end. I hoped this would set her up to understand my discipline regime from a very young age, but, for an astute child, she's proving an extremely slow learner. She's now approaching five, still gets sent to either the hall or her room, but now the sound of a tongue-out raspberry can often be heard as she heads out the door. She never has been one for the full-blown, lie-on-the-floor, screaming tantrum, but she sure can find my Achilles heel when it comes to answering back. I don't remember ever speaking to my mother in the way she speaks to me, and she's not even five. It's not as though I'm a soft touch either – I really am the Hitler of the discipline world, and when I really lose my rag I can manage to make even Sarah with a flooded bathroom look like a complete pussycat. All too frequently I turn into a shaking mess, inarticulately bellowing my planned punishments whilst practically frothing at the mouth. Molly manages to maintain an air of disdain throughout it all and gives me a distinct look of 'For God's sake, Mother, get a grip.' I frequently find myself in bed at night dissecting the day and coming up with my next plan of action for how I am going to get it right next time. My latest is a three-tier volume of discipline. I start by explaining why I don't like whatever it is she is doing and ask her if she understands. If she carries on, I'll then raise my voice one level and firmly say that I don't like telling her twice and, if I have to say it again, I'll be shouting and she'll be in her room. If I hit level three, I take on a remarkable resemblance to the cartoon character Captain Caveman as I release yet another bloodcurdling bellow and frogmarch her upstairs. Unfortunately, we are already reaching level three far more often than I would care to admit. The trouble with Molly and me is that we are just too similar. We are both so headstrong and determined, yet extremely sensitive underneath. We are both the sort of people who have a plan and just cannot control ourselves if things don't go exactly as they should. It's because of her hypersensitive personality and astuteness that I always had a no-smacking policy. With Molly, rejection by isolation was always far more painful.

I also spent most of my life telling her not to smack other children, so I knew that she would rapidly throw that back in my face if I ever dared to smack her. The line 'Do I ever smack you? No, well don't smack other people' always seemed to have so much power to it. But then Alfie was born, the girls started to bicker constantly and achieving the school run on time became mission impossible. Trying to get all three dressed, breakfasted and out the door on minimal sleep finally tested my patience to the limit in week four of Alfie's life. Ella and Molly were particularly hellish this day, with one or other of them bursting into tears every couple of minutes throughout the entire breakfast and dressing process. Alfie decided that he was not happy to let go of my boob for even thirty seconds without screaming the whole house down, and, as the stress mounted, David decided to pop back in from the farm to offer his own little pearl of wisdom. As I strapped a screaming Alfie into his car seat whilst insisting that a whining Ella could walk the whole eight steps to the car that she was demanding to be carried, Molly decided to burst into tears yet again. She didn't know whether to have her hair in the bunches I had put in or a ponytail. What if her friend Alice had a ponytail and she had bunches? You'd have thought she was talking about a funeral arrangement not a hairdo the way she howled. 'Does something hurt?' I asked. 'If not, don't cry . . . talk.' This was probably at least the sixth time I had needed to use this line that morning, so I was now on an extremely short fuse. As I reached the car, all three were still going at fever pitch for their own personal crisis, be they boob requirements, carrying needs or bad hair days.

It was at this point that David decided to add his little gem: 'May I suggest you get up ten minutes earlier to save all this hassle.' My fuse finally burnt out and the bomb went off. I could have swung for any one of the four of them, but poor Molly was in for a direct hit as she chose this precise moment to let out another howl about her hair. 'Does something hurt?' I bellowed. 'No,' came the reply, just as I lifted her school dress and flesh met flesh as I smacked her thigh. 'Well, now it does,' I said and bundled her into the car. She was stunned into total silence, as were the whole family and I suddenly took on an uncanny resemblance to Basil Fawlty. 'Good, good,' I chirped. 'Everybody's happy now, Molly's got a good reason to cry, something does hurt. Lovely, lovely,' I cheerfully spouted as I drove to the school. Having dropped off two totally bemused children at the school and playgroup maintaining a manic grin throughout, I then got back in the car, with a now sleeping Alfie, put my head on the steering wheel and burst into tears. Not only had I failed in my no-smacking policy, I had said 'good' with such pleasure after inflicting my first-ever physical punishment!

Ella, I have to say, has been far less complex, far less vocal and therefore given me far fewer guilt trips when it comes to discipline. She was extremely aggressive to others when she was a toddler, though. In fact, during her brief spell at nursery, she was nicknamed 'WWF' (World Wrestling Federation) because of her phenomenal ability to wrestle any child off the nursery rocking horse. But she just looked totally bewildered when I made her say sorry to others and quite happily made all of the appropriate gestures, even though she clearly didn't understand or care why she had to. She also doesn't really care about being isolated and quite happily goes to her room whenever she is naughty. She almost sees this as a treat because that's where her dummies are so she can go for a surreptitious midday suck. I'm sure that if she could vocalize as well as Molly could at her age she'd be saying, 'Suits me, I'd wanted to go to my room anyway. See you later,' as I sent her packing. This would totally infuriate me, but because she's silent she gets away with it. She'll then quite happily trudge down again and apologize with a chirpy 'Forwee' to whoever without a second thought. Life must be much easier in her little world than it is in Molly's. Molly would have to weigh up whether the situation warranted an apology or whether she should argue her case some more. She would have sat upstairs worrying about how cross I was, whether I still liked and loved her, and what other people thought of her. Ella would have sat up there, sucked her dummy, undressed her teddies whilst humming 'Baa, Baa, Black Sheep', without even considering the reason why she was up there in the first place.

Ella has managed to do the full-blown public tantrums to perfection, though, but this is something that really does not faze me. I certainly would never pass judgement on the parent of a tantruming child, especially if they weren't giving in to that child. Maybe I'm naive, but I just assume that's how everyone's brain works, and I tend to remain completely unflustered as she rolls around the floor. Having said that, I must admit I was embarrassed recently when Ella decided to lie on the floor, kicking and bellowing, next to the chocolates I had refused to open for her in WH Smith. I had taken my usual calm approach of saying, 'I'm not going to change my mind, so when you've finished being a baby, I'm down here.' I then went and acquired a riveting fascination for a packet of Bic biros a short distance away from her. Unfortunately, before she realized quite how ineffective her tantrum was, a well-meaning old lady had scooped her up and was heading for the tills to hand her in. I could see the desire to call social services in her eyes, as she heard me casually calling from the plastic pens section, 'Just leave her there. She's with me, thank you.' She replaced my uncontrollably sobbing child on the floor next to the chocolate shelf and looked decidedly down her nose as she passed me. My embarrassment manifested itself in anger at Ella for putting me in such a position. I aborted my shopping trip, unceremoniously dumping her in the buggy and walking at such a pace back to the car that her head was practically G-forced to the back of the buggy seat. Once again I found myself spitting and snarling totally impractical punishments such as, 'That's it. You're never having chocolate again in your whole life!' as I manhandled her into her car seat, started the engine and wheel-spun my way out of the car park in true 'boy racer' style. Ella by now looked petrified and progressed to the silent sob stage. She remained subdued for the rest of the day, and it wasn't until bath time that I realized she had a temperature and was rapidly plummeting with a stinking cold. Once again I found myself guilt-riddled as I kissed my children good night and wondered if I would ever get it right. But perhaps the reality is that there just isn't a 'right'.

Lyndsey

* * *

As Bethan settled into nursery life, I was quietly happy that the potty training was going to be a shared experience. I was looking to the nursery for some guidance on when we should embark on this next milestone and how the hell we were to do it. When the right time was going to be was a question that lingered at the back of my mind, and, having heard tales from friends with older children and read articles on the subject, it was something that filled me with dread. It seemed as if the precise time of this act were crucial: get it right and the potty training could be done and dusted within a week, but get it wrong and you could be facing weeks or, in Sarah's case, months of frustration. What I did pick up was that it wasn't something that I would need to worry about until Bethan had at least turned two, so as that birthday came and went I started to look for signs that the task of potty training should commence. As it turned out, Bethan made the choice to relieve herself of her nappy only a couple of months past her second birthday. One evening when I came to collect Bethan from nursery, her key worker suggested that I brought a few spare pairs of pants and clothes the next day, as Bethan had decided that this was it. She, too, wanted to wee on a toilet like her friend Laura.

Now let me just explain that Laura was a full four months older than Bethan, and Bethan certainly looked up to her in more ways than one. If Laura could use a toilet, then so she should, too. I felt that it was doomed from the start, and I was sure she wasn't ready for it. The nursery staff disagreed and said that we might as well give it a go if she was willing, as that, apparently, is half the battle. It all got off to a brilliant start in that first week, with only a couple of minor accidents, but, as soon as the weekend came, with Laura nowhere to be seen or copied, Bethan reverted to wetting her pants almost continually. So with much fuss the pants came off and the nappies went back on. I put it down to a dodgy start and decided to broach the subject of delaying the potty training with the nursery staff once more. But back at nursery Bethan came home with dry pants, and the nursery staff were so excited that she had cracked it that I didn't dare suggest a reversion to nappies. Come the next weekend, though, I spent my entire three days off mopping damp patches on the floor and changing wet clothes. It felt as if Bethan were teasing me just to make sure I had a full failed parent score when I returned her to nursery on Monday. In my defence, though, I would like to say that I felt it was more important to do some activities *outside the bathroom* during our time together, and it appeared that nursery was one long toilet run. When Laura needed a wee, Bethan was toddling along, too, and successfully went. In addition, the nursery also insisted that the 'potty trainers' be taken to the toilet at least once an hour. So, all in all, Bethan never had a chance to wet herself with all the toing and froing to the toilet. At home I couldn't contend with this level of vigilance, so it felt as if the whole messy business took forever to sort out. But, just as I'd been led to believe, the penny eventually dropped, and soon we had the weeing aspect all sorted.

The poos, on the other hand, were a dodgier story altogether. It was the intense expression on Bethan's face as the strain started that I had to be extra vigilant for. As soon as I spotted this, I'd scoop her up and run for the nearest toilet, pulling her pants down as I went, in a totally undignified fashion. Perhaps it was these sudden movements and reluctance to be catapulted through the air whilst mooning that led to Bethan's next trick emerging. She decided that pooing in private was the only option, but sadly did not pick the more conventional privacy of the toilet. Instead, she opted for sneaking off to a quiet corner or behind the curtain, or indeed anywhere that was out of sight so that she could perform in her pants alone. This then became a game of vigilance on an entirely different scale. Instead of simply spotting that change in facial expression, first I would have to find the child. As soon as it went quiet, the child hunt would be on, as I'd run around the house desperately searching her favourite haunts to try to catch her before her pants caught the poo. As soon as she was located, she would be eeked out and once again hurled into the toilet. Her aversion for the use of the toilet for number twos hit rock bottom when we all went to a birthday party at Andrea and Bruce's. It was a summer's day, and all the children were naked in the paddling pool. Clearly Tim and I were not on the same level of daily exposure to groups of semitoilet-trained children all being together, but I tried not to be too protective as I let Bethan paddle in the pool that all the other children had weed in. None of the other Fat Ladies looked at all perturbed by the hygiene levels of the water, so I happily took my lead from them. Tim, on the other hand, looked totally horrified at the prospect of his little princess paddling in urine and encouraged her to play on Max's new slide instead. Tim had never really had to deal with many embarrassing moments with respect to Bethan's toilet habits before that day, so what happened next certainly was a baptism of fire – or should I say faeces. Just as Bruce was serving up the spicy sausages, Bethan decided to lay claim to Max's slide by depositing the biggest log you have ever seen right on the top of it. For his angelic Bethan to do something so totally undignified in public was a mortifying moment for Tim. Fortunately for me, I was nowhere to be seen, having timed my trip to assist in the kitchen perfectly. So Tim had to roll up his sleeves and deal with the offending matter, not to mention his daughter, who had by now sat in it and slid down the slide. When I returned to the scene, Tim was chasing Bethan around the garden with a packet of wipes whilst apologizing profusely to Andrea and Bruce for the soiling of the brand-new birthday gift. The rest of the Fat Ladies and their partners were all thoroughly enjoying this spectacle, offering absolutely no assistance whatsoever as they positively whooped with laughter at poor Tim's expense. I have to say that I learnt my lesson from my husband's nightmare and made sure that Bethan kept her pants on for all future summer parties that year.

Given all the travelling around we do in the car, I had always dreaded the day when we would be travelling with a nappy-free Bethan. At least when toddlers are still in nappies the journey doesn't need to be interrupted for those inevitable toilet stops that prolong the tortures of journeys with children even more. For a while after she was out of nappies, if we were going on a long trip, I would encourage Bethan to wear 'pull-ups', purely to remove the 'I want a wee wee' equation from the trip. Having the opportunity to quite simply reply, 'Fine, do one,' was ideal. We got away with this for a while, and as long as we didn't call them nappies she was quite easily persuaded to put on the travelling pants. But to be fair to her, though, Bethan could last as long as me and, until she was four, she would nod off in the car and not wake until the car stopped anyway, so toilet stops weren't too much of an issue. We finally had to concede that our big girl really did not need travelling nappies any longer and let her stick to her pink cotton Barbie pants instead. Eighteen months after the last pull-up was binned, journey disaster finally struck. Shortly after Caitlin was born, we headed off for a holiday in France. We set off on our way to Dover for the cross-Channel ferry, but having been caught up in traffic we were cutting it very fine, to say the least. Just as my blood pressure was rising as I tried to calculate exactly how many miles per minute we needed to cover for us still to be able to catch the boat, Bethan piped up with that dreaded phrase, 'I want a wee wee.' She didn't just want a wee wee, she needed one so badly she was beside herself. There was absolutely no way she could hold on for the extra half hour until we reached the port, but if we stopped the car for even one of the precious minutes I had calculated we would be in danger of missing the ferry. Then I recalled a tactic a friend of mine had used in a similar situation: use one of the baby's nappies. So there we were hurtling down the motorway, Bethan still strapped in her car seat, but now with pants removed, skirt hitched up and sitting on one of Caitlin's newborn nappies. Well, the friend who had advised me of the tactic either had a baby with far bigger nappies or a child with a far smaller bladder capacity because all I can say is that an extremely miserable Bethan had to spend the rest of the journey sitting on a decidedly damp car seat! We did sit her on a jumper to make the journey more comfortable, and it brought back memories of the towel on milk-soaked baby car seat of earlier years. Writing this reminds me – I must wash that car seat cover!

Tantrums are something we haven't had to deal with when it comes to Bethan. Yes, there have been the very odd occasions where she has lost the plot, but, nine times out of ten, left to her own devices she calms down after a few minutes, then comes to sit or stand next to me. We'd then find out what all the noise had been about, and the situation would be resolved. This certainly doesn't make Bethan a perfect angel because what she didn't do in the world of tantrums she made up for in her ability to object to the dreaded car seat. Invariably, the worst time was collecting her from nursery when she was tired and not wanting to cooperate, and it took all manner of persuasion and a bit of muscle to get her eventually strapped in. I didn't realize the strength that Bethan had, even as young as a toddler, until she and I came face to face with the car seat. Some days were worse than others in that just getting her through the car door was a nightmare, and I'd have to prise her fingers from the door frame as she shouted and screamed as loud as she could just to make sure that all and sundry could hear her objections. Once the obstacle of the door was overcome, the battle of the straps and getting her body out of the rigor mortis, joint-locked position into a more flexible mode to lower her into the seat began. Sometimes it took nothing short of pinning her down like a wrestler with my shoulder whilst avoiding injury from fighting limbs as I frantically tackled the straps to lock her in. Hot, sweating, flustered, stressed out and, if an audience was on hand, mortally embarrassed simply does not begin to cover the emotions I felt. I'd have been at work all day missing my little girl, embarked on that journey back to her dying to scoop her up into my arms, then only minutes later I'd be taking on the skills of Big Daddy purely to get my child to come home with me. I always felt that the nursery staff and other parents must have wondered what kind of hell home life was for Bethan for her to be so desperate not to want to get in the car. But at least I knew it wasn't personal because she carried on the same trick with other people, too. On one occasion, my parents had kindly offered to collect their granddaughter from nursery, as a nice surprise. Bethan managed to create such a scene that even the combined wrestling skills of both my mum and my dad could not beat her. Poor Mum had to admit defeat and go back into the nursery to ask one of the staff to help get her grandchild into the car. This was probably the only time in her life that my mother had been belittled by a child, so needless to say she was not too keen to repeat the performance. After that, she, too, dreaded taking Bethan anywhere in the car for fear of the carseat-hating monster rearing its ugly head.

Thankfully the car seat tantrums were relatively short-lived, although eighteen months of body bending didn't feel 'short-lived' at the time. But when I look at the whole picture up until now, that has been the only grief Bethan has given us. Now she has started school, and life seems to be changing. She has definitely become more cheeky, and we are entering a new phase in life called 'Backchat'. At the moment, this can be controlled by saying that I am going to talk to her teacher about her manners, which is enough to send her into a stream of apologies. I'm just hoping that the power of the teacher threat remains so effective until she has grasped the fact that backchat simply isn't Bethan. Having got off so lightly with the terrible twos and threes with Bethan, once again I find myself wondering whether our little Caitlin is going to give us a rougher time or be a carbon copy of her sister. Fingers crossed for the latter!

Andrea

***

I will start by holding my hands up to being the soft touch out of the four of us when it comes to dealing with children. Hilary is definitely the Fat Ladies' Hitler. Sarah, when driven to it, can be nearly as frightening. And as for Lyns, with angel Bethan, she really hasn't a clue what discipline is! If I ever have to raise my voice to any of the others' children, then you immediately hear them say, 'If Andrea had to shout, then you must have been really naughty.' I don't have a problem at all with my boys being told off by one of the others, though, because, as much as I don't dish it out myself, I'm not averse to them getting a decent ticking off. I have no idea why I have turned into such a soft touch when it comes to parenting. I was brought up very strictly, and I have no complaints about this. Although I must admit that I did resent all three of us being punished when an admission wasn't forthcoming, as it was always either my brother or sister who were the culprits.

Bruce has always been the voice of discipline in our house, and I know that, if I don't get a grip and become stricter once

I'm on my own, I will suffer in years to come. I do keep trying, but I must admit it is a struggle, so I'm putting it off now until we have moved. My plan then is to lay down some stricter rules about teatime, bedtime and general manners. Yet another resolution to try to achieve when I move!

Max was such a brilliant, cheerful, placid baby that I hoped he would stay that way through the toddler years, too. He didn't even object to the mouthful of ever-descending teeth, but just got on with it with his luminous red cheeks being the only evidence of the latest gum eruptions. Mind you, this may also have been down to the fact that every time he even gave a hint of teething I had him on the maximum Calpol dose plus hourly squirts of Calgel. He was probably so pain relieved he couldn't feel his own face, let alone his gums. No wonder the poor lad dribbled so much. It must have been like one long mouth-numbing trip to the dentist, but it did the trick. As all the others dealt with month after month of nose-rubbing babies who didn't sleep at night, a rosy-faced Max just smiled and dribbled his way through the whole experience.

Then he hit the toddler years, and it is fair to say that Max absolutely hated being two. It was as if he felt the whole world was against him, so he walked around with a permanent scowl on his face when he was in anyone's company other than family. The entire year was all pretty embarrassing really. You could count on one hand the number of times he smiled or spoke to anyone outside the house, and generally I spent the whole year apologizing for my son's rudeness, as he either bit people's heads off or stuck his nose in the air and ignored them if they had the audacity to say hello to him. At home he was funny, chatty, smiley and great to have around, but, as soon as someone else appeared, so did Max, the antisocial scowler.

Despite the fact that he was an early talker, he seemed to lack the ability to comprehend that, if I didn't have something, I couldn't give it to him, and so the full-blown explosion would occur. These did not then generally let up until that 'something' had been acquired. If it was chocolate he wanted and there was none in the house, it didn't matter how many times I explained or showed him the empty treaty cupboard. 'I want it, though,' just kept being screamed at me nonstop for what seemed like a lifetime. I generally dealt with these situations by simply remaining calm and patient, and just letting him rant and rave – although if I could get a bit of peace by giving in, I would regularly go that route as a first option. Hilary, being the complete opposite, having Molly who did understand and respond when she was told something wasn't available, found my approach to Max totally frustrating. At times I wasn't sure who was the biggest kid out of the two of them. But on a four-hour car journey from

At times I wasn't sure who was the biggest kid, Max
or Hilary . . .

hell when Max was nearly three, I finally decided that Hilary could beat Max hands down on the wind-up stakes. About an hour before home, stuck on the motorway, Max announced that he wanted juice to drink and not the water we had offered him. We didn't have juice and so the tantrum started. I then made the mistake of threatening Max that I would throw away the McDonald's toy he had just acquired if he didn't stop screaming and hitting out at the other children. I say this is a mistake because I really should learn not to make threats, as I am absolutely useless at following them through, even when I am not driving, let alone when I am. Half an hour later, Max still screaming and me still calmly making the same threat, Hilary lost the plot. Suddenly her seat belt was undone, she dived through the back, whipped the toy out of his hands, wound down her window and held it out saying, 'Now, will you listen to Mummy? . . . Stop scream-ing!' This form of discipline was totally alien to Max and so his volume went up tenfold as she then feigned throwing it out of the window and quickly hid it under her car seat. Max hit apoplectic pitch just as I dropped an apologetic Hilary and her children off at their house, leaving me to deal with my uncontrol-lable son for the rest of my journey home . . . Thanks, pal.

Fortunately, once Max hit three, he almost immediately stopped the full-blown tantrums and has even begun to quite enjoy Hilary's wind-ups now. He can still be quite moody at times and is best ignored when he just isn't in a sociable mood. Sam certainly hasn't hated being two quite as much as his big brother. He didn't develop the antisocial scowl anyway, but, boy, can he tantrum, too. Sam's tantrums are always connected with being tired or waking from a daytime nap. When he wakes up in the morning after a good night's sleep, he is as cheerful as anything. He comes running in so excited that it is morning and time for his hot milk. However, when he wakes from a daytime nap, he is always in the foulest mood and generally likes to greet me by lying on the floor, kicking and screaming for at least half an hour. If I try to go near him, he lashes out; if I give him hot milk, he throws it across the room, then screams louder for it. I have tried all sorts of different techniques to deal with this and have realized that I just have to ignore him until it wears off, and he then comes and gives me a big cuddle as he sobs and drinks his milk. He then chats away, totally oblivious to the commotion he has just caused. When Sarah rang during one of these post-nap nightmares, she thought he had suffered some major limb loss injury from the wailing in the background. I could hear concern for his welfare in her voice, but I have to admit that I am now totally immune to these wobblies and barely appreciate they are happening if we're at home and nobody else is around. Having said that, I am looking forward to this stage ending, as it's always a bit of a worry when I'm out and about, and he dozes off in the car. These displays in public really aren't a pretty sight.

My namby-pamby approach to discipline may have meant that my boys have given me a particularly hard time, and admittedly they still do, but it has paid off in one respect. I am assured by everyone that they always behave impeccably for other people. The other Fat Ladies frequently tell me what a pleasure my boys are as long as I'm not there. I suppose I should be grateful for this. With the current stress in my life, however, if I have an after-school sulky Max combined with a post-nap screaming Sam to contend with when the only thing I have to look forward to when I've tucked them up in bed is an evening with my estranged husband, I have to admit that I wish I, too, could be party to the pleasant treatment from my boys and that it wasn't saved solely for the pleasure of other people's mums.

As for toilet training, I think the others have covered this quite thoroughly. Max got the hang of it all incredibly easily, especially for a boy, so I'm told. Sam was similar to Bethan in that he'd sneak off to do a poo, but, unlike Bethan, he'd drop his pants, leaving evidence behind in whatever secret location he'd chosen. It was a bit like playing on one of my Sunday morning park football pitches and having to avoid the dog poo as you slid into a tackle. Sometimes the only evidence of a poo having been deposited somewhere by Sam was the telltale brown buttocks. On some occasions, he would pull his pants back up, which meant we might not know of the occurrence until bath time, but often he took the opportunity to strip at the same time. I'm not sure which I preferred, going on a search for a day-old poo wasn't great, but when your naked two-year-old climbs onto your lap for a cuddle and leaves a skid mark on your jeans when he slides off again, that really is revolting. I've lost count of the number of times I've sniffed skid marks on me to ascertain if it's chocolate or poo!

Sam was always a baby who didn't like sitting in a stinky nappy, but this certainly wasn't out of a deep-rooted desire to be clean, like his brother. When he was about eighteen months old, I loved listening to him through the monitor in the morning. He would wake, then chat and play happily in his cot for about half an hour before he'd call out. This eavesdropping on my contented son was one of those mothering moments I loved. Then one day I discovered exactly what carnage he could create in that time zone, and the magical moment became a nightmare. Having enjoyed my listening in, I decided to find out quite what this fun game was he was so enthralled in. As I opened the door, the first thing that hit me was the smell. I was then faced with a de-nappied Sam who had completely redecorated his room, cot, self and bedding with the contents of his nappy. In true Rolf Harris-style, he had smeared brown patterns across everything in his reach. I was just waiting for him to pipe up, in a thick Australian accent, 'Can you see what it is yet?' as he grinned with pride at his creation.

Despite Max being nearly five now, one aspect of toilet

training I've still not tackled is standing-up wees. Max, with his obsession with cleanliness, has never even attempted to take aim and always opts for the failsafe sitting position. Sam, by contrast, loves to wee around the toilet. He stands and vaguely points his hips in the right direction, but hasn't yet mastered the need for hands to assist in directing the flow. If I'd known Bruce and I were going to separate, I'd have got him to cover this long ago because I really haven't a clue what tips to give them. How the hell am I supposed to know the best way to hold their todge and whether there are different approaches to dealing with a dribbler rather than a shooter wee? This will have to become a training task for weekends with Daddy, I think.

Finally, whilst on the subject of willies, what better subject to end on than erections. Both of my boys would constantly surprise me from a young age when I took their nappies off and would be met with a miniature stiffy. Neither of them played with his willy as a baby, and I am not sure when their minds worked out that this was a pleasurable experience, but both of them have sussed it out now. Max recently expressed his first sexual urges to Bruce and me when he was having a shower. He suddenly said, 'When I am waiting to see who gets Rosie, I get really excited and my willy goes all tingly and sticky-uppy.' I will quickly explain that Rosie is a teddy bear that each child in the class takes it in turn to take home for the night. The teacher draws a name out of a hat to see who wins the bear for the night. Bruce and I caught each other's eye and rapidly had to bite our lips, desperately trying not to laugh at his revelation. 'Really, Max, that's nice,' I managed to squeeze out in a high-pitched, wobbly voice as Bruce ran from the room giggling. Fortunately there won't be a 'Rosie bear' when he goes up to year one, so hopefully this 'first love' will soon die. Poor Max, he certainly won't thank me in later life for putting in print the fact that his first desires were for a brown, furry bear!

Ground, Swallow Me Up!

Here goes for all the moments when you look up to the sky and ask yourself, why me? It may be those classic moments when our children have said or done something that leaves us totally speechless and rapidly turning crimson. It may be those situations we manage to inflict on ourselves as we face the often frightening and unpredictable world of being a mother.

Prior to having children, we all had a vast degree of control over our everyday lives and our destiny, but that all rapidly went out the window. 'Never work with children or animals,' they say in the film industry – and how true it is, too. Once children are on the scene, you never quite know what will happen next. Everything can appear to be going totally to plan, and then, like a bolt of lightning, 'it' happens . . . whatever 'it' is. Your perfect world is instantly turned into disarray, and you're either left in a numbed, shocked state of total disbelief or searching for that metaphorical hole to curl up into and wait for the whole embarrassing nightmare to pass.

Here are a handful of the bolt-of-lightning 'it' situations that motherhood has managed to throw us into and how we attempted to crawl our way out of our ground-swallowing holes.

Sarah

* * *

As I remember some of these hideously embarrassing moments, I realize that the majority of mine have occurred round and about the high street of where we live, which is what makes them all the more embarrassing, I suppose. If they had happened anywhere else, they simply wouldn't have made such an impact on me because I wouldn't have been so concerned about people that I don't know seeing me in these predicaments. However, maybe I should take heart in the fact that at least the people in my home town know me already and will hopefully be laughing *with* me, rather than *at* me, during these earth-swallow-me-whole episodes.

When Jack was three and a half, I felt that the need for the buggy board permanently attached to Eloise's pram was probably a little overkill, so I decided to introduce him to the use of his feet. I felt sure that, by this stage, the original novelty of the buggy board, which was designed to be a 'big brother' mode of transport when his sister was born, was no longer necessary. So, one day, we ventured out without the buggy board attached and, after a little initial hesitation, Jack thought he'd give this new 'walking to the shops' lark a bit of a go. After all, the bribe of a gingerbread man as a special treat at the supermarket was always worth any challenge. We started off well, and he managed to walk all of the 500 yards to the shops, without complaining, but the fun started as soon as we reached the supermarket. Jack had obviously grown bored with the shopping trip which had, in fairness, included a ten-minute wait in the post office queue and a browse in a gift shop, so by the time we reached the supermarket he obviously felt he needed to spice things up a bit.

As I was selecting some apples from the fruit counter, thinking that Jack was still obediently holding on to the pram handle, I was broken from my train of thought by a shriek from a passer-by: the poor woman looked like she had seen a ghost. I turned to find the pram behind me, with Eloise smiling happily in the seat, but Jack nowhere to be seen. On closer inspection, I realized that Jack had not only clambered into the shopping tray, underneath the pram, but had also turned himself into some kind of pram monster who was growling and grabbing unsuspecting passing ankles. Clearly this poor elderly lady had been his first victim, as she was passing innocently by with her shopping trolley. Seeing how pale and petrified the woman looked, I instantly swung into the mode of being overly apologetic and

Much to my horror, Jack the pram monster was grabbing the
ankles of unsuspecting passers-by

hideously embarrassed by my son's offensive behaviour; I even offered to replace her 'American tan' tights which were now severely laddered. She nervously accepted my apology and went on her way, but, judging by the way she sloped off up the vegetable aisle, jumping sideways at least two feet from any prams advancing towards her, I think Jack may have inflicted lasting damage to her nerves. I then had the nightmare situation of meeting her from the opposite direction in every aisle of the supermarket afterwards, and I found myself muttering, 'I'm so sorry,' each time we made eye contact. I have to admit that I was also struggling to hold back a smirk as my pram monster continued to growl from the undercarriage throughout the shopping trip. I didn't deprive him of his gingerbread man treat, but did regret giving it to him whilst he was still firmly embedded in my shopping basket. Once we were through the checkout, he decided that he would rather stay exactly where he was for the return journey home. I had a devil's job trying to prise him out from underneath the pram so that I could fill the basket with my shopping. Even with a gingerbread man to protect, he managed to keep such a grip on the pram frame that I thought he was going to need to be surgically removed. After a certain degree of extremely public spitting and snarling from both Jack and myself, and a huge dose of brute force, I managed to drag an indignant and very stroppy Jack all the way back along the high street. Perhaps I had been rather premature in the disposal of the buggy board after all.

Having overcome the huge hurdle of stopping my son from growling and ankle grabbing in the supermarket, I then came face to face with his use of foul language. I am always stunned at children's ability to absorb information like sponges and to regurgitate it in the most appropriate context, but why it is that this is done with such ease with bad language and is such a struggle with basic manners is something I'll never understand.

Jack's use of expletives has made me wince on many occasions, not least when it has been in front of his grandparents or our neighbours. I'd like to think that we're bringing our children up to use language intelligently, and hence I scold Tim mightily whenever he lets rip with swear words in front of them. I take heart in the knowledge that my friends know that I don't use the more revolting swear words, so anything gross uttered from Jack's lips can only be copied from his father! Still, that doesn't really help when I'm in a public place and nobody knows me from Eve. And so back to our hometown high street, where I had to face my second ground-swallowing experience. I'd just collected Jack from school, and he was happily walking along beside me, holding on to the buggy and chatting away about his day. Suddenly, midway through the blow-by-blow account of his lunch-break antics, he just disappeared from sight – face first on to the pavement. I do realize that there is absolutely nothing funny about your son falling flat on his face, but for some reason the 'Now you see me, now you don't!' aspect of his fall prompted me into hysterical laughter. The way he fell was somewhat reminiscent of Del Boy falling through the bar in that classic *Only Fools and Horses* sketch, but still that is no excuse for my unsympathetic reaction. I did stop to help him to his feet, but he bounced back up like an angry little troll before I had the chance. He was so indignant that I could possibly be laughing at his expense, and then I made the grave error of suggesting that he may have tripped over his own feet, which was just too much for him to bear. He was Mr Angry by this stage and proceeded to kick the hell out of my handbag, which was hanging down the side of the buggy. 'I didn't fall over my feet,' he yelled, 'I fell over your *bloody* handbag!' And this he yelled several times over in order to make absolutely sure his stupid, giggling mother had got her facts straight. I was still laughing as the sudden realization hit me that I had, in fact, produced a perfect clone of my husband;

'Dolly the Sheep' was nothing in comparison to 'Jack the Tim'. He even had the same irritation in his voice as Tim would have had should he have tripped over my handbag on the stairs. If it hadn't been for the fact that we were standing right beside a crowded bus stop at the time, I might not have regained my composure until we got home. But seeing the stunned faces turn to stare at the scene we were causing in the middle of the pavement, I felt I had to do the shocked, admonishing mother bit. After all, I would be shocked to hear someone else's four-year-old talk to their mother like that! 'What dreadful language, Jack. Where did you learn language like that?' I spluttered before rushing round the corner with Jack in tow, still booting the stuffing out of my handbag. I only hope that no one in the bus queue had previously fallen victim to the 'pram monster'!

Tim hasn't yet experienced a bad-language embarrassing moment, which really isn't fair as he is quite clearly Jack's trainer in this arena. So, I was quietly pleased when Jack successfully plummeted his dad into a huge, ground-swallowing hole with another skill he has acquired: guffing. Tim quite often works from home, but has not yet mastered the fact that, if you have a study upstairs at home, with no door, it is nigh on impossible to keep children away. To be fair to Tim, though, on this particular occasion, I wasn't doing my best to 'keep the children away', as I was engrossed in a chat with Andrea in the kitchen. Radio blaring, good gossip under way, and I was oblivious to Jack's shaking of the bottom-stair gate and bellowing, 'Dad, let me up. I need a wee!' Tim wasn't just working from home; he was, in fact, in the middle of a conference call with about twenty people, including lawyers, accountants and bankers. The combination of being ignored and being desperate for the toilet made Jack scream all the louder, so much so that someone on the end of the telephone line commented, 'Someone's not happy!' Tim remained silently embarrassed, feeling safe in the knowledge that no one would be able to identify exactly which participant on the call had such an unruly child. Tim's concentration was being tested to the limit by this background interruption and so, irritated by the fact that I wasn't taking things in hand myself, he ran downstairs, phone under chin, and let Jack up the stairs to the bathroom. The finale came when, just as Tim bowed his head to help him down with his trousers and pants, Jack let out a rippling guff that reverberated straight into the phone's mouthpiece. Conversation in the conference call drew to an abrupt halt as the speakers wondered who on earth had the front to break wind in the midst of such a business meeting. Tim desperately hoped that his anonymity would prevail, as he continued to contribute to the call, and, to his knowledge, no one ever suspected Tim Groves's three-year-old son to be the unexpected gate-crasher on the call. Strangely enough, Tim now gives me plenty of advance warning of my need to take up my motherly duties when he is about to make an important phone call.

Eloise so far hasn't let me down too much in public, although she is already showing tendencies, like her brother, of nonconformist behaviour, so I ought to be prepared! I had been pleased with the way her language had been developing so well until last month, when I wished she hadn't been able to speak at all. We were attending one of Jack's school assemblies, which involved a lot of singing by the children and a speaker who had been invited to talk about an East European children's charity. We all listened attentively for the first fifteen minutes of this speech, but, by the time he had notched up half an hour, even the more patient parents amongst us were beginning to yawn. How the teachers manage to ensure the children sit still when even the grown-ups are fidgety is beyond me. Anyway, at this stage Eloise had decided that she was tired of clambering over Andrea's and my legs, and was getting fed up with me persistently reminding her to mind my pregnant stomach. Totally out of the blue, she suddenly declared to everyone within a five-metre radius of our seats, 'My want to suck your boobies, Mummy!' at the same time as trying to rip open my shirt and stuff her hands down to my chest. As I felt the colour rise up my cheeks, I could hear the tittering around me as all eyes turned to watch this welcome change in entertainment. Andrea's eyes were on stalks as she struggled to believe what Eloise had just dared to shout out loud. Even my muffled attempts to divert her attention towards the children and tractors on the speaker's slideshow didn't have any effect whatsoever. She had already seen enough of those and was a little girl with a mission to thoroughly embarrass her mother in a hall filled with parents. My biggest fear was that people would presume, on hearing Eloise's outburst, that I was still breastfeeding her – a two-year-old with a full set of teeth and capable of groping her way to her midmorning snack. And at the same time as me being obviously pregnant – ugh! Although that may well suit some mothers, for me the thought is utterly repellent. I felt like standing up at the end of the assembly to put the record straight for friends and strangers alike: 'Just for your information, I am not still breastfeeding my daughter, and her earlier request must have been provoked by books that I have been reading to her recently to prepare her for the birth of her baby brother or sister. Thank you.'

Hilary

* * *

The big lesson that I have learnt in these first few years of parenthood is that 'Do as I say, not as I do' just does not wash with young children. Some of my greatest ground-swallowing moments have occurred because of the haunting repercussions of my own actions. The first that springs to mind was in a picture frame shop. 'Don't touch them, Molly,' I had repeatedly told her. 'If you break the glass, then I will have to pay for it and it will costs weeks and weeks of your magazine and treaty money.' Everything went downhill from there – Alfie started crying, Ella was singing the 'Grand Old Duke of York' as she marched through piles of precariously stacked frames and Molly was on a mission to find a pink frame in amongst a stack of multicoloured frames. My ability to concentrate on what size, colour and shape frames I wanted for my various pictures was tested beyond its limits. So I scooped up the frames I had already chosen with one hand, whilst manoeuvring Alfie's pram and grabbing Ella as she marched past with the other. At this point, my elbow caught the end of the shelf, causing a handful of frames to fall to the ground. As I quickly put them back on the shelf, I noticed the glass had cracked in one, but surreptitiously slipped it between two undamaged ones and headed for the till.

I was so certain that Molly had still been ensconced in her passion for pink, but how wrong I was. Just as I was paying, Molly chirped up, 'What about the one you smashed, Mummy? You have to pay for that one, too.' I desperately tried to ignore her as I fumbled in my purse to find the correct money so I could make a speedy exit. 'Mummy,' she shouted, 'did you hear me?' I could feel the colour rising up my neck, and I avoided all eye contact with the lady at the counter. 'But you have to pay if you break something, Mummy. Don't forget, will you?' Transaction complete, beetroot-faced, I left the shop. But that was when my real embarrassment started. Molly was not going to drop this one. She wanted to understand the rules of life, and she needed an explanation as to why in these circumstances I was allowed to hide something I'd broken and not pay for it. I just didn't have an answer. I couldn't even plead that I had forgotten because she had so eloquently reminded me and at such a volume, too. After a few minutes of talking complete chomp as I tried to string words together into some kind of justification for my actions, I eventually had to concede defeat and admit that I was wrong. I felt suitably chastised by my four-year-old daughter and extremely guilty. I'm just glad she didn't drag me back to the shop with my head held low to 'apologize to the nice lady'.

Molly's crystal-clear communication has got us into some difficult situations on more occasions than I would care to remember. She developed the words and thoughts, but was decidedly lacking in the diplomacy aspect of communication. Dealing with this in confined spaces is when I really struggle; Molly's most magical moment was in a lift. The doors opened when we still had four more floors to travel and in stepped a woman – or was it a man? It was one of those situations when, even as an adult, we struggle not to stare as our brains rapidly try to compartmentalize what the eyes are seeing. This person was about six foot and wearing a shirt and jeans, which gave no clues as to what sex they were. They appeared to have breasts, or was it fat? And they had a moustache, or was it a need to invest in some Immac? There was just no way of telling. Just as my brain reached this point in the thought process, Molly's mouth opened, and all her thoughts came flooding out in the form of unanswerable questions addressed to me. And so they just kept on coming for the remaining four floors of our journey. 'Mummy, is that a lady or a man?' This was her opening question and what the hell was I supposed to say? 'I don't know' was the only answer in my head, and how rude would that be? Mind you, it would be even worse to take a fifty-fifty guess and get it wrong. When I didn't answer this one, she decided to try to work it out . . . out loud! 'It looks like a lady, but she's got a moustache. Women don't have moustaches, do they? How silly. Perhaps it's a man then, but men don't have boobies.' I tried desperately to give her my 'death glare', which is saved for all those public occasions when there is a need to communicate: 'Stop it now or all hell will break loose.' But this just confused her completely. She wasn't doing anything naughty, after all. 'Why are you giving me that look, Mummy? What have I done?' Once again I could feel those blotchy red patches flaring on my neck as I longed for this seemingly lifelong ride to end. That fourth floor couldn't arrive quickly enough for me to escape the confines of the lift.

Ella, with her own little language, so unrecognizable to the untrained ear, has not been able to inflict too many nightmares on me. My biggest issue with her is how young the giggle factor of toilet talk has started. This is clearly because of the influence of her big sister, who has started school and discovered just how hysterical the words 'poo', 'bum' and 'willy' are. Fortunately, when Ella shouted at Molly from the sanctuary of her seat in the supermarket trolley, nobody else appeared to understand that my angelic little two-year-old, with her butter-wouldn't-melt blonde, wispy curls, was in fact calling her sister a 'poo bum smelly pants'.

Due to the ever-present entity of Molly's bowels, poo and botty burp talk does feature quite greatly in our family. As I mentioned earlier, Molly's bad guts could produce aromas that an entire rugby squad would be proud of, and they were the sort of smells that lingered in the air for hours. The gases were so strong they were almost visible. Well, the most embarrassing moment in my parenting career so far centres on one of these mind-blowing botty burps. I had gone for a doctor's appointment for something fairly trivial like a throat infection, and I had to take Molly in with me as she was only two and a half. She sat at my feet quite happily playing with the statutory moth-eaten teddy from the doctor's toy box, while the doctor turned to print a prescription. It was at this moment that the old, familiar waft penetrated my nostrils. Now, believe me, to the unfamiliar nose, it would not seem plausible that such a smell could be emitted from an innocent two-year-old, and so I immediately wanted to make it clear to the doctor exactly who had dropped this clanger in his surgery. 'Molly,' I said in a loud enough whisper to ensure he heard, 'have you done a botty burp?' At this point, she should have given an affirmative reply. I would then have been able to apologize on her behalf, and we would have escaped with only a minor ground-swallowing hole. But, oh no, I was destined for a drop as deep as the Grand Canyon. Molly indignantly retorted, 'No, I have not, Mummy. It was you. Don't blame me for your botty burps.' My entire existence had plummeted to depths I did not know existed. I didn't push her to own up in case it turned out to be the doctor himself who had dropped it, and anything else I said would just make me look even worse. And so I left the surgery knowing that the GP thought not only that I was revolting enough to have dropped a Newky Brown guff in his surgery, but also I was low enough to push my toddler to take the blame, albeit unsuccessfully. As soon as we were outside, I asked Molly again if it had been her, and she quite happily took ownership of it then. 'Why did you lie in there, then?' I asked, to which she replied, 'It smelt horrible. I didn't want the doctor thinking it was me.'

On a slightly different note, I am someone who likes to know exactly what is happening and when, and credit myself with a vast degree of organization. The downside of this is that I do tend to lose the plot easily when I mislay things. This may not sound ground-swallowing, but it certainly is time-swallowing – especially when children were introduced into my world and I realized that I could, in fact, make a career out of looking for things. Those frustrating, frantic searches for everyday items have now become the main focus of many a day of motherhood. No longer when I lose something can I work my way back through all the logical places it may be. Logic goes out of the window, which may also be exactly where that mislaid item is. Recently

I lost my prescription sunglasses. Driving is a nightmare in the summer without them because my eyes have become so used to the tinting that I can't see a thing without them; I was not a happy bunny. The search started with all the sensible places such as in the car, work surfaces and coat pockets, to no avail. I then had to step the search up to level two and look in all the less-than-logical places they may have been moved to such as the bathroom, kitchen drawer or outside by the swing. By the time I had done this, my frustration was mounting. Simultaneously, Ella's excitement kicked in at the prospect of the hours of fun this hide-and-seek game could provide. Desperately trying to remain calm, I very firmly asked Ella, 'Have you seen my sunglasses?' 'Yef,' she replied, 'my fink they in toy tubboard.' And so we emptied the toy cupboard, again to no avail. In Ella's eyes, the game was now hotting up, as were my anxiety levels. 'Erm,' she said, 'how 'bout wif your pots and pans?' Every lid on every pan was removed to check for hidden contents. We found the earrings I'd lost last week in the wok, but no glasses. After a couple more Ella zones were searched, I was close to exploding. The frustration levels were so high I wanted to cry. 'I know,' she said, and I could see the lights come on in her little mind as she dragged me to the playhouse in the garden. As I sat on the floor, plastic pots and pans and Velcro vegetables all about me, wondering what the hell I was doing with my life, Ella miraculously produced my sunnies from the depths of her doll's pram. We both were so triumphant and sang a quick rendition of 'If you've found your mummy's glasses, clap your hands.' But, as I ducked my way back out through the door still feeling the elation of success, I looked at my watch and it suddenly struck me. I was now judging my day's achievements by a successful conclusion to an hour-long search for an item that shouldn't have gone missing in the first place. I'm sure I was in control of my life once upon a time.

All this paled into insignificance, though, when I was recently told by a friend of her worst motherhood nightmare. Her two daughters both had friends around to play, and so she decided to do the decent thing and ask the mother of these friends around, too, for a bit of a 'let's get to know each other' cuppa. She spent the morning ensuring her house was immaculate, bought in some home-made cookies which she thought she could pass off as her own and really felt quite satisfied with the idyllic image she was going to portray. The guests arrived, and everything was going swimmingly. The children went off to play in the sitting room, and the cookies were going down a treat. Then one of the children came in carrying a spoon from the play kitchen with something ominously brown on it. Her mind was racing as she leapt to her feet, saying to the other mother, 'You stay here. I'll just check the children.' As she turned the corner into the sitting room, there, splat bang in the middle of her cream carpet, was the biggest human bowel movement you have ever seen. Protruding from this delightful sight from various angles were four sets of plastic knives and forks, one for each child. Not only had someone dropped their knickers to lay this log in the middle of her carpet, but also they had all been carving it up and serving it to their teddies. As she stood there staring in total disbelief, she heard the approaching footsteps of the other mother and quickly scooped up the poo with her bare hands; hiding it behind her back. Hearing this tale made me realize just how far I still have to go in the grand scheme of ground-swallowing moments. Having to hide a dissected turd in your own home, and not even knowing whether it is the turd of your own offspring, has to be the ultimate moment of motherhood when you look up to the sky and simply ask, why!

Andrea

* * *

From what I have been told, I was an absolute nightmare as a child, always being the one who asked in a very loud voice at the supermarket checkout, 'Mum, you know you said I was in your tummy, well how did I get there?' My poor mum recalls numerous occasions when she went bright red and had to try to tactfully give me a suitable answer in front of amused onlookers. My mum wasn't the only one who suffered as a result of my comments, as a biology teacher found out when I was dared by everyone in the class to ask her what an orgasm was at the age of about thirteen. Never being one to turn down a dare, I willingly obliged. The teacher blushed and said she would tell me at the end of class. It backfired a bit, though, as I then had to squirm through a one-to-one teaching session on the technical definition of the joys of sex. So, with this history, I probably deserve two boys who drop me in it all the time.

I'm not sure if I somehow inflict embarrassment on myself, but I certainly could easily fill this chapter single-handed. Ground-swallowing occurrences are almost a daily feature of my life, so I shall stick with tales from just one week's holiday.

Last summer, Bruce and I took the boys to the same Spanish resort as Hilary and David. We had our own villas, would spend our days as separate families and then meet each evening at the beach. This worked brilliantly because all day we could use the threat of not meeting Molly and Ella if the boys misbehaved, then all evening the children played on the beach right in front of the restaurants whilst we had a relaxing evening meal. Every evening one of the highlights would be to visit the sand-sculpting artist and check out what his latest masterpiece was. These were massive pieces of work that took him a couple of days to complete. The first few days, we watched the beach gradually evolve into a fantastic portrayal of the Simpsons vegging out on their couch, then he commenced work on the Last Supper. Over the next couple of days, Jesus and his disciples were carefully carved, with hours and hours of work going into the finer detail of each of their biblical faces. On day five of our holiday, we arrived at the beach and could see in the distance the proud artist having his photograph taken by the collecting crowd in front of his completed work. We decided to let the children have a play on the beach's climbing frame before wandering along the front to see the finished sand scene, but Sam had other ideas. Suddenly I realized he was no longer on the climbing frame, but was in fact hurtling at high speed towards the back of the Last Supper. I don't think I have ever run so fast, and running on a soft beach is neither easy nor a pretty sight. I did a full-blown goalie dive and caught Sam just as he mountaineered the back of Jesus' head. Jesus was left decidedly bald at the back, but at least his face was still in one piece. It's bad enough having to apologize when your toddler runs through the middle of someone's sand castle. But somehow saying 'Sorry about that' whilst scooping up some sand, bashing it into a ball and sticking your finger in to make eyes a nose and mouth just wouldn't have been becoming for the Lord Jesus himself. Especially in Catholic Spain. If he had to demolish someone, the least he could have done was to go for Homer or Bart . . . Why Jesus?

The next night we decided to ignore the beach and opted for what we thought would be the less risky option of a barbecue at our villa. Full of plumptiousness, we were all relaxing on the balcony dining area – Hils, David and Bruce necking the wine, whilst I enjoyed my statutory Pepsi Max. Then Hilary heard a splash. 'Someone's in,' she yelled, as she flew down the steps to the pool with Bruce in hot pursuit. I leapt up and looked over the balcony and saw an image which will stick with me forever. There in the depths of the floodlit pool was Molly's face pleading up to me as she desperately tried to surface. I didn't actually give myself any time to think, but instinctively jumped off the balcony on to the grass, lay down and hauled her out. As Hilary rounded the corner, ready to dive, she was met by the sight of Molly and I both crying from the shock, in a soggy heap by the pool. I could see her brain connecting as she realized quite how I had got there so fast. Having made this life-threatening rescue of her daughter, I was expecting a hero's welcome from Hils, but, oh no. 'You stupid stupid bloody woman,' is in fact what I was greeted with. 'You could have bloody killed yourself.' Then she, too, started to cry. I looked back at David on the balcony, who it has to be said had barely reacted at all, and realized just how far I had jumped. It suddenly struck me how I really did have to change my kamikaze approach to life and start thinking before I acted. Hilary and Bruce were on their way, Molly's life really was not in immediate danger and yet I had risked leaving my children motherless to save her. It would still have been nice to get a thank you, rather than a bollocking! I think we all felt a bit guilty and totally petrified by the 'what if' element. It really struck a chord as to how quickly your life can change. If Hilary hadn't heard the splash, Molly would have died. By the end of the night, even I had had an alcoholic drink and our adrenaline levels had subsided. As they left, Hils, albeit belatedly, did thank me for saving her daughter's life!

On our final night, we decided to return to the beach; the destruction of a sand-sculpted Jesus was now far more preferential to the loss of life. But for some reason, none of us was in a particularly good mood. I'm not sure if it was end of holiday blues, but Hilary and David were snappy with each other, and Bruce looked like he was chewing a wasp all evening. The meal's atmosphere was not helped by the fact that Bruce decided to choose this moment to insist our boys should eat vegetables and began forcefeeding Max courgettes. When Max started to cry, the onus was then put on me for being such a disgraceful mother who never cooks vegetables. We let the children down from the table to play on the beach, and Hilary and David successfully defused the situation by initiating a completely different conversation. The atmosphere was just rising from chilled to tepid when Max came over and announced that Sam had done a poo in his nappy. Now I have to say that I didn't find my actions at all ground-swallowing, but the wasp Bruce was chewing finally stung, as he was totally mortified by my response. I casually waltzed off to the edge of the beach, wipes and a spare nappy in hand, and lay Sam down on the promenade for a swift nappy change – which incidentally wasn't a pooey one. Bruce, however, was horrified, and I returned to the table to find a ranting, disgusted husband, head in hands going on about the levels to which his wife plummets the Bettridge name. I was unable to get a word in to clarify that it had in fact only been a wee because he was fuming. The fact that I would have changed a poo in the same way is immaterial, of course! As far as he was concerned, I had committed the worst sin and I had no excuse. Well, if the atmosphere was slightly chilled before, it was now positively freezing. This is when true friendship showed itself, though, as Molly arrived only minutes later to say that Ella had done a poo, too. Hilary stood up like one of the Three Musketeers as she strode to the beach, whispering to me as she passed, 'I wouldn't usually do this, but this one's for the Fat Ladies.' She then proceeded to publicly change Ella's nappy, which was pooey, in exactly the same place I had. I immediately forgave her for telling me off for saving Molly's life; she had truly redeemed herself.

My final ground-swallowing moment was not actually on this holiday, but on a clothes-shopping trip in preparation for it. This is one that will stick with me in life as my big 'Why me?' moment.

As Sarah said earlier, I now do all my clothes shopping by Internet or mail order, and here's the reason why. I thought it was embarrassing enough when Max reached the age he could walk and the big game in the changing rooms became lifting the cubicle curtain to expose me. He somehow mastered the art of always raising the curtain when I was in the most embarrassing position. His favourite was when I was attempting to squidge my boobs into a new mammoth-sized sports bra. He always timed his 'ta-da' curtain pull to perfection with this one. Obviously, in an all-female changing room this was not the end of the world, but I would get all flustered as I tried to conceal my bulk and retrieve the curtain all at once.

On one occasion, though, I would have been grateful for a mere 'ta-da' exposure. I had taken in a T-shirt and some trousers to try on for the holiday. I'd just stripped down to my bra and knickers when I realized that I could no longer hear Max. I peeped my head out through the curtain and, in a strong whisper, started to call him. 'Max?' The whisper went up a level when there was no reply. 'Max?' Still no reply – my adrenaline was pumping. I grabbed the T-shirt and ran from the changing rooms as I yanked it over my head. I catapulted into the store in that full-blown panicked mother mode yelling, '*Max, where are you?*' Max was nowhere immediately visible, so true panic set in as I darted between the racks of clothing wearing nothing but a T-shirt, knickers and socks. Max, of course, was very close by hiding under a rack of coats, but it wasn't until my panic subsided as I dragged him out of his hiding place that I realized quite what a commotion I had caused. It appeared that the whole store had come to a standstill because of my semi-streaking lost child incident. I know the looks I was getting were all of sympathy, as they always are when anyone hears that note of high-pitched panic signalling a mother missing her child in a public place. But as I sidled back into the changing room and wedged Max in the

*I darted between the racks of clothing wearing nothing but a
T-shirt, knickers and socks*

corner of the cubicle while I put my clothes back on, I couldn't
help but think, it could only happen to me – and in my skanky,
greying white pants, too!

Lyndsey

* * *

Somehow, my embarrassing moments pale into insignificance in
comparison to everyone else's. The stories I was going to tell
now seem barely ground-denting, let alone swallowing. I thought
it was fairly mortifying when I was left in the ladies' changing

room in a high street shop and Bethan piped up with 'Mummy, why are you having a wee wee?' just as I dropped my trousers. She then pulled back the curtain to make sure that everyone had a good look at my bottom, as I was bent double struggling to get my feet out of the trouser legs. Of course, all eyes were on me as the other females in the communal part of the changing room had been alerted by Bethan's comment, and by the looks on their faces it was almost as if they truly believed that I was indeed having a wee. But the flustered, curtain-retrieving embarrassment this caused is barely worth a mention in comparison to Andrea running round the whole store in a similar state of undress. And as Andrea insists that I point out, she had a lot more bottom to expose, too! Then there was the time in the toilets when, while we were washing our hands, a lady who had been in the next cubicle joined us at the hand basins. Bethan turned to me and said, as clear as a whistle, 'Mummy, why does that lady have a silly hat on?' I looked at the lady apologetically, thinking to myself that Bethan was quite right, it was a silly hat, and hauled Bethan out of the toilets as quickly as I could before she could do any more damage. But, once again, in comparison to Molly's inquiries about someone's persona in a public lift, my public toilet incident was hardly a harrowing ordeal. So does this make my daughter some kind of saint, I wondered, but then I thought of all the embarrassing incidents she has saved up for her dad . . . the little sweetheart.

Tim has only taken Bethan to the doctors on two occasions in her short life, and both times he has come out vowing never to return with his little girl. The first time they were sitting in the waiting room next to a lad who was about eighteen years old. Tim had come straight from the office and was wearing 'work' trousers which were tailored at the front, rather than being straight like a pair of jeans, and so they 'puffed up' over the crotch when he sat down. No doubt you can guess what's coming next. Bethan asked quite clearly, 'Daddy, why is your willy poking up?' Tim didn't know where to put himself as the lad next to him smirked. 'It's my trousers, darling. The way I'm sitting.' 'No, it's not, Daddy, it's your willy. I've seen it poking up before.' Tim, not wanting to carry on the conversation, avoided his first instinct, which was to make a bolt for the door. He stood up and, in doing so, removed the said protrusion of material over his crotch, so at least anyone who had overheard would realize it really was his trousers and he wasn't the surgery pervert getting a bit too excited about his pending appointment. In a desperate bid to avoid eye contact, he made an overinterested bid to examine the contents of the toy box with Bethan, who made no further reference to his genitalia. Every second seemed like a lifetime as he crouched there willing the doctor to call them in and pull him out of this public humiliation. It didn't help that out of the corner of his eye he could see the teenage lad positively relishing his predicament.

The second time he took Bethan to the doctor's was when she was about three and a half. Now, when I took or, indeed, take Bethan anywhere, I ensure that before we leave home I ask her to do a wee, or at least try, so that we won't be caught short while we are out. Bethan has the terrible habit of leaving it to the last minute to say she needs to go to the loo, and unless there is a toilet in the near vicinity you may soon find that you have a crisis on your hands. Tim, on the other hand, never even thinks about this and always complains that I overdo the 'go to the toilet before we leave' routine. So it came as no great surprise to me when I heard that for once he had experienced exactly why I badger Bethan so much about going to the loo before we go anywhere. There he was sat in the doctor's room and, with Bethan's examination over, the GP was explaining the different creams and potions required for her ailment and what order they should be applied. Bethan started tugging his arm. 'Daddy, I need a wee.' 'Okay, darling, just a minute,' he said, continuing to listen to the doctor. 'Daddy, I need a wee,' the voice said a little louder. 'Okay, we're nearly finished.' The doctor was taking his time writing out the script. 'DADDY, I NEED A WEE!' she shouted, but this time it was accompanied by a frantic desperation to get her tights down and, as Tim watched in horror, her pants were already around her ankles. The penny finally dropped. In order to save the huge embarrassment of Bethan emptying her bladder there and then on the thick-piled carpet of the doctor's room, Tim scooped her up, grabbed the prescription from the doctor's hand with his signature still wet and made a bolt for the door. As he flung open the doctor's door, all eyes from the waiting area spun round to be greeted with Bethan's bare bottom, followed by Tim holding her at arm's length. God knows what they thought had been going on in the consultation room, and Tim certainly doesn't intend ever returning to find out. He just hoped that nobody from the willy-protruding visit had also been there for this one!

But the best earth-swallowing experience for Tim was when he picked Bethan up from nursery one evening. As a preamble, I have to explain that Tim is a very observant individual and takes note of people's clothes and hairstyles, both men and women alike. In fact his favourite pastime, other than Welsh rugby, is buying clothes, for himself and me. As they were leaving the nursery, Steven's mum was entering to collect her son, and it has to be said that she is a very pretty lady and always well dressed, so I'm not surprised that she didn't go unnoticed. Tim obviously felt in touch with his feminine side that day and, as Bethan and he walked down the path hand in hand, he said to her, 'Steven's mummy is beautiful, isn't she?' Well, that started Bethan off on her favourite topic, as he knew it would. She was off into a world of princesses being beautiful and how she would like to be a princess and describing the clothes she would wear.

Now Bethan is a bit of a dawdler, especially when she is in princess mode and needing to explain details to you, so it was no surprise that, before they reached the end of the path, Steven was already out of nursery and racing past at full speed with his mum in hot pursuit. Just as she was coming level with Tim and Bethan, Bethan shouted out, 'Bye, Steven. My daddy thinks your mummy is beautiful.' Tim couldn't believe what he was hearing and that his daughter had unbeknowingly dropped him in it from a great height. He reckoned that this beat both doctors' experiences hands down on embarrassment levels. He was immediately plummeted back to the days of schoolboy crushes, when your mate tells the stunning sixth-former that you're in love with her, as you cringe into your school bus seat. Whilst Steven took it all with a pinch of salt, I think his mum was a bit taken aback, but, fortunately for both her and Tim, Steven was still going at full speed, so she embarrassedly overtook them without needing to exchange any social niceties. Meanwhile, oblivious to the awkward situation she had put her father in, Bethan carried on where she had left off in the land of princesses. Tim learnt his lesson and so far has never made the mistake of sharing his thoughts with his daughter again.

Waving Goodbye – Off to School

'Enjoy them. Before you know it they'll be off to school.' How many times do you hear people say something like that when you are nervously clutching your first-born and every hour seems like a lifetime? Yet, here we are five years on, and it seems like only yesterday that we were hearing those irritating little ditties from well-meaning folk on the high street. The past five years have just disappeared, and it's impossible to believe that we have all now packed our precious first babies off to school. So here's what happened, from choosing schools to dealing with the challenges of both learning and playing. The emotions, both ours and theirs, the struggles and the juggles – all are covered here.

Then, of course, for us comes that whole new phenomenon of having time. For some of us, this was just a reduction in the offspring head count for the daylight hours, but for others it was time completely to ourselves again. So what do we do with that first taste of freedom back into the adult world?

Andrea

* * *

Because of the way our childcare went with Max, we never actually went through that big 'first day' emotional milestone. This was because Max had been going to a local private school for four days a week since he was two and a half. He was packed off, complete with uniform, plimsolls and snack, right from day one. This wasn't because Bruce or I had some desire to get him into the private education system from such a young age, but purely down to childcare. Now this is perhaps not the best way to choose a school, I acknowledge, but it is exactly what happened. We didn't go looking around several local schools weighing up the pros and cons. We simply went for the one that was walking distance from the police station, had breakfast club, after-school club and, wait for it, the huge plus of holiday care.

When Max was just over two, we decided that, much as he loved his childminder, he needed to spend some time with children his own age. We opted for the school that takes them from two to eighteen, rather than put him in a private nursery, only to move him when he had to start school. We lived in a village at the time, and I was keen for him to attend the village school when he reached the statutory age, but Bruce wanted him to stay at the private school. My concerns were mainly that he would be the only one in the village who didn't go to the local school and how this may affect him socially as he grew up. However, he settled so well into the school nursery, followed by kindergarten, that when the time came for him to move into transition, or reception class as other schools call it, I didn't even contemplate the option of swapping schools. The fact that he was in a class of nine compared to a class of over thirty was a swaying factor it has to be said, and, in hindsight, thank heavens we didn't swap him because we are now about to leave the village anyway.

For the first couple of years, Max regularly attended breakfast and after-school clubs on the days that I worked, and he did not seem to mind at all. In fact, he liked breakfast club so much that he was gutted on my days off when we had breakfast at home. Once he was old enough, I was also allowed to take part in the 'kiss and ride' scheme, which basically meant that I drove to the entrance of the school where a teacher would unload Max and I would drive off again. Fantastic! I might have felt guilty about subjecting my son to all these extra activities at such a young age if it hadn't been for the fact that Max loved it. He thought he was so grown up and really didn't give me any grief at all about the whole process. It wasn't until Sarah, who has Jack in the same school, told me of something Max had done in a school assembly that I had my first guilt pangs of never being there for him. I hated the thought that my little boy was the one who didn't have his mum at school events or in that sea of smiling faces in the playground after school. So when I returned to work after Sam, I reduced my hours again. This time, rather than taking more days off, I opted for working my hours around the school runs as much as possible. Being able to do at least some of the drop-offs and pick-ups, and take time off for the occasional assembly, was perfect.

Still, I don't think my absence had ever bothered Max. Well, the advantage of having the coolest mum in school has certainly helped to ease any anxiety it has caused anyway. Being the local police officer, part of my role is to give talks to the local schools, and Max's school is one I am regularly asked to visit. When I first did these talks, it was fairly daunting. As adrenaline-pumping as frontline policing can be, I have to say that standing up in front of a bunch of five-year-olds is just as big an ordeal. I'm now used to the standard questions which always come up: 'Do you have any guns?' or 'Have you hit anyone with your stick?' Fortunately, I haven't yet had anyone say, 'My dad was taken away by you once,' as that would be a bit tricky. Max loves it when I come to school, blues and twos all a-go on my police car as I pull up on the school playground. You can see his whole body puffed up with pride when the whole school squeals with excitement as they crowd around. He's also a great volunteer to try out the handcuffs when all the other children are feeling shy. It's definitely a pretty impressive perk at this age, having your mum as the local policelady, but I'm sure he won't be nearly as impressed when he reaches teenage years. It won't be nearly as cool to have a copper for a mum then.

Having gone through state education myself, I had no idea what to expect of the private system. It definitely does have some pluses, with the class size being an obvious bonus. They also have swimming lessons with the school, which has been great. Max has come on in leaps and bounds with his swimming since he hasn't had me sitting on the sideline. It's amazing what they can do when you're not around that they'd wimp out of if you were. One aspect of his schooling that I am not so keen on is the amount of homework he is expected to do at such a young age. He is given writing and reading every day, and it is a real effort to motivate him to sit down and concentrate after a full day at school. It always hangs over us like an after-school black cloud, which I hate. Maybe it's my soft-touch parenting again, but there are so few hours between school and bed that I hate having to initiate extra battles in that short zone of *my* time with my boys.

Sam has now joined Max for three days a week at school in the nursery department, but he rarely needs to do the breakfast and after-school clubs because of my reduced work hours. On the odd occasion that I might be delayed at work, Sarah is always on hand to help out for half an hour or so. Bruce is keen that the boys stay where they are for their school lives and I have no objection, but I am totally relying on him paying for this, as it is not something I am going to be able to afford on my salary. My main priority is that they are both very happy wherever they go, and at the moment they are. Max occasionally has a grumble in the morning, when I have to kick him out of bed. But he genuinely enjoys going to school, to such a degree that when school holidays are coming to an end he actually cheers when I tell him we are going back to school the next day. Sam is gutted on the two days that he doesn't go to nursery and always wants to pop in to his class to say 'hi' when we drop Max off.

Due to my shift pattern, when I'm working on a Saturday night, it means that I now get a day off in the week when both Max and Sam are at school. I have to say that these days are absolutely heavenly. I usually get two a month, and what I do with them varies from packing the day up with things like gym, food shop, trip to Ikea, meeting friends or studying for Open University, to having a total slob-out day. These involve me taking the boys to school, coming home to go back to bed for a nap, then lounging about the house checking my e-mail with Sky Sports on the television. I must say that the 'slob' days are becoming less frequent at the moment, though, with the big house move being imminent. One thing I don't do on these treat days is waste them on something as boring as housework or ironing. It helps that I have a cleaner and ironing lady, and I'm not sure what I will do when I move because I certainly won't be able to afford such a luxury then. I may have to consider staying up past my usual 9 p.m. watershed to do these tasks, rather than spoil my special days off.

There is one thing that I always try to do on my treat days and that is to spend a little bit of time, on my own, with Ella. I was dead chuffed when I was asked to be godmother three times in the space of a year to three of my best pals. Sadly, two of them have moved away from the area since then, so Hilary's Ella is the only one I see on a regular basis. Ella and I definitely bonded from day one, and with her endearingly appalling pronunciation she was never going to get her tongue around calling me 'Andrea', so I have always been her 'yaya'. I love spending the odd hour with her, even if she just joins me on my DIY runs to B&Q or comes with me to pick the boys up from school. Whatever happens from now on, I'll always aim to keep a slot for her in my treat days.

Lyndsey

* * *

The nursery that Bethan was attending happened to be in the grounds of an infant school, and many of the children in the nursery were transferring from there straight into the school. It was an ideal situation for a local working parent, as the nursery their child had always been to then took on the role of gradually introducing them to the school, then continued to care for them through the breakfast and after-school clubs. When Bethan was three, she moved up into the preschool group and soon became accustomed to her friends starting to go to big school. Bethan, on occasion, would be allowed to walk with the key worker taking the children to school in the morning or collecting them for lunch or 'home time'. It was inevitable, then, that Bethan longed to join her ever-increasing band of friends in the big school next door. Unfortunately, for both her and us, this was never going to be practically possible. The nursery and school were not only ten miles away, but also in a different county to us. This meant that, even if we did want to make the journey, in the interest of continuity, she probably would not have been accepted as we lived so far out of the catchment area. Bethan was destined for our local village school, which was less than a mile away from our house.

As the conversations about her wanting to go to school became more frequent, we began to go for a stroll down the leafy lane for her to see her big school. Our neighbour's children also attended this school, which was a huge bonus in swaying her interest. Bethan wanted so much to play with her friend next door, who was going to be in the year above her, that soon she longed for the day that she could carry her Barbie lunch box and join in with the big boys and girls, leaving her much-loved nursery behind. However, the one disadvantage about the local school is that it has no pre- and after-school clubs, so once again I felt the tug between work and childcare moving into a new dimension. We were going to have to face the fact that we would no longer have the luxury of 8 a.m. until 6 p.m. childcare and start considering how we were going to juggle the shorter school day of 8.45 a.m. until 3.05 p.m., never mind the school holidays.

When Bethan was a young baby, and I was still tearing my hair out about leaving her for such long days at a nursery, I can remember my colleagues and friends saying, 'Just wait until Bethan starts school, then it gets even more tricky.' Little did I realize how true that was. I couldn't imagine it getting anything other than easier once such a huge percentage of the day was taken care of by the education system. The other factor that worried me was the thought of not being around at the end of the school day, for at least the first few weeks, to settle Bethan into school. I didn't like the thought of a childminder dropping or collecting her in those important early weeks. I was feeling that as a parent I would be failing her, and I so much wanted to be there for her for this milestone in my little girl's life. But then there was light at the end of the tunnel. After the long years of waiting to fall pregnant and thinking what a nightmare the age gap of four and a half years was going to be, fate dealt us a kind blow. The timing was now perfect. I was going to be off on maternity leave for the term Bethan started school, the whole of the first summer holiday and for at least a month of the start of the next school year. The childcare issue was pushed to the back of my mind, at least until after Caitlin was born.

The transition from nursery to school was a bit too 'cold turkey' for my liking and something I did worry about. I thought we would be offered visits, then half-days, then full days, like other schools. But instead it was a couple of two-hour sessions, then straight in to the full five days a week. It didn't help that Bethan managed to go down with chicken pox after the first of these visits, so she missed the second one altogether. I couldn't believe it. After all those years of exposure to outbreaks of chicken pox at nursery, she decides to go down with it just three weeks before starting school. Furthermore, Caitlin was only two weeks old and had been kissed, cuddled and no doubt 'saliva'd' all over by an unsuspecting chicken pox virus-infected big sister. My concern for Bethan's entry into the education system without enough preparation was somewhat overshadowed by my concern for Caitlin. Despite assurances that Caitlin wouldn't contract it whilst I was breastfeeding, she did get three whole pox two weeks later, but thankfully that was it. Hopefully this means that they are both done now, chicken pox box ticked for life.

And so the big day arrived. Bethan could not contain her excitement. In fact, she woke up earlier than she had on any Christmas morning and, by seven o'clock, she was stood by the front door, breakfast eaten, coat on, Barbie lunch box in hand, raring to go. It was all I could do to tell her that her teacher was probably still in bed and that she had to wait another couple of hours. Tim had decided he would also like to take her to school on her first day, and so the teacher was faced with the whole Lawrence family: mother, father and five-week-old baby sister, as well as Bethan, of course. I had often wondered what that first day would be like. At nursery, in the mornings, Bethan always needed us to pass her over to someone for a cuddle of reassurance, and this was a habit she kept up right until her last day there. This was not a problem in the nursery environment as the carer-to-child ratio was so high, but I was concerned that the teacher at school would not have the time or inclination to do this with every child, even with the small class number of twelve. But Tim and I were almost aghast as Bethan eagerly hung her

'Bethan, your teacher hasn't even woken up yet!'

coat and PE bag on her peg, put her book bag in the red box and ran to sit on the floor in front of the teacher. We must have looked a sorry sight. I had at least expected a moment of hesitation, or the need for a cuddle of reassurance. But, no, absolutely nothing – my little girl had grown up overnight. Her teacher must have seen the looks on our faces and asked for Bethan to at least give us a wave goodbye, which she did happily, but almost with a dismissive, 'Okay, you can go now.' Well, it was a huge mixture of relief and an anticlimax at the same time; we felt positively redundant.

And so Bethan has never looked back. She loves school, and the added bonus of finishing at 3.05 p.m. is like a daily treat for her after her long days at nursery. When I hear the other parents saying how tired their children are now they're in school, I just smile sympathetically as I think of our Bethan practically bouncing off the walls with her reduced hours. I wondered whether having a new baby sister and me being at home would have complicated the issue by introducing a hint of jealousy, but it has never been questioned. School was something she had been looking forward to for at least eighteen months, and she was going to enjoy every minute, no matter what exciting new things were going on at home. Looking back, I wonder whether part of Bethan's easy transition to school has been because she has been used to the disciplined environment of a nursery, but I think it has been a combination of this and her personality.

With Bethan starting school and a new baby on the scene, it has certainly been not so much a juggling act to fit around the school day, but more one of careful planning to try to get the sleeps and feeds in the right order. I find that if Caitlin hasn't had some decent sleep before collecting Bethan, we are in for a nightmare few hours over tea, bath and bedtime. Basically, once Caitlin sees her noisy, excited, big sister, she refuses to give in to sleep in case she misses out on something, or maybe its her way of showing how delighted she is to see her and has missed her through the day. A bonus for me, with this age gap, is that I find myself at home once more, alone with a new baby. It's like being a first-time mum all over again. I can give Caitlin some one-on-one time all day without having to worry about an older sibling. The postnatal social life is a little bit restricted this time round, though. Fat Ladies' lunches now have to be cut short for me to make the 45-minute drive home for the end of school pick-up. I've even had to miss out on my puddings on some occasions!

Now that Caitlin is born and Bethan is in school, I must think again about my return to work and the childcare issue. Having now experienced the school run, I know it is going to be a logistical nightmare to get Bethan to school and Caitlin to nursery, in a different location, if I'm still to get to work at a reasonable hour. It seems that the most realistic option is for a nanny to come to the house. That way we don't have to worry about getting the children to a childminder, who would then have to get Bethan to school with Caitlin in tow, then do it all in reverse at the other end of the day. Although I realize this is the only sensible option, it still doesn't sit comfortably with me, as all my arguments for dismissing the idea of having a nanny when Bethan was born still exist. I still would prefer Caitlin to be in a nursery environment rather than with a stranger in my home. Of course, the alternative would be for me not to return to work and to try to set myself up in a job with more flexibility around the hours of the school day and holidays. And so this is where I leave this chapter, having entered a new era in the space of a couple of months – Bethan at school, a new baby at home and a big decision to make about what to do next.

Hilary

* * *

After all our complicated childcare arrangements during Molly's first few years of life, her entry into the school system was comparatively remarkably simple. Both David and I grew up in villages, but did not go through the whole village school experience. This is something we both felt we missed out on in life, as it also meant missing out on local children's friendships. We therefore decided it was important for our children to go this straightforward route into education. Molly went to playgroup from two and a half; this led to a silky smooth transition to nursery at three and a half, followed by an equally well-planned pass to reception class at four and a half. And all of these places were in the same school grounds, with the same network of teachers and pupils.

This should all have been incredibly straightforward and stress-free, but Molly has always been keen on a good worry and certainly didn't want to let this simple system deprive her of a serious stress-out! It all started in October before she was due to start school in January. She started having nightmares and even wetting the bed. These nightmares were always about seemingly trivial aspects of going to school. 'What happens if I don't eat all the dinner, where do I put the scraps?' 'What happens if I hurt myself in the playground, who will help me?' 'What happens if I need the toilet in the middle of a lesson?' 'What if no one wants to play with me in the playground?' You name it, she worried about it. In the middle of the night, the best I could do to alleviate these fears was brush over them with an, 'I'm sure you'll be okay,' and 'It's ages until you start school. Let's worry about it then.' From the bleary-eyed, semi-conscious zone of 3 a.m., I thought these were all pretty logical, coherent and sympathetic responses, but they frustrated the pants off poor Molly. She clearly thought that I was not giving her concerns the attention they warranted and angrily retorted, 'It won't be okay and it's not ages anyway. It's three months away. My birthday was three months ago and that wasn't long ago, so you're wrong, it's actually very soon, Mummy!' Well, that was me told: sympathetic parenting skills, two out of ten, could do better. We ended up making a list of all her worries, which I promised we would take into nursery and have answered if she was still worried about them by the time her nursery class broke up for Christmas. It was an instant stress release for her. To see her anxieties being put down on paper meant that she was being taken seriously, and I wouldn't forget. Sympathetic parenting skills: nine out of ten. Well done, Mummy. Much better effort.

By the time January term started, all Molly's concerns had

been answered and she was gunning for it. The actual education part of the school day had never been an issue for her; she was desperate to learn and settled straight in to this. The two parts she had worried most about prior to starting school were school dinners and playtimes, but these rapidly became the highlights of her days. Molly and I are up there in a very short list of people who love school dinners. As a child I was the one who longed for liver and onions day because I got to eat everyone's. Prunes for pudding day was the best, though. Forget being destined to wed a tinker or a tailor, I ended up with so many stones I even left the beggar man and the thief behind. Perhaps the farmer comes after that! I had a huge sense of *déjà vu* when Molly returned each day from her first week at school proudly wearing a smiley sticker on her school jumper. It turned out that these were awarded to all the children with clean plates. She has now been at school for over a term and we have not yet had a sticker-free day; that's my girl!

The other gene I have passed on is a love of playground games. Nothing could beat an hour of Stick in the Mud or What's the Time, Mr Wolf? Although playing tag with the climbing frame being 'home', where you couldn't be got, was always a firm favourite, too. Well, Molly greets me each day with a rundown of her meal, followed by a list of lunchtime games. I feel great pangs of envy as she talks me through the memories of my playground days, and we have been known to have a quick game in the garden after school. Unfortunately, as it's only two months since I had Alfie, I do struggle to fit under Molly's legs to set her free when we're playing Stick in the Mud, but I can win What's the Time, Mr Wolf? every time. After all, each one of my steps is about six of Ella's or Molly's – not that I'm competitive!

I didn't ever experience the huge emotional pang of having the proverbial apron strings snapped as I released my precious daughter on to the educational path in life. I think I was so

*As much as I love playground games, it is a bit of a struggle
to fit under Molly's legs!*

preoccupied with getting her into the classroom without an
Oscar-winning 'distraught child' performance that I didn't have
the chance to think about how I felt. Molly never did master the
art of entering nursery without howling the place down as her
fingers were prised off my trouser leg. If she doesn't take up
amateur dramatics in later life, her talents will be wasted. Her
howling was always a means to an end, the end being the satisfying
position of being the one child allowed to sit on the teacher's
lap. She would have had every ounce of my sympathy if I'd
thought there was even a hint of genuine nerves. But it drove
me up the wall because I knew exactly what her game was, and
I took on a Nazi approach to nursery drop-offs! I must have
looked a complete dragon as I shook my devastated-looking
daughter from my trouser leg and made a run for the door.

I longed for a child like Max, who had happily waved his
mother off with a quick kiss and a skip in his step pretty much
wherever he was left, for all his preschool life. Well, finally I

have got just that. When Molly started school, I feared the dropping-off fiasco would start again, so I laid down plans to nip it in the bud. I had just introduced her to pocket money, largely because I was fed up with the constant 'Can I haves' when we were out. The fact that most of these requests were for useless bits of pink plastic, loosely disguised as toys, didn't help either. So I decided to give her £1-a-week pocket money, which she could save up for whatever pink plastic rubbish she wanted. At the time she was starting school, she was absolutely desperate for a £2.99 pink umbrella, with sequins, of course. I explained that now she was a big school girl she would get 20p of her pocket money for every day she happily waved goodbye as she went into school. This meant she would still get £1 on the Saturday if she'd had a really good week, but it would be 20p less for each day she didn't manage a tear-free school drop-off. I wasn't sure if she'd understood this concept, but it's amazing how quickly a child catches on when a pink umbrella is at stake. 'So it will take me a very long time to get my brolly if I cry going into school every day, but it won't take long at all if I go in happily.' You can't beat a bit of bribery and corruption to steer your child through life. Highly frowned upon, I'm sure, but it worked for me. She has not had one single 'wobbly' going into school since then, and needless to say she was soon the proud owner of the most horrendous brolly I have ever seen!

The new emotion I did experience when I started waving Molly off to big school was, in fact, one of anger when I picked her up again. That sounds awful, but it was the big 'I am' schoolgirl attitude that she came home with that really wound me up. She started shouting at me, being irritated by things I said and even started mimicking me. The cheek of it! It was as if she'd had a personality transplant the second I'd let her out of my clutches and into that school. Just as I was thinking that I had in fact produced a she-devil and not a human at all, I was invited to a school mums' night out. It was such a relief to discover that most of the mums, especially those who had girls, were experiencing the same premature pubescent attitudes. One term later and this monstrous Molly is beginning to fade away, but give her even one inch and the monster still rears its ugly head. Luckily the monster in me is even uglier and more scary, so I still have control at the moment. What the hell happens when the real puberty zone starts is something I am not looking forward to finding out.

I may not have experienced the tearful mum 'first school day' bit, but I certainly made up for it at the first school assembly. It was mother's day, and as I squatted on my miniature seat in the school hall I had absolutely no idea that I was about to experience a total emotional roller-coaster ride. When Molly's class filed onto the stage and I saw my shy little girl hiding behind her classmates, I felt that first tingle come over me. But when they started to sing, so loudly and proudly, 'Don't forget to tell your Mum you love her', that was it for me . . . blub city. And I didn't have so much as a baby wipe, let alone a tissue on me. The combination of sheer pride and joy at seeing my big school girl, combined with sudden images of Emily singing such songs at her school, but with no Annette in the audience, was all too much. I was so embarrassed, though. The other mums all around me looked so 'in control' of their emotions, and I was sure they'd be writing me off as a complete drama queen. I even had to resort to wiping my streaming nose on my sleeve, leaving the telltale sleeve snail trail I give Molly so much grief about. It turned out that all the other mums were equally struggling to get a grip of themselves, and I now go to these things reassured that I'm not the only blubber and armed with the essential pocket pack of tissues.

The making of friends bit for reception mums is nearly as traumatic as the making friends bit is for the five-year-olds. In fact, I think it's even harder. We all spent the first few weeks trying to spot some friendly faces who looked like they might want to chat, then gradually sidled over and started talking. It's here that I realized just how little personal identity you have when you are meeting people for the first time as someone's mum. You are no longer Hilary, learning disabilities nurse and farmer's wife, you are just 'Molly's mum'. I love finding out what the other mums are in their real lives. It's a bit like playing misfits. I've even discovered an ex-*Vogue* model hidden in our playground midst.

And so, before the first term was over, so was my five-year prohibition on alcohol. School mums evening sessions have started, which has introduced a whole new aspect to my life. With Alfie being such a good sleeper, I can feel the old pre-parenting Hils re-emerging as breastfeeding ends. Late boozing nights and the need for a gallon of water and a couple of aspirin in the morning are no longer a thing of the past, but are rapidly becoming a feature of the future. So it seems that the milestone of Molly starting school has got a lot to answer for.

Sarah

* * *

Thankfully this process of 'waving goodbye' seemed quite gradual for me, beginning with taking Jack to the crèche in Spain, then the sports centre crèche back in the UK, then eventually starting him at preschool nursery at the age of two and three-quarters, for three mornings a week. Nevertheless, that very first morning that I left Jack at his preschool nursery, dressed in his regulatory sweatshirt and jogging pants uniform, I walked home feeling quite bereft. No little hand to hold, no buggy to push, no chatter to listen to. It was the best I could do to stop myself pointing out planes in the sky and birds sitting on rooftops to an invisible person beside me. Walking back into an empty, silent house without the usual clamouring for the television or something to eat from the little person normally beside me was such a weird experience. To begin with, I was at a bit of a loss to know what to do as I transformed from the full-time mum, constantly at the beck and call of a child, into a woman with free time to do with whatever she wanted! The habitual rush to get the washing hung out or the dishes done before my attention was diverted to a tractor puzzle or an emergency rush to the toilet all of a sudden wasn't necessary. For the first time in almost three years, I could stop and have a cup of coffee and read the newspaper, something that I had got completely out of the habit of doing. Knowing that I was only a couple of months off my due date with my second baby, I knew that this time was going to be precious. The notion of being able to use these 'free' mornings to do things such as have my hair cut, meet friends in town for a relaxing caffe latte or indulge in something as decadent as a pedicure (especially as I hadn't seen my feet under my expanding bump for several weeks) was actually quite exciting!

Despite the first few mornings when I had to rely on the nursery teachers to literally prise Jack from my neck in tears, screaming, 'Mummy, Mummy!' for all his worth, Jack quickly settled very happily into his new routine. Although it has to be said there was always the odd morning when I had to physically manhandle him into his little nursery uniform and then coerce him into walking up the road under the guise that he was going there 'to tell the teacher that we wouldn't be able to go today'. What I found brilliant was that children do at nursery and school all those activities that as an FTM (full-time mum) I always felt I should do with my child and always felt guilty that I didn't, either through never getting round to it or through just not wanting the mess and the hassle! Playdoh, painting, cutting and pasting, planting bulbs, playing in the sandpit — all were activities that Jack just loved. The pride with which he brought home his artwork was matched only by my joy at being able to display these little treasures all over the kitchen wall knowing that I hadn't had to clear up any mess at all to achieve them.

Although I say that it was a 'gradual' process, I was still astonished at how quickly the issue of schooling came around. When Jack was born and we faced the prospect of living abroad for an indefinite period, I decided to register his name at one of the local private schools here in the UK, just to make sure that, whatever the next three to four years held in store for us, we would at least have a place secured for him at a reputable local school. As it turned out, we moved back just around the right time for Jack to start at the nursery part of this school. What I hadn't reckoned on, though, was the fact that, at the age of two and a half, Jack was now expected to have an assessment in order to secure his place. Our £50 deposit, which we had paid three years previously, was not sufficient to simply just 'get him in'. Having already paid this deposit, I decided I might as well take him along for the assessment, more out of curiosity than anything else; however, I did have reservations over what they would really be able to determine from two hours with a bunch of toddlers, at a time when most of them would normally have been having an afternoon nap. On arriving to drop the children off, the parents were given an introductory chat, and I got the distinct impression that I also was under some sort of assessment. It felt as if I were being vetted as a respectable enough parent!

After a guided tour of the school, which I have to say is very similar in tradition and values to the school that Tim went to, and that is probably why we like it so much, I felt nonetheless spurred on to viewing other schools in the town — private and state alike. It seemed such a huge decision to be making so early on in Jack's life when getting it wrong and ending up with a son who was unhappy at school from a very young age might mean that we would be paying the consequences for years to come. In the end, we chose to send Jack to another fee-paying school in the town. We liked the relaxed, nurturing and caring atmosphere that it offered to young children when they start the preschool nursery at the age of two and a half. That for me was essential – that Jack should have a basic grounding in emotional security in a confidence-building environment from the word go, as well as a gentle introduction into the education system, seemed a good combination that this school appeared to have. He would also be able to stay at the same school until he was eighteen if we so desired. And, on top of all of this, of course, was the fact that Andrea had already chosen to register his buddy Max there, albeit for a whole range of completely different reasons!

At the time Jack started, a term before Eloise was born, the payment for three mornings a week was more or less equivalent to any other type of nursery in the town. Now that he is full time, however, the reality of 'school fees' has kicked in big time. On a couple of occasions, Tim has picked up the Visa bill choking, wondering if our cards have been stolen, but then I reassure him that it's the fees that have gone through that month! Fortunately, I have availed myself of the school's excellent second-hand uniform shop, which sells clothing at a fraction of its brand-new price; otherwise I think Tim would have needed resuscitation the month I bought Jack's blazer and duffle coat. And what we do for one child, we'll want to do for the others: we're already hoping that Eloise will start at the preschool nursery after the summer holidays, just before our third child arrives. So maybe we are destined for a future where Visa bills will need to be hidden from my husband in the interest of his continued good health!

As Max and Jack have moved up through the school, their uniform has changed from jogging pants and sweatshirts to full-blown grey trousers and smart blue-striped blazers, and this suddenly identifies them for me as little schoolboys, as opposed to kindergarten toddlers. Snaking out into the playground at the end of the school day, with their rucksacks on their backs, which are almost as large as they are and certainly as heavy (with sports kit and reading folders inside), they look so grown-up. Appearances can be so deceptive, and I have to remind myself of this regularly. The expectations I sometimes place on my little man are often well above his five years, and I have to remain conscious of how young he really is and that I should be treasuring his innocent years instead of pushing him to grow up too fast. Very soon he really won't want to come rushing up to me in the playground for a big kiss and a hug at the end of the school day – very soon it just won't be cool to display affection for your mum in public . . . I dread that day.

A very positive thing that I have found with Jack going to school is the discipline. One of Jack's teachers recently told me that she had guessed that he was visibly sussing her out at the beginning of term, just to see how far he could push her and to see how little effort he could make in the classroom and get away with it. With her years of experience of children's foibles, she had noted Jack's stubborn nature early on, and she said to me, 'Don't worry, as soon as children work out that school and home are working together, they soon apply themselves!' I remember thinking that it sounded like we were all part of one big experiment and that the children eventually realize that they, too, are just a cog in a very big machine – the sooner they knuckle down and get on with it, the better. I'm depending on this teacher's apparent wisdom proving correct so that my discipline regime with Jack at home will become easier. I can only hope! However, this added dose of discipline can have its drawbacks in that, at the end of a school day, especially a rainy one when they have been stuck inside all day, Jack comes home like a wound-up spring. Having been subjected to school rules the entire day, it's almost as though he needs a half-hour of foul-mouthed rebellion once he's home to rediscover his inner status quo. I don't mind admitting that that half-hour can test my patience to breaking point.

Another test for my patience is Jack's homework. The word 'homework' has become a dirty one in our house now: the mere mention of it brings me out in a cold sweat and transforms Jack into the angry little troll character that sprung about in the high street, shouting obscenities at my handbag more than eighteen months ago. I still haven't found the magic formula (if indeed it even exists) for getting Jack to apply himself to doing his homework quickly and without fuss. I've tried Tim's approach of sitting him down as soon as we walk in the door after school, with no television until it's done. I have also tried the allowance of television, with a drink and biscuit, to let him chill out straight after school. But then all hell breaks loose when I dare to turn it off and declare in a smiley Zippy from *Rainbow* fashion, 'Homework time!' I recently thought I was coming down with a very bad throat infection until I remembered shamefacedly that the day before I had practically screamed myself hoarse at Jack to sit down to do his homework, which is not something I'm proud of. Strangely enough, as desperate as Jack and Max are to avoid doing their set homework of half an hour every night, Molly is as desperate to actually do *any* at all! I called Hilary one day last week, just after tea time, and our conversation was punctuated with her spelling words out to Molly, who was typing up a story on the computer, something which she had decided, alone and unprompted, that she wanted to do. Oh, for the diligence of a little girl – I only hope Eloise takes after Molly and not her older brother when it comes to schoolwork, otherwise I'll be having to have my hair dyed every week instead of every six!

The prospect of soon 'waving goodbye' to Eloise, at a slightly younger age than Jack, fills me with every emotion in the book. I recognize that she is ready for the more social environment of nursery life and will undoubtedly thrive in it. I know that it makes sense for her to have settled in before her younger sibling is born, but I cannot help but want to hold on to my little girl at home for that bit longer. I suppose the baseline is that I am not wanting her to grow up. Seeing how quickly Jack has moved up through the preschool, reception and transition classes already, I want the pace of life to slow down a bit. Now that our years are divided into school terms and holidays, the passing of twelve months suddenly only seems half that. That is one reason why I am looking forward so much to having our third baby later this year – to give me the opportunity to relish every single moment of new motherhood all over again, before I'm faced once more with the life-speeding process of schooling. However, if I keep up this mentality towards mothering, I'll end up being a mother of ten, and Tim will need to open an extra Visa account just to cover the education costs!

So What's Next?

Six months have already passed since we wrote this book, and it will be another six months before it goes to print. So by the time you are reading this, our precious first-borns will already be at the end of year one in school! Time, once you are a parent, just goes so fast. So, here is an update on what has happened in our lives over the past few months and what our plans are for the future.

Hilary

* * *

Alfie is now eight months old, still sleeping well and basically incredibly easygoing. He is due to be christened next month and is having Lyndsey and Sarah as his godmothers. Ella will be starting nursery school at the same village school as Molly next month. She is currently receiving speech therapy in a desperate bid to help her to be understood by others before dressing her up in her smart school uniform. Molly is rapidly losing her pubescent attitude and becoming a little girl with exactly the same sense of humour as her mother.

So, what's next? Now that is a question I simply do not know the answer to. All my life I have always been a bit like a small business and had an ongoing five-year plan in my head. For the first time ever, my five-year plan is currently a bit of a blank sheet. This surely must mean that, for the time being, I have reached a point in my life where I have achieved all that I set out to achieve and much more. I'm happily married and still holding down a job in my chosen career, albeit very part time. I feel that my family is now complete, and everything in life is pretty hunky dory – well, nothing that a bit of extra cash wouldn't sort out anyway, and who doesn't feel that? I know that this is a high-risk position for everything going pear-shaped emotionally. After all, if you don't have a mission to strive for, life can become stagnant very quickly, and I'm not the sort of person who likes to stand still for long. For this year, though, having Alfie and writing this book are plenty of extras, and I'll start setting myself some new targets next year. One idea I have up my sleeve is setting up a baby and children's equipment store in a unit on the farm. So, maybe a new business will be my next great venture: watch this space.

Andrea

* * *

Max, Sam and I moved into our new house in Berkhamsted four months ago, and we have all settled in remarkably well. The boys have taken it all in their stride and, although they miss Bruce, they love their regular weekends with him and, importantly for me, they always love coming back home. I have been far too busy to even contemplate feeling lonely or depressed about my situation so far; I'm just hoping it will stay that way. I have been decorating nonstop for the first few months, and my masterpiece has been a full-on Arsenal bedroom for the boys, which I love almost as much as they do! I have also retired from playing football after fifteen years and taken up hockey instead, which I am thoroughly enjoying. There's nothing like a whole new circle of friends to help make a fresh start in life.

What the future holds I'm not sure, and any certainties I had about my life have definitely disappeared because of the events of the past year. I have settled into my new role as a community officer and would like to remain doing this for a few more years yet. Although financially it may be tempting to increase my hours once Sam starts school, I am hoping I won't have to do this, as I would like to use any spare days to continue with my studying. Having almost completed the first year of my Open University degree, and thoroughly enjoying it, I intend continuing with this, and if successful this would gain me a degree in about five years time, just before I reach forty. I've no idea what I will do with it if I ever do finish, but it's a goal I am enjoying working towards.

As for my future, well, at the moment all I know for certain is that I will still be mad about Arsenal, still be fighting the flab and still have two boys I adore. Other than that . . . who knows?

Lyndsey

* * *

I have returned to work on a three-day week following a wonderful maternity leave, and I find myself back on the roller coaster of juggling career, children and life in general. Our childcare dilemma was resolved on a shopping trip when I bumped into one of the carers from Bethan's old nursery who had joined the nanny circuit. As we exchanged news, I introduced her to baby Caitlin, and I explained my dilemma in finding a nanny whom I could trust to look after our two girls. As luck would have it, she told me of a friend of hers who had also been at the nursery and, more importantly, whom I (and Bethan) knew and liked, who was looking for a new nanny position. I contacted her straight away and, after a long chat, she agreed to come to work for us on my return to work. I have now been back at work for two months, and both Caitlin and Bethan have settled with her really well – I can go to work knowing that they are happy.

Bethan is now in her second term at school and is loving every minute of it. Her teacher refers to her as a 'little princess', and Tim and I are so proud of her many achievements in such a short space of time.

But the biggest issue for me at the moment is my nine-month-old cherub and her refusal to drink from either a bottle or a cup, other than a few sips here and there. 'That's okay, Mum,' she must be thinking, 'I'll make up for it at night.' And so I am back to four-hourly breastfeeds during the night. It is like having a six-week-old baby again, and, if I am honest, I am finding it tiring and frustrating. As a result, it is making my return to work very difficult, both emotionally and physically. This was a baby who slept through the night from when she was three months old until she was six months, and then it all went downhill. At first we put it down to growth spurts and teething, but, without a tooth in sight, perhaps we simply have a baby who just isn't going to sleep through the night. Added to this is the fact that she's not drinking any milk during the day, so I do feel the need to keep up this nightly vigil. I fear the next few months, or dare I say years, are going to be hell.

So what's next? I am enjoying the balance of only working a three-day week whilst having time for my family, and I hope to maintain this for the foreseeable future. But my main ambition, call it a pipe dream if you like, is to return to having a solid block of eight hours of good-quality sleep!

Sarah

***

Our third child, a baby girl called Pippa Mary, was born four weeks ago. She had us guessing when she didn't arrive punctually on her due date like the other two, but I can forgive her that because she arrived in the quickest time. We got to the hospital just before the afternoon school-run traffic jams. Pippa was born two hours later, and we were back at home eating fish and chips by 9 p.m. Jack and Eloise could have been forgiven for thinking that Mummy had just popped out to the shops and bought a 'pink' one from the baby shelf. If only it were that easy.

Jack is still at the same school as Max, still detests his homework and is still testing my patience on occasions, but is becoming more and more grown-up by the day. He is taking his role of 'big brother' to two little sisters very seriously, which is so lovely to see. Eloise started at the nursery in September and, although she is by far the youngest there, hasn't looked back from the minute she walked through the door on her first morning. As we predicted, she's thriving in the sociable environment of nursery and is already displaying her cheekiness with the teachers by leaving out the Mr or Mrs, and calling them just by their surnames. Acceptance of her new little sister has ranged from utter denial to overzealous hugs and kisses, but fortunately she hasn't yet asked me when Pippa's going back.

Tim is now working in London for a telecommunications company. So far foreign travel has been kept to a minimum, which I'm very chuffed about, particularly at the moment whilst Pippa is so young. I need to be able to pour out my domestic nightmares to him at the end of every day and to have him there in the mornings to sympathize over how few hours of sleep I have had during the night.

With our family now feeling 'complete', I am looking forward to the fun of being an FTM for a few more years, before exploring a different way of spending my days. Once all the children are in school, my hope is to set up a small business selling an eclectic mix of old furniture and gifty things such as homemade cards and cushions, perhaps with a coffee shop out the back! But, in the meantime, I will content myself with making things out of old French fabric that I'm finding in the depths of rural France whilst tackling our renovation project there. Other than that, I would still like to go down the adult education route, maybe studying psychology further. But I'll wait until Pippa is at least a few months old before investigating that one.